CW00567162

Love You to Death

Crissy Calhoun

Love You to Death

the unofficial companion to

the Vampire Diaries

season 3

ECW Press

Copyright © Crissy Calhoun, 2012

Published by ECW Press
2120 Queen Street East, Suite 200, Toronto, Ontario, Canada M4E 1E2
416-694-3348 / info@ecwpress.com

All rights reserved. No part of this publication may be reproduced, stored in a retrieval system, or transmitted in any form by any process — electronic, mechanical, photocopying, recording, or otherwise — without the prior written permission of the copyright owners and ECW Press. The scanning, uploading, and distribution of this book via the Internet or via any other means without the permission of the publisher is illegal and punishable by law. Please purchase only authorized electronic editions, and do not participate in or encourage electronic piracy of copyrighted materials. Your support of the author's rights is appreciated.

LIBRARY AND ARCHIVES CANADA CATALOGUING IN PUBLICATION

Calhoun, Crissy
Love you to death, season 3 : the unofficial companion
to the Vampire Diaries / Crissy Calhoun.

ISBN 978-1-77041-119-7
ALSO ISSUED AS: 978-1-77090-335-7 (PDF); 978-1-77090-323-4 (EPUB)

1. Vampire diaries (Television program). 1. Title.

PN1992.77.V34C343 2012   791.45'72   C2012-902731-6

Typesetting: Troy Cunningham
Text design: Melissa Kaita
Cover design: Rachel Ironstone
Cover image: Crissy Calhoun
Author photo: Lee Weston Photography (LeeWestonPhoto.com)
Printing: Trigraphik | LBF   5   4   3   2   1

Interior photo credits by page: vi, 3, 17, 23, 66, 73 © Andrew Evans/PR Photos; 12, 34 © Janet Mayer/PRPhotos.com; 30, 110, 120, 160 © Tina Gill/PR Photos; 41 © The CW Network/Bob Mahoney/Landov; 49, 91 © Emiley Schweich/PR Photos; 54 © David Gabber/PR Photos; 77 © Glenn Francis/PR Photos; 83, 96, 137 © The CW Network/Quantrell D. Colbert/Landov; 104 © Robin Wong / PR Photos; 115 © Joshua Tousey/PR Photos; 123, 187 © J. Miller Tobin; 139 © Tatiana Davidov/PR Photos; 146 © Glenn Harris/PR Photos; 153 © MavrixPhoto.com/ Keystone Press; 173 © Joshua Butler; 179 © Price Peterson.

The publication of *Love You to Death — Season 3: The Unofficial Companion to The Vampire Diaries* has been generously supported by the Government of Ontario through Ontario Book Publishing Tax Credit, by the OMDC Book Fund, an initiative of the Ontario Media Development Corporation, and by the Government of Canada through the Canada Book Fund.

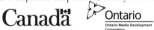

PRINTED AND BOUND IN CANADA

Contents

"In a town full of witches, werewolves, and vampires..."

If you asked a random person on the street for a description of *The Vampire Diaries*, you might hear about the love triangle — a girl and the two vampire brothers who love her. But ask *The Vampire Diaries* fandom or a cast member or *TVD* writer, and the answer you'll get could involve any number of things: Breakneck pacing and twists. Thousand-year-old hybrids. Grief and isolation, and perseverance in its wake. Teen drama with supernatural stakes. An exploration of the importance of choice. Shirtlessness. Family, family, family. *The Vampire Diaries* — like Caroline Forbes — has always been more thoughtful and interesting than it appears on the surface. It's no kiddie pool. And that's why I am quite happily back here again: writing my third *Love You to Death* companion guide on a television series that to the uninitiated doesn't require this amount of ink spilled. But we know better.

As the series has grown and changed since its now wonderfully idyllic-seeming pilot back in September 2009, it's slowly and surely gained in both critical reception and popularity. While recognition of *TVD*'s accomplishments is not likely to be forthcoming from the Emmys, there are other ways it's recognized; beyond the Teen Choice and Saturn Award nominations, the fans make their voices heard with moments like Nina Dobrev's People's Choice Award in 2012. Not only did fan votes win her the award, she was on the ballot thanks to them, making Nina the first write-in nominee and winner. Season 3 marked the first *Entertainment Weekly* cover for *TVD*, and

while the story and photos focused on the love triangle and shipper wars, the three collectible covers were a milestone for The CW series. Another sure sign of a devoted fandom is the proliferation of conventions: big-time convention company Creation Entertainment joined the con party with official *TVD* conventions in the U.S. in 2012, and Europe's and Australia's cons kept the cast jet-setting during their time off.

In the ramp-up to the season 3 premiere, the series promised to look both forward and backward. Fan favorites Kayla Ewell and Malese Jow made a cliffhanger return in "As I Lay Dying" and would feature in the first arc of the new season. In interviews leading up to the September 2011 premiere, showrunner Julie Plec touted the upcoming year as the "Season of the Originals," promising viewers more of the Original family we learned about in the tail end of season 2. But the big character moment everyone was keen to see was Stefan's — and Paul Wesley gave us something to look forward to by promising sweet, heroic Stefan would return as a "freaking nutbag." How could we resist that?

Just as the series has evolved over the years, so have my companion guides to it (though hopefully we're not in nutbag territory . . .). What was covered in the first two volumes is not rehashed here, and careful readers will notice that the format of the episode guide is slightly different. I've grouped all the song-by-scene information at the back of the book (page 162) so that it can function as a handy-dandy music reference. And since we all love to interpret the significance of which cast member delivers the opening "Previously on *The Vampire Diaries*" line, I've added it in to each episode's details. (Gone are a few sections: "Bite Marks," "The Diabolical Plan," and "Meanwhile in Fell's Church," R.I.P.)

Each episode's write-up begins with a bit of dialogue that stood out for me either because it captures the episode in a pithy few lines . . . or it was just too well written not to acknowledge. From there, I provide an analysis of the episode, looking at its main themes, the character development, and the questions it raises, followed by these sections:

COMPELLING MOMENT Here I choose one moment that stands out — a turning point, a character standing up for herself, a shocking twist, or a long-awaited relationship scene.

CIRCLE OF KNOWLEDGE In this section of the episode guide, you'll find all the need-to-know info — the details you may have missed on first watch, character insights, the cultural references, and motifs or recurring elements. Often, an episode's title is a play on another title (of a film, book, song, etc.); those are explained in this section.

THE RULES Any work of fiction with a supernatural element has its own particular spin on how that world operates. Here I catalog what we've learned about what goes bump in the night.

HISTORY LESSON The only class at Mystic Falls High School that ever got considerable screen time is history. History, both real and fictional, is important in this series — and for the characters' back stories, the town's history, and subtle references, "History Lesson" is your study aid.

PREVIOUSLY ON THE VAMPIRE DIARIES History repeats itself in Mystic Falls, and here I outline the incidents, motifs, and key moments that are revisited or echoed in each episode. Included at the back of the book is a quick refresher on the previous seasons' episodes (see page 215), which I refer to by title in this section and throughout the book.

OFF CAMERA Here we leave the fictional world behind to hear what the cast and crew have to say about filming an episode; sometimes I provide background details on a guest star, director, or other filming details.

FOGGY MOMENTS Elena, surprised by Stefan in the cemetery in the pilot episode, tells him the fog is making her foggy. "Foggy Moments" is a collection of confusing moments for the viewer — continuity errors, arguable nitpicks, full-on inconsistencies, and mysteries that may be explained later.

QUESTIONS *TVD* fans *love* to theorize about what will happen next or what motivates a character. In this section, I raise questions about characters, plotting, and mythology for you to consider as you watch the season unfold.

Make sure you watch an episode *before* reading its corresponding guide — you will encounter spoilers for that episode (but not for anything that follows). Within the pages of the guide, you'll also find short biographies of the actors who bring the recurring characters to life as well as sidebars about other elements of the show and about its influences. I've updated the timeline included in my first companion guides to include season 3's info on the past thousand years in the *TVD* universe.

Finally, in the interview section, I'm thrilled to have four whip-smart, insightful members of the *TVD* family: director J. Miller Tobin, editor/director Joshua Butler, TV.com photo recapper and internet hero Price Peterson, and executive producer/writer/showrunner/genius Julie Plec. Four different perspectives on the series, which I hope will provide a nice counterpart to my pages of heartfelt rambling.

Speaking of . . . if there's something you think I missed, or that I completely read your mind about, drop me at a note at crissycalhoun@gmail.com, @reply me on Twitter (@CrissyCalhoun), and/or stop by my Facebook page at Facebook.com/CrissyCalhoun. Being a part of *The Vampire Diaries* conversation is just about my favorite thing ever, and the *TVD* family has come to mean a great deal to me personally. So thanks for reading, and for letting me to spend so much time in Mystic Falls.

xoxo
Crissy Calhoun
July 20-12

Show me a hero and I will write you a tragedy.

— F. Scott Fitzgerald (*The Crack Up*, 1945)

Episode Guide

Season 3
September 2011–May 2012

CAST Nina Dobrev (Elena Gilbert/Katherine Pierce), Paul Wesley (Stefan Salvatore), Ian Somerhalder (Damon Salvatore), Steven R. McQueen (Jeremy Gilbert), Kat Graham (Bonnie Bennett), Candice Accola (Caroline Forbes), Zach Roerig (Matt Donovan), Michael Trevino (Tyler Lockwood), Matt Davis (Alaric Saltzman), Joseph Morgan (Klaus)

RECURRING CAST Nathaniel Buzolic (Kol), Jack Coleman (Bill Forbes), Torrey DeVitto (Dr. Fell), Alice Evans (Esther), Kayla Ewell (Vicki Donovan), Daniel Gillies (Elijah), Claire Holt (Rebekah), Malese Jow (Anna), Marguerite MacIntyre (Sheriff Forbes), Sebastian Roché (Mikael), Susan Walters (Carol Lockwood), Persia White (Abby Bennett), Caspar Zafer (Finn)

> *Damon (to Elena): Stop looking for him.*
> *Stop waiting for him to come home. Just stop. Stefan is gone*
> *and he's not coming back. Not in your lifetime.*

3.01 *The Birthday*

Original air date: September 15, 2011
Written by: Kevin Williamson and Julie Plec
Directed by: John Behring
Guest cast: Dawn Olivieri (Andie Star), David Gallagher (Ray Sutton), Cherilyn Wilson (Samara), Sarah Cooper (Keisha), Lilly Roberson (Sofie), Diany Rodriguez (Claudine)
Previously on *The Vampire Diaries*: Paul Wesley

It's Elena's 18th birthday: Caroline throws her a massive party, Damon tracks down his brother, and the birthday girl's wish actually comes true.

When season 2 of *The Vampire Diaries* ended, Stefan had sacrificed himself to save his brother, agreeing to be Klaus's wingman in exchange for some precious werewolf-bite healing blood. With "The Birthday," we meet Stefan two months into his sentence and he's not the man who left Mystic Falls. He's a ripper. The horror-movie-style opening sequence lets us know that Stefan's heroic act has made him a villain: he kills those two women at Klaus's command and, before the day is done, has tortured a werewolf and killed Andie Star, who he used to be concerned about. The writers make it clear from the top: this is not your season 2 *TVD*.

The jump ahead in time is one of many ways this episode signals a new beginning for the series; most notably "The Birthday" marks Elena's official entry into adulthood as she turns 18. But hitting this milestone day on the calendar doesn't mean the past will be easily forgotten. In Mystic Falls, the characters struggle in various states of limbo until they ultimately force themselves to choose between letting go or holding on. Despite trying their darndest to be normal and boring, their attempts to cover up the messy truth fail when they pretend to be something they're not. Elena sucks at being the chipper birthday party girl, Jeremy's mundane existence at the Grill is punctuated with ghostly visitors, Caroline and Tyler can no longer deny their physical attraction, Alaric feels like a fraud acting as a guardian to the Gilbert kids, Damon has been hiding his search for his brother from Elena, and Stefan's ripper act

isn't as convincing to Klaus as he thinks it is. Even Klaus himself puts on an American accent, telling the suspicious Floridian that he's not a serial killer.

While no one has an easy time letting go of the past, for Jeremy, it's ever present. His past is literally haunting him and he's been holding on to a huge secret all summer. Until he opens up to Matt after the party, he is alone with a terrifying reality: Anna and Vicki appearing to him as a result of Bonnie bringing him back to life. Jeremy's been playing at normalcy, but judging from his reluctance to get out of bed and his pot-smoking at the party, he's regressing to his season 1 stoner self instead of dealing with his supernatural problem. In the same way that Elena is drifting, purposeless except in her hunt for Stefan, Jeremy is in a kind of limbo, just like Vicki and Anna. Matt describes Jer as on a "downward spiral" and himself as "out of it"; neither one knows where they fit in the new supernatural normal. Though Jeremy opens up to Matt, Matt isn't ready (or sober enough) to hear that Vicki's ghost is real and not imagined, a product of Jeremy's grief.

While Jeremy's exes interrupt his phone conversation with his current ladylove, Bonnie, Matt has to deal with watching his own ex dance around a relationship with his best friend. Matt reminds Caroline that she and Tyler are supposed to be, like, mortal enemies; as much as this werewolf and vampire duo act like everything's normal, they're actually quite subversive with their inter-species relationship. The tension between these two supernaturally horny teenagers is palpable, and the payoff a racy kickoff to season 3. But Werewolf Road and Vampire Boulevard may not meet again if Carol Lockwood has anything to say about it. Though Sheriff Forbes has changed alliances — she's feeding information about vampire attacks to Caroline and company to help them find Klaus and Stefan — in the wake of her breakthrough with her daughter in "As I Lay Dying," the acting mayor of Mystic Falls is still maintaining the old founding family philosophy: vampires are the enemy.

The self-proclaimed "chaperone teacher from hell," Alaric Saltzman has been living in his own limbo: on the couch for the two months since Jenna was killed in the sacrifice, drinking excessively and feeling like a bad role model and an unfit guardian to Jeremy and Elena. In a heartbreaker of a scene, he tells Elena it's time she take care of herself, and he leaves, a man broken by the relentless tragedies he's suffered. Alaric may have moved out, but he hasn't moved on; his grief and disconnection just have a new address. Though Elena still has her little brother (and his adorable birthday drawing), she feels very much on her own, holding down the Gilbert fort and holding on to hope that Stefan will come home — in her lifetime.

In "As I Lay Dying," Elena told Jeremy that they had to start going through the motions of their lives, so that at some point it would feel normal again. But, in addition to mourning Jenna over the summer, Elena seems to be stuck in a kind of Stefan-less limbo. It's no wonder that Caroline is concerned about her friend not living her life. As Elena insists on tracking down Stefan, clinging to the possibility that he's alive and not already one of Klaus's innumerable victims, there's an interesting tension set up between her and Damon: they are at odds despite sharing the same goal. Damon is just as single-minded and determined to find his brother. But he has a second, contradictory, motivation: protecting Elena. By keeping his intel from her, he's shielding her from the truth about Stefan's murderous deeds, letting her hold on to the idealized Stefan, the Stefan she loves who would never dismember and reassemble victims. Or kill Andie in a "cool" way just to drive home his point to his brother.

But, having witnessed a murder firsthand, by the end of "The Birthday," Damon's faith in his brother is shaken, if not destroyed. Stefan had been Andie's defender and, while it seems like Damon's "complicated dynamic" with his "fake compelled girlfriend" was on *slightly* more equitable terms than last we saw them, the safe bet would have been on Damon killing Andie one of these days, not Stefan. In a quiet moment before the raucous party, Damon returns Elena's necklace to her, the symbol of the "good Stefan" and of the love shared between Stefan and Elena. But by the end of the night — after Andie's death and Stefan's insistent growl that Damon let him go — Damon loses it with Elena, finally coming clean to her about what Stefan's done, that those are his victims up and down the eastern seaboard, not Klaus's. In a small but telling gesture, Elena clutches her necklace: she wants to hold on to her faith in Stefan.

Alone in Stefan's room, Damon tears up the place that stores all of Stefan's memories, revealing how upset Damon is by Stefan's dark turn. Though it wasn't his choice, Damon is the *cause* of Stefan losing himself. It was to save Damon's life that his little brother gave up his identity, his values, and the woman he loves. Stefan is trapped in a kind of purgatory, he's descended into a dark prison guarded by the biggest (and potentially indestructible) baddie of all time. No wonder Damon's drinking champagne before breakfast.

This true introduction to Stefan the Ripper is masterfully done. Villainous but sympathetic, Stefan straddles the roles of romantic hero and gruesome imaginative killer with subtle gradations in Paul Wesley's performance that reveal Stefan's internal conflict. In a very deliberate moment, Stefan delivers Damon's "Hello, brother" line from the pilot — signaling the role reversal between the Salvatores from season 1 to 3 — and it's Stefan, not Damon, who racks up an impressive body count while Damon is left to cover up his brother's bloody tracks. It's more than a little bit cool to see the transformation from the Stefan we know and love to this unflinching killer. But as much as Stefan plays his part as Klaus's dutiful henchman, it's clear to Klaus, if not to Damon, that Stefan is doing just that — playing his part. He hasn't truly given in to his dark side; it's serial killing by numbers. Though Stefan's not following his moral compass, he's still holding on to it; his love for his brother and for Elena is buried but burns bright. Stefan acts like he's enjoying himself — "It's a little bit cool, no?" — but his duties are a burden, not the pleasure Klaus wants them to be.

As if leashed to Klaus, Stefan can only escape as far as the bar's parking lot. Stefan knows the truth of Damon's warning — that it's a fine line he's walking — and his façade is breaking as Klaus's words ring true: every time he feeds, the blood makes it easier to give in to the Ripper. It's a testament to Paul Wesley's command of his character that he can bring us to very different places with Stefan in this single episode — from murderous rampages to desperation in his wordless phone call to Elena. She *knows* it's him though he can't speak to her, and she says just what they both need to hear: never let go. This show is never more accomplished than when it goes to dark twisted places while maintaining its firm grasp on the emotional heart of the story, the motivating forces that drive its characters to such extremes.

Isolated but hopeful, Elena remains unwavering in her faith rather than accept reality; she'll never stop fighting no matter how dire things are. And with Klaus now one step closer to enacting his master hybrid plan, it seems like things are going to get a lot worse before they get better.

COMPELLING MOMENT Elena and Stefan's phone call. From that crack in Elena's voice to the way Stefan holds back his tears and says nothing, it's a short scene that's powerfully emotional and beautifully performed.

CIRCLE OF KNOWLEDGE
- Damon quips that Stefan could be "alive and well and living in Graceland," Elvis's Memphis, Tennessee, estate. Like Elena whose hope for Stefan's safe return is unwavering, some Elvis die-hards still believe the King lives on.
- In response to Elena's glum birthday girl attitude, Damon references the 1963 Lesley Gore song "It's My Party," where the birthday girl is thrown over by her boyfriend and says she'll cry if she wants to.
- The pins on Damon's Stefan-tracking map are in Alabama, Georgia,

North Carolina, Tennessee, and Virginia. The newspaper articles are from fictional Tennessee papers: one from Memphis, another from Sylva (which is actually in North Carolina) and reference is made to Meeman-Shelby Forest Park, near Memphis. The article "Body Discovered at Drive-In" includes this quote: "What kind of sick [expletive deleted] chops somebody into pieces and then puts them back together for someone to find?" The answer is provided by Damon's stickie note: Stefan.

- Klaus lets Stefan leave to deal with his brother in a test of trust proven by Stefan's return. It's a moment that nicely contrasts with another Original's relationship with one of the gang. In "Klaus," Elijah allows Elena to tend to Jenna, and she proves the value of her word when she returns to him. Here, instead of being tentative allies like Elijah and Elena were then, Klaus and Stefan are master and slave.

- R.I.P. Andie Star, Action News. Though it seems as though she spent her final days exercising a little more independence and control over herself (if that get-the-champagne-yourself moment was any indication), Andie's murder is one that Damon may feel culpable for, despite not actually being her killer. Because Damon wanted someone to feed on, she was vervain-free and therefore vulnerable to Stefan's compulsion and attack.

THE RULES Unable to compel a werewolf, Klaus resorts to torture, but he leaves handling the wolfsbane to Stefan. As a hybrid vampire-werewolf, both vervain and wolfsbane are poisonous to Klaus. To turn Ray into a hybrid, Klaus is trying the usual human-to-vampire three-step transition: Klaus feeds the werewolf his blood, kills him, and, presumably once Ray resurrects, he'll be forced to drink human blood.

PREVIOUSLY ON *THE VAMPIRE DIARIES* In this season 3 premiere, there are a number of echoes of the pilot episode: a grieving Elena forces herself to face the day, she prods her brother into at least going through the motions (getting him out of bed and off to work) and helps out her slightly inept guardian (Alaric now, instead of Jenna). Jeremy is back to feeling morose and smoking weed to avoid his problems, while Elena's not into partying though Caroline is gung ho ("Pilot," "162 Candles"). The photo of Elena and Stefan dates from before she knew he was a vampire; it was taken on the day he gave her the necklace ("Friday Night Bites"). Though Stefan gave her that necklace, Damon has had some key moments with it, as he does here in "The Birthday": he put it on Elena in "Fool Me Once," and he returned it to her at the end of "Rose." Damon escorts Elena down the stairs in a moment that recalls when he stood in for Stefan at the Miss Mystic Falls pageant ("Miss Mystic Falls"). Damon trashes Stefan's room like he did in "Lost Girls," but instead of that gleeful destruction, it's more of a breakdown akin to Stefan's own in "History Repeating."

OFF CAMERA David Gallagher plays hybrid–guinea pig Ray Sutton; Gallagher is best remembered as Simon in *7th Heaven* and was more recently seen in *Super 8* as the stoner, Donny. He actually auditioned for both the Stefan and Damon roles on *The Vampire Diaries*, and the producers were happy to finally find the right fit for him on the show with Ray.

For the first released scenes of season 3, the producers chose a great teaser: the clip shown at San Diego Comic-Con in July 2011 was of Elena getting an eyeful of Damon wearing nothing but bubbles.

The phone call at the end of the episode was Kevin Williamson's idea, and when he outlined it to Julie Plec, as she related to *Entertainment Weekly*, "I started to cry. I was like [in weeping voice], 'That's the best thing I've ever heard in my entire life.' And then he started to cry. Because that's what we do, we get each other going, because we're complete saps. . . . There's something about seeing Paul Wesley trying not to cry that is so sad. So he just nailed it. That's one of my all-time favorite moments emotionally." It was also one of the most difficult season 3 scenes for Paul Wesley to film. Shot on location, a group of fans had gathered across the road (on public property) to watch the filming, and unfortunately they were directly in Paul's eyeline and trying to get his attention. It was a big distraction for the actor, and he modestly credited the editor, Sean Albertson, with pulling together such a powerful scene from the performance he gave.

FOGGY MOMENTS While it's believable that Alaric *still* can't operate the coffee maker after two months of living at the Gilbert house, it's incredible that, after Elena takes over, the coffee brews in a matter of seconds. On Damon's tracking-Stefan wall, the newspaper article with the stickie note that reads "Neck Wounds" is actually a sports report about a local baseball team. Klaus tells Ray that he's the first werewolf he's come across "in many moons." But in "The Sacrifice," Klaus had Tyler lined up as his werewolf to sacrifice; has he forgotten about him, or is Klaus more interested in Ray's pack than a lone Lockwood wolf?

QUESTIONS

- Will Damon tell Elena that Stefan killed Andie?
- Where is Katherine?
- Vicki asks Jeremy to help her. What does she need him to do? Are she and Anna on a ghostly quest together?
- Does Carol Lockwood know better than to turn to Sheriff Forbes for dealing with her outed vampire daughter? Will people ever quit it with the surprise attacks on Caroline?

> *Alaric: Know what you're doing there?*
> *Elena: No, I don't.*

3.02 *The Hybrid*

Original air date: September 22, 2011
Written by: Al Septien and Turi Meyer
Directed by: Joshua Butler
Guest cast: April Billingsley (Paige), David Gallagher (Ray Sutton), Jason Mac (Derek), Kelly Sutton (Anchor Woman)
Previously on *The Vampire Diaries*: Nina Dobrev

Elena leads Alaric and Damon on a hike through werewolf-filled woods on the night of a full moon in a quest to find Stefan . . . who doesn't want to be rescued. Tyler shows his mom the monster in him.

No one would call *The Vampire Diaries* a comedy, but when it goes for funny moments, man, does it ever deliver. In "The Hybrid," an episode that explores determination in the face of mounting obstacles, our heroine is tossed off a cliffside into a lake in mid-sentence and you can bet that doesn't slow Elena Gilbert down. In a continuation from the season premiere, her focus is on saving Stefan, and Elena's refusal to give up on "lost causes" eventually wins over Damon and Alaric. All three accept the risk involved in this attempted rescue op; with werewolves and Klaus roaming the woods on a full moon, and a ripper who doesn't want to go home, it's not the most surefire of half-baked plans. But the importance of their connections to each other — Elena's love for Stefan, Damon's for his brother, and Alaric's for both Elena and Damon — overrules any pesky sense of self-preservation. Beyond the bickering trio of would-be rescuers, it's an episode full of failed attempts: bitten Stefan is at Klaus's mercy again, Carol thankfully realizes the flaw in her plan, and Klaus fails spectacularly with his bleeding-from-the-eyes hybrids.

Elena isn't a total failure though. Easier than dragging Stefan from Klaus's side is reminding Alaric who he really is. Since leaving the Gilbert household, Alaric's been boozing it up, eating pizza, and passing out (pants open, boots on, shirt off). You could practically smell his rank apartment through the TV. While Elena uses the specific info Alaric has about Stefan and Klaus in Tennessee as an excuse to come over, what Elena really needs is Alaric's help and support, both as a weapon-making vampire slayer and as a friend and confidant. It's clear from their bantering in "The Hybrid" that these are two people who *know* each other. They've lived through crazy supernatural trauma and adventure together, they've mourned Jenna and worried about Jeremy, they've been annoyed and frustrated by Damon but ultimately care deeply for him, and they share the weird connection to Isobel. Alaric is already Elena's pseudo stepfather (as her birth mother's former husband) and stepped up as the adult-of-the-house after Jenna died. But when Elena gives him John Gilbert's ring and he finally accepts it, Alaric becomes an honorary Gilbert.

On their trek through the Smoky Mountains, Elena not only helps Alaric rediscover his purpose, but she leads Damon to a place where he's able to rediscover his own. It takes Stefan ripping the heart from a "hybrid zombie mountain man" for Damon to realize the truth of what Elena had told him that morning: Stefan would never give up on them, and they owe it to him not to give up either. The bond between the Salvatore brothers means that even when they're at odds, each would die saving the other; after Stefan killed Andie and told him to let him go, Damon felt that connection had been cut. But Stefan's actions speak louder than his words.

With so many ties to loved ones cut, Jeremy had been drifting, unsure of what to make of his spectral visitors. But with Vicki's request for help, Jeremy has a goal and purpose again. He seems more like his season 2 self, when he was involved in the gang's plans, as he springs into action, roping Matt into a world he keeps fighting to stay apart from. Given the piles of boxes of Vicki's stuff in the garage, it's evident that Matt just can't let go of his dead sister; his raw grief still sits right there on the surface, the possibility of contacting Vicki too painful to pursue. But ignoring grief won't make it go away, and the same holds true with ghosts: Vicki makes her presence known to Matt, and ultimately he reaches out to Jer and helps him contact Vicki. Despite the emotional risk, and the danger inherent in communication between the living and dead, both Matt and Jeremy feel bound to Vicki, a girl they both loved and understood better than anyone else.

Matt makes the distinction that Jeremy understood who Vicki was more than anyone else and loved her in spite of what others judged in her as "bad." It's a crucial lesson for Carol Lockwood in this episode, as her son reveals his true self to her and radically alters her closely held beliefs. Last season, when Brady and Jules were torturing Caroline, Tyler failed to stand up for her in a life-or-death moment, but here he wastes no time in confronting his mother despite the risk involved in outing himself. Instead of starting a fight with Carol, the leader of the anti-vampire council, he opens up to her as his mother and leads her to acceptance with a little monster show-and-tell. He counts on her unconditional love for him, and she does him proud by understanding that being a "monster" isn't what she once believed. If only all coming-out moments went this way!

Not all is so rosy in "The Hybrid": while some characters find strength and purpose in their connection to loved ones, others suffer the consequences of isolating themselves. Bill Forbes, a character Caroline fans were once eager to meet, proves to be emotionally distant; after the cliffhanger reveal that he is Caroline's dad, his earlier comments to Carol seem incredibly icy. Though he may live out of town, he is harboring some old-school Mystic Falls attitudes towards vampires.

Even when you're the oldest, meanest vampire in the history of time, the best-laid plans can go awry, and for Klaus, there is no greater failure than that of his much-ballyhooed hybrid army. His desire for an army so great that he'd be invincible seems to be about more than just self-preservation; once his rage has passed, Klaus seems almost broken. The price of being feared and powerful is isolation, and in Klaus's insistence that Stefan *enjoy* himself and stop whining, it seems that Stefan's true part to play is as much companion as foot soldier to the Original hybrid. It's incredibly entertaining to watch Stefan act the sullen, mouthy, put-upon underling to Klaus's leader. But by episode's end,

Stefan has obeyed Klaus's order to "lose the attitude" (at least temporarily); he supplicates to Klaus and is shown mercy — in the form of blood in beer. Klaus calls Stefan his only comrade, and it seems that next on his To Do list is getting Stefan to lose that self-loathing, brooding thing that Klaus can't abide.

Stefan could learn from the warning in Klaus's example; Stefan is isolating himself from those who keep his humanity alive (his brother and Elena) in order to protect them from Klaus. When the two brothers meet in the woods over a hybrid heart, Damon sees through Stefan's denial of late-night phone calls to Elena. Paul Wesley's a great actor, but Stefan? Not so much. Without saying much of anything, Stefan manages to give his brother purpose: he admonishes him for allowing Elena so close to Klaus (who still believes she died in the sacrifice), and Damon seems to be newly committed to protecting her while simultaneously finding a way to deliver Stefan home to her. But what will happen to Stefan as Damon continues to fill his former role in Elena's life? His "insufferable martyr" instincts mean isolation, and there's an even greater danger to Stefan if he loses the very people who make him human at heart.

Elena may be the impetus for much of the action in "The Hybrid," but Damon is the one forcing *her* to confront her feelings. Last episode, Elena called the "deathbed kissy thing" a goodbye, a relatively uncomplicated characterization of a fraught moment, but her conception of it could easily unravel if she continues to be more conscious of all the things Damon makes her feel. It's a messy situation, and one she readily admits to Alaric she's not in control of. Her Gilbert stubbornness and determination may not help her out in this situation.

COMPELLING MOMENT Elena bringing Alaric back into the Gilbert family fold.

CIRCLE OF KNOWLEDGE
- No Bonnie in this episode.
- In the season 2 DVD commentary for "Masquerade," Julie Plec and Kevin Williamson joked that in season 3 Carol Lockwood should drink more, and here she is starting her day with a glass of whiskey.
- Ray's werewolf pack gathers in the Smoky Mountains, a range along the Tennessee–North Carolina border, part of the Appalachian Mountains. Home to bobcats, coyotes, foxes, and the occasional mountain lion, that area is wolf-free — save for the supernatural variety.

- Matt tells Jeremy that he doesn't remember the last moment he had with Vicki before she was a vampire, when she was still his sister. . . . Seems like Matt hasn't let go of his perception of vampires as monsters, believing that vampire Vicki was no longer his "real" sister. That feeling likely extends to Caroline, that she's no longer the "real" Caroline with whom he fell in love.

THE RULES As a werewolf, Tyler has a keener sense of taste than humans, and he can detect the vervain laced in with the coffee at home and at the Grill. Making further use of his excellent online research skills, Jeremy discovers that family members and personal items help make a connection between the living and spirits. Because he was brought back from the dead, Jeremy can see and hear the ghosts, while Matt can't. In addition to making the lights flicker, the ghosts can move physical objects: Vicki's ghost sets the framed photo upright, and one of the ghosts smashes the backdoor at the Gilbert house.

Klaus's attempt to create more hybrids fails: instead of being "true hybrids" like him, he winds up with shivering, suffering, rabid, not-a-werewolf, not-yet-a-hybrid creatures, who die quickly. But, like Klaus, they can turn into wolf form even when the full moon is not at its apex (unlike a werewolf that only turns during the full moon).

HISTORY LESSON Stefan scoffs at Klaus's failed hybrids, calling them "some master race." It's a loaded term tied to Nazism, eugenics, and (closer to Stefan's own past in Civil War–era Virginia) slavery in the American South. Then, it was used to describe a white slave owner in relation to the person enslaved (the "master" to the "slave"), as well as in a boastful way to distinguish Southerners ("the master race") from the Northerners. Stefan's use of it is appropriate in both contexts: Klaus believes he's creating superior creatures, ones that will be dutiful to him (Stefan terms them slaves, while Klaus spins them as comrades or soldiers), and with this "master race," Klaus will have a loyal force so powerful he will be forever unchallenged. He will be the master of the master race. But his attempt is an utter, foaming-at-the-mouth failure.

PREVIOUSLY ON *THE VAMPIRE DIARIES* Unable to leave Klaus (or, at least, not without dire consequence), Stefan watches and listens as Damon and Elena passionately bicker, as Damon hustles her into Alaric's car; it's a nice echo of "The Sacrifice" when Stefan was trapped in the tomb with Katherine, listening to them fight in their heightened, emotional way. At the end of the episode, when Damon appears in Elena's room, she asks him if he's drunk; in "The Return," he was and, after she refused his pushy come-on, he snapped Jeremy's neck. When it comes to the ladies Tyler dates, Carol Lockwood is super judgmental: she compares Caroline to a prostitute in "The Hybrid," and back in "Family Ties" called Vicki Donovan trash. Bill Forbes makes his *Vampire Diaries* debut after only being mentioned in previous seasons: in "Family Ties," we learned that Caroline's dad had left Liz and had a boyfriend named Steven, and in "Let the Right One In," before the storm took Caroline on a dark detour, she was headed off to celebrate Steven's daughter's birthday. Raised to believe such things, Liz once felt the same way about Caroline's vampire status as Bill Forbes does, telling Matt in "The Last Day" that they're "monsters."

OFF CAMERA The childhood photo of Vicki and Matt (and a giant present) is actually of Kayla Ewell and her little brother. "My youngest brother, my real brother, looks so much like Zach — blond hair, blue eyes, same height," Kayla explained to HollywoodLife.com. "When I sent [the production team] the photos, they said, 'Instead of trying to superimpose Zach's head on these pictures, can we just use your brother?' [My brother] is so stoked. He keeps calling me, like, 'So, when do I premiere again? When am I on?'" Playing a ghost was a strange experience for Kayla Ewell: she had to be very aware of everything around her, so as not to touch it, as she didn't want Ghost Vicki to interact with the physical world in a way outside the "rules."

FOGGY MOMENTS Why didn't Damon just snap Ray's neck when he was all tied up and not yet turned into a wolf?

QUESTIONS
- Are Klaus's hybrids failing because Elena is still alive? How did Klaus successfully turn into a hybrid if her resurrection is the problem?
- Will Jeremy tell Matt what Vicki told him? Will he admit that he's also seeing Anna? What did Vicki mean about "coming back"?
- Why *is* Klaus keeping Stefan around?

> *Klaus (to Stefan): Thank you — I had forgotten*
> *what it was like to have a brother.*

3.03 *The End of the Affair*

Original air date: September 29, 2011
Written by: Caroline Dries
Directed by: Chris Grismer
Guest cast: Enisha Brewster (Young Gloria), Shane Callahan (Liam), Charmin Lee (Old Gloria), Christine Lekas (Lila)
Previously on *The Vampire Diaries*: Joseph Morgan

Klaus brings Stefan to Chicago to relive the Roaring Twenties, and Damon and Elena are in hot pursuit. Caroline's dad tortures her.

"You'll know when I want you to know." Klaus promised Stefan in "The Hybrid" to reveal his purpose when he was good and ready, and in "The End of the Affair" Stefan and us viewers at home finally understand why Klaus never considered sacrificing him in lieu of Jenna in "The Sun Also Rises"; why he demanded his service in exchange for saving his brother's life in "As I Lay Dying"; why Klaus objected to Stefan's faking-it attitude in "The Birthday." They used to be the best of friends, delightfully devilish "brothers" together in an era made famous for widespread indulgence in bad behavior.

In a series that loves a good flashback episode, "The End of the Affair" is its most stylish trip back through time, and one that doesn't skimp on story in the presence of all that sparkle. Across the various narrative threads, the episode explores torment in the name of love — from the physical torture of a daughter to "fix" her, to the cruel dismissive words from Stefan to Elena, to the titular end of the affair back in the '20s when Klaus cut both himself and his sister off from their beloved Ripper Stefan. In a delightfully strange parallel, both Elena and Klaus have lost the Stefan they once had and want nothing more than their memory of him to be real again, for who he was to be who he is — and neither one of them is happy. Can a person be changed? Can the old self be brought back?

The flashback allows us to experience firsthand why Klaus has such a vested interest in Stefan: we get to witness his ripper skills and see the friendship as Klaus did. The good-boy vampire Elena fell in love with used to *want* to be Klaus's wingman — and he was great at it. But more significantly, both

men were happy to find brotherhood with each other, having lost that with their actual brothers. As the audience is exposed to the past, these memories of true friendship are also a revelation to Stefan, who can't remember his own history. The episode plays with ideas of memory, weaving the flashbacks and present day scenes, and by doing so it explores the concept of an unstable identity, which has been the heart of Stefan's struggle since season 1. Is the real Stefan the one Klaus remembers or the one Elena knows? Can Stefan be

The End of the Affair

The End of the Affair is the title of a 1951 novel by Graham Greene, which has twice been adapted for film, in 1955 and in 1999. The story centers on the love Sarah (played by Julianne Moore in the '99 version) has for her husband, Henry (Stephen Rea), and for her lover, Maurice (Ralph Fiennes). Using flashbacks between the years of World War II and the aftermath of the war in England, the story explores the nature of love, faith, and jealousy in the affair between Sarah and Maurice and its titular end. As in "The End of the Affair," the story moves back and forth through time and shifts between characters' perspectives to reveal forgotten or misunderstood moments. Sarah believes that she must cast off Maurice, end things in order to save him. She believes he has died in a bomb blast, and she makes a promise in prayer to end the affair with him if only he lives. When he does, she rejects him. She acts out of love, like Stefan with Elena and Damon to protect them from Klaus, and Klaus does with Stefan (and in a twisted way, Rebekah) to protect them from the mysterious man the Original siblings run from.

But left in the dark about her true motivation, Maurice believes that Sarah's love for him has died, and he becomes bitter and fueled by jealousy. Maurice thinks of his neediness and obsessive behavior as signs of the ferocity of his love; Sarah, on the other hand, firmly believes that love is a kind of faith, something everlasting even if it cannot be expressed. She says, "Love doesn't end just because we don't see each other." It's a important sentiment for many characters in this episode of *The Vampire Diaries*: Klaus has been dragging Stefan around for months, hoping that the brotherly love once shared between them will bloom again; Rebekah and Stefan's love didn't die but was forced into hibernation by Klaus compelling his comrade and daggering his sister; Stefan pushes away Elena to protect her from Klaus. Both Sarah and Maurice experience a feeling of death in living without the person they love and having to repress that love.

There is also a parallel in the coda of the film, which emphasizes the bond that exists between two men who love the same woman and who lose her. In *The End of the Affair*, the husband, Henry, and the lover, Maurice, become friends. The brothers Salvatore both love Elena, but will hopefully never have to let her go as Henry and Maurice must let go of Sarah.

sure of who he is when he's spent the last 90 years with a significant piece of his memory missing?

As is often the case with *TVD*, the audience is aligned with Elena's point-of-view: we thought we knew what the good ol' ripper days were like. We had witnessed the events of "Under Control" and "Miss Mystic Falls," "The

Dinner Party" flashback as well as a few of Stefan's recent kills. We could handle it. But there was something delightfully different about the Stefan of the '20s; it's no wonder that Rebekah fell in love with him or that Klaus was his number one fan. His confidence, his control, his relish in twisted torture made him a villain that another villain could admire. (And, oh, the tuxedoes.) With a mixture of fascination and delight, Klaus watches Stefan compel that man to drink his wife's blood. Stefan's the kind of "sick freak" Klaus could open up to, and Stefan returned that confidence, telling him about his ritual of recording victims' names to later relive the kills. When you're a thousand years old, that kind of kinship must be hard to find; Klaus seems earnest when he thanks Stefan for his companionship (before compelling him to forget it). In the past, they were two of a kind — relishing the fun, the power, the solidarity of brotherhood — and it speaks to the deadliness of the threat posed by that mysterious man Klaus was running from that he was willing to let Stefan go . . . but never forget him.

"The End of the Affair" doesn't rest on just one amazing backstory revelation, but introduces us to a much-anticipated character: a new Original, little sister Rebekah. A firecracker who makes her grand entrance by *licking the blood off Stefan's mouth* (and later telling him to put a sock in it), Claire Holt's Rebekah commands attention and we understand why Stefan fell for her. Klaus warns Stefan that Rebekah will love him and then leave him, but Rebekah shows a commitment to Stefan that even Klaus didn't expect; tired of running, Rebekah chooses love — a vampire's greatest weakness — and is daggered for punishment. It's an interesting glimpse into the Original sibling dynamics: these two were clearly on the lam together for ages, but Klaus treated her like his subordinate to be commanded, not his equal. He does not accept willfulness in his family members, as his coffin collection attests. Klaus was himself made to feel like an abomination for being half-vampire, half-werewolf, and that makes his "elitist" comment about Rebekah having pure vampire blood seem to stem from his own feeling of inferiority. But Stefan helps him to realize that being near invincible is not something to be ashamed of, but to be proud of. He's a king. What a good pal that Ripper Stefan is.

Bill Forbes' could take a page from the Ripper's diary when it comes to acceptance. He can't change Caroline, no matter how determined he is to "fix" her. Like trying to train the "ultra-violence" out of Alex in *A Clockwork Orange*, Bill tries negative association, conditioning Caroline so that the thought of human blood will be connected with searing pain, forcing Caroline to repress her monstrous thirst for blood. He reminds her, and us, that her ancestors were staunchly anti-vampire (and quite ingenious to put vervain in the ventilation system of that torture chamber), and that her existence as a vampire is a blight on the family name that must be fixed or removed. Caroline tries to get her dad to understand that she doesn't hurt anyone, that she handles her urges, just as she ultimately was able to convince her mother. Candice Accola again breaks our hearts — with her screams of agony as Caroline is burned again and again, and with her vulnerability and brokenness at the end of the episode as she mourns her lost connection with her dad. Her father "got" her, and now he hates her. Bill wants to force her to be what she *used* to be (human), but she can only be who she is, a moral vampire; how is that any worse than being an immoral human? Bill believes he's hurting her because he loves her, but thankfully Liz models what love in action should look like. Fiercely protective of Caroline, Liz Forbes is *totally* making up for her subpar sheriffing of days gone by. While it's incredibly difficult to watch Caroline tortured (again) these scenes are stunningly filmed and scored, and provide a nice visual counterpoint to the glitz of the 1920s flashbacks.

With a vastly different approach, Elena, too, is trying to "fix" a vampire she loves and finds herself unsuccessful at the end of the day. Bill Forbes tried to repress the monster in Caroline, but Elena's trying to bring back the human in Stefan. And she's way out of her league. In the past Elena's done her best to keep up with the insanity thrown her way, and when Stefan went off the rails in season 1 she managed to bring him back to himself. But her old tricks fail her. He is stronger, much deeper into the darkness, and the stakes are higher. Elena skims through Stefan's diary and decides that saving him from his ripper self is still a possibility because of Lexi's past successes. But more than ever, Elena's faith in Stefan seems naive and his cruel words crush her, seemingly signaling the end to their love affair. But again, that torment stems from love. He emphasizes that things have irrevocably changed between them, because he has murdered so many times. And though Elena *knows* that, it's unclear if she truly understands.

In a scene that was so completely rich with symbolism, the two separate sides of Stefan are trapped together: Elena hides in the closet, clutching his diaries, up against the list of his victims' names and bottles full of human blood. He will have to choose which part of himself to free and which to let go of, and, in that tense moment, he protects Elena from being discovered. As Damon says to him, "Good? Bad? Pick one." When Stefan orders Elena to stay away from him, he is still protecting her from Klaus — preventing the Original from discovering that she's alive and exacting revenge, from hunting down her necklace. But the already complex situation got even more nuanced with his memory restored: Stefan now knows all of what he once felt for Klaus, that brotherhood and kinship, and all that he felt for Rebekah. Even the necklace has an unknown history of its own: it's not just the symbol of Stefan and Elena's love, but a millennium-old artifact given to Rebekah by the Original Witch that possesses some magical property. Will this trip down memory lane change Stefan?

COMPELLING MOMENT The revelation that Klaus and Stefan were once the best of friends. It's such a brilliant twist, one that seemed to come out of nowhere but made past events and characters' motivations click perfectly into place.

CIRCLE OF KNOWLEDGE
* No Bonnie, Matt, Jeremy, or Alaric.
* Damon says Klaus and Stefan are not in Chicago to meet Oprah; *Oprah*, the longest-running daytime TV series, was filmed in the Windy City for 25 seasons before its end in May 2011.
* The diary entry that Damon began reading to Elena continues, "I feel alive again. There are no rules here. Nothing matters anymore. Chicago is a place teeming with life and pulsing with people I have only imagined meeting, drinking with as well as enjoying. There is a woman who is so intriguing. She has lovely [. . .] hair and is such a [. . .] dancer. AND [. . .]" Presumably Stefan goes on to say this lovely lady, Rebekah, is a vampire.
* Bill Forbes tortures Caroline in an attempt to make her repress her vampire instincts. What he's doing is a form of aversion therapy: a patient is simultaneously exposed to the stimulus (in Caroline's case, human blood) and to a negative sensation (the burning sunlight) in order to develop a fixed association in the patient's mind between suffering and the stimulus. Once the association is strong enough, the patient ceases that behavior to avoid the suffering. In real-life modern aversion therapy,

Claire Holt as Rebekah

"That character was obviously meant to make a splash. I mean, when we introduced her she gets to walk in and lick blood off Stefan's mouth. Hello. Her entrance was pretty powerful," said Julie Plec of Claire Holt's debut as Rebekah. "She has this great presence. She's a mean girl without being unlikable, she's tough without being too aggressive, she's vulnerable without being a sap. Everything about her is so fun to watch. [Claire] also happens to be a very nice person offscreen, which is always a bonus."

The future Original sister Claire Rhiannon Holt, born in 1988 in Brisbane, Australia, was a competitive water polo player in her teen years, studied tae-kwon-do, and loves sports. Claire took acting classes during her teen years at Stuartholme School, as well as privately. It was just one year after she graduated in 2005 that she landed her first big role, one she's still widely recognized for: Emma Gilbert, the accidental mermaid in the Australian kids show *H2O: Just Add Water*, which had a huge audience — 100 million viewers in over 100 countries. Her experience playing competitive water polo and her love for swimming helped her during the physically demanding shoot of playing a mermaid. After leaving her fish tail behind after two seasons of *H20*, Claire relocated to the U.S. and landed roles in a couple of movie sequels, *Messengers 2* and *Mean Girls 2*, and an independent film *Blue like Jazz* (released in 2012). She returned to TV with recurring roles as Emily's love interest Samara in season 2 of *Pretty Little Liars* and Rebekah on *The Vampire Diaries*.

Luckily for the Australian transplant, her friend from *H20*, Phoebe Tonkin, also made the leap to Hollywood and landed a role on *Vampire Diaries* sister show *The Secret Circle* as the delightfully badass Faye. But before Claire was cast as Rebekah, there was a chance the girls would share the small screen again. Claire explained, "At the beginning of the year [2011], I had tested for another pilot that Kevin Williamson had created, and so I did a bunch of auditions for that. It was *The Secret Circle*, with my best friend, Phoebe. It would have been a little reunion, but that show is perfect for her and I love *The Vampire Diaries* and we're both super happy with how things have turned out, so it's great." Meeting a new member of the Original family was a big deal for the *TVD* fandom, but Claire has more than proven she can hold her own opposite her onscreen brothers.

milder negative associations are more frequently used — bad smells, tastes — to combat addiction issues, but in the mid-20th century electric shocks were used. It's an ironic choice for Bill Forbes: shock therapy was used on homosexuals in an attempt to "cure" them of what was

judged as perverse behavior. But as Caroline tells her (gay) father, "That's impossible. Daddy, you can't change who I am."

- Gloria's first song is the standard "St. James Infirmary" (famously recorded by Louis Armstrong in 1928), an appropriately morbid choice for a vampire-infested club. The song's narrator goes to the St. James Infirmary to find his girl lying dead on a morgue table, "so cold, so sweet, so fair," before describing how he'd like to be outfitted for his own burial.

- Damon tells Elena he was also in Chicago in the 1920s, indulging in a few Daisy Buchanans of his own. In *The Great Gatsby* (1925), Daisy is a blond as beautiful as Rebekah and the object of Jay Gatsby's affections. *TVD* has referenced *Gatsby* before: in "Haunted," Carol Lockwood dressed up as Daisy Buchanan, and in "You're Undead to Me," Stefan named the book as one of his favorites. Perhaps he had a subconscious inkling that, like Gatsby, he spent the Roaring Twenties with a good pal named Nick before the raucous times came to a crashing end.

- In order to delay the revelation that Elena's necklace was once Rebekah's, it is tucked into the neckline of her dress in her first scene.

- As we learned in "Klaus," the Original vampire's name is actually Niklaus, and in the '20s he went by "Nik." That choice allowed the writers to let Elena read Stefan's 1920s diary without her clueing into the fact that Stefan used to be besties with Klaus.

- In "The Last Day," Klaus told Damon that he'd heard about him, "the crazy, impulsive vampire." In all likelihood, it was *Stefan* who told Klaus about Damon.

- In a classic *Vampire Diaries* structure, the episode is bookended, this time with Katherine. In the opener, she mocks Damon by telling him she's lurking outside his window, pining away for him. In the final flashback, she is doing just that to Stefan in the 1920s, and in the present she is tailing him and Klaus in Chicago.

THE RULES With herbs and spells, Gloria has managed to slow down the aging process and extend her lifetime. Gloria needs the necklace the Original Witch gave to Rebekah in order to contact her; as previously established, a personal artifact helps a witch (or someone like Jeremy) make a connection to the dead. Gloria reminds us that spells have loopholes. The curse, which was placed on Niklaus by the Original Witch, may have a loophole as yet undiscovered that is preventing him from successfully creating hybrids. Rebekah knows that the dagger won't work on Klaus because of his hybrid status (and she didn't coat it in white oak ash anyway), but she still stabs her older brother with it.

HISTORY LESSON Klaus takes us back to his time with Stefan in Chicago in the 1920s, an era often resurrected onscreen thanks to its romance, high stakes, and great style. The 18th Constitutional Amendment, enacted in 1920, led to the Prohibition era in the United States, which lasted until 1933. While the consumption and manufacture of alcohol were prohibited, an organized crime racket sprung up to fill the demand for bootlegged booze; in Chicago, the Outfit crime syndicate was soon run by Al Capone, the most notorious gangster of all. Since this is *TVD*, instead of a mob-controlled bar, Original vampires hold court in a speakeasy, but they're still subject to an aggressive police raid. Despite Prohibition and the extreme punishments for breaking the law, hundreds of bars stayed open in Chicago, often outfitted with a peephole on the door (as we see when Stefan enters) and no signage out front. Jazz music spread through these speakeasies, and different societal groups mixed and mingled in a new way. It was a period of social change, and women got the vote in 1920 with the 19th Constitutional Amendment. Rebekah wonderfully encapsulates all the shimmer and boldness of flappers, the era's famous women whose then-shocking fashion was only one way in which they threw off societal expectations of female behavior. Rebekah approaches a strange man, is sexually aggressive, isn't afraid to speak her mind, dates outside her "class" (with a non-Original vampire), and stands up to her older brother — qualities familiar for a modern woman, but daring for those in the 1920s.

PREVIOUSLY ON *THE VAMPIRE DIARIES* At the 1960s Decade Dance in "The Last Dance," AlariKlaus told Elena and Bonnie that he loved the '20s — the style, the parties, the jazz; he left out the bromance with Stefan. The first name on Stefan's victim list is Giuseppe Salvatore; it was his father's blood that turned him ("Blood Brothers"). Elena tries to replicate the move she had success with in "Miss Mystic Falls": while embracing Stefan, she pulls a vervain dart on him. But this time Stefan catches her. *Fool me once . . .* Just as Rose, Trevor, and Katherine were on the run from Klaus ("Rose," "Katerina"), Klaus and Rebekah are on the run from someone themselves — the mysterious man who shows up at the end. In "Masquerade," Katherine told Stefan that she spied on him and Lexi in Chicago in 1987 (at a Bon Jovi concert, naturally); here she spies on him in the Windy City far earlier than that.

OFF CAMERA Young Gloria is played by Enisha Brewster, who began her professional career in musical and theater productions in Atlanta; she played Etta in the 2011 *Footloose* remake. Charmin Lee brings modern-day Gloria to life; best known for her role on *Girlfriends* as Maya's mother, Charmin has been acting in film and television since the early '90s.

FOGGY MOMENTS The time it takes a vampire to burn to death in the sunlight varies, depending on plot necessity. In "Know Thy Enemy," Isobel went up in flames almost instantly and died (and most of her skin was covered under her coat), but here Caroline is able to survive long doses of daylight. (Maybe because Caroline's personality is made of pure sunshine?) The necklace Elena wears was originally Rebekah's. In "Rose," Elijah looked at it and then yanked it off Elena's neck (so he could compel her). Shouldn't he have recognized it, if his sister always used to wear it? Klaus compels Stefan to forget about him and Rebekah, and it works — but how does it work with the events that Stefan recorded in his diary? If he read the Klefan-era entries, would Stefan immediately forget their contents and chalk up the holes in his memory to ripper blood-binge blackouts?

QUESTIONS

- How will Rebekah fit in with 21st-century Klaus and Stefan? For her, no time has passed; presumably she's as in love with Stefan as she was the moment Klaus killed her. Will she forgive her brother for daggering her? Or will she remove the daggers from her other family members who didn't choose Klaus's side?

- Who was the man looking for Klaus and Rebekah? When Rebekah is waiting for Stefan, Klaus says to her, "Do you want to die? We have to move," meaning that whoever "he" is, he has the ability to kill an Original. And when he asks Stefan about Klaus and Rebekah, he compels him, suggesting that he is himself an Original.

- Does Katherine realize the significance of the necklace? Did she know the whole time (i.e., during season 2's events) that Nik and Stefan used to be "brothers"? That Stefan and Rebekah were an item? What is she up to in following Klaus and Stefan?

> *Caroline: Daddy? I'm gonna be okay.*
> *Bill: You're a vampire, sweetheart. I don't think you'll ever be okay again.*

3.04 *Disturbing Behavior*

Original air date: October 6, 2011
Written by: Brian Young
Directed by: Wendey Stanzler
Guest cast: Charmin Lee (Gloria)
Previously on *The Vampire Diaries*: Paul Wesley

Gloria forces Stefan's secrets from him, Damon misbehaves at a Lockwood bar-becue, and Bonnie returns home to a haunted boyfriend.

Bill Forbes may be the least popular guy in Mystic Falls, but his presence has brought an important idea to the forefront of the series: his experiments in behavioral modification (on himself and on his poor daughter) raise the question of whether or not someone *can* change, whether willfully or by force. How powerful is the mind in either repressing or overpowering innate urges and emotional impulses?

Bill is able to resist Damon's sloppy compulsion and, over in the Windy City, Stefan fights with all his power to resist Gloria's magic — to keep the secret that Elena has the necklace and that the doppelgänger lives, two pieces of information that Stefan is desperate to hide from Klaus. There are certain truths Stefan can't help from revealing, and his love for Elena is one of them. In a harrowing witchcraft torture scene, Gloria draws the truth from him despite his valiant fight. His humanity is his downfall: it's what always keeps him from being a master manipulator like Katherine. She wanted in on Stefan's diabolical plan, and judging by how it's turned out so far, he could have used her help — and not just to save his life. Never shy to "switch Salvatores" like her doppelgänger is, Katherine has her own master plan afoot.

In the aftermath of Stefan's cruel dismissal of her in Chicago, Elena is holding it together under the watchful eyes of Alaric, Damon, and her two best friends. Instead of facing her emotions — her grief over the Stefan situation, or the ever-changing Damon dynamic — Elena is compelling herself to pretend everything is peachy-keen. Led by the always-blunt Ms. Caroline Forbes, in "Disturbing Behavior" Elena is forced to face her emotional reality. She knows she's trying to fit Damon into the Stefan-shaped hole in her life,

Jack Coleman as Bill Forbes

Born in Pennsylvania, Jack Coleman began his professional career working in the theater in New York, before landing gigs on soap operas. After a year on *Days of Our Lives*, Jack took over the part of Steven Carrington on *Dynasty* and stayed in the role for five years until 1988. The gay character "was quite daring at the time," said Coleman to *TV Guide*, but the portrayal now "seems unbelievably quaint." Throughout the 1990s and early 2000s, Coleman worked on many series, TV movies, and films. He described that string of roles: "I don't play a lot of convicts or Mafia guys. I'm usually a professional, a doctor, lawyer, banker . . . that kind of thing. . . . There's nothing worse than playing a milquetoast. I'm happy to play a jerk, and I'm happy to play a bad guy. It really is fun to be able to play somebody who has a dark, sinister side." Jack gained a whole new following in 2006 with his role on *Heroes* as Noah Bennet — better known as HRG, or Horn-Rimmed Glasses. As the sinister man on a mission sidetracked only by the soft spot he has for his super-powered daughter, Claire (Hayden Panettiere), Coleman created a memorable character. That success led to other high-profile gigs — *The Office*, for example — once *Heroes* wrapped in 2010. From *House* to *The Mentalist*, *Entourage* to *Criminal Minds*, Coleman continues to pop up on TV screens, and his time in Mystic Falls might feel familiar as he plays father to another blond cheerleader with supernatural abilities.

and at the same time is terrified of what kind of person she would be if she admitted that she's attracted to Damon. Elena keeps her emotions under very tight control — how else can she weather the tragedies and trauma thrown her way? — and while questions of who she wants to be, and who she wants to be with, are banging down her door, Elena doesn't seem ready to tackle those big questions of identity. It's challenging enough to make chili for the barbecue.

While she's not ready to change herself (or acknowledge the change that's already taken place), she does try to make Damon behave according to her idea of right and wrong (and she has the law on her side: murder = bad). There's a push and pull to their relationship, and Damon follows in his tradition of pushing back hard when he feels he's being forced to be someone he's not. He isn't Stefan; he *likes* being a vampire. He loves feeding and hunting and terrorizing; his satisfaction is palpable when he drinks from Bill Forbes after far too long sipping on blood bags. In season 2, Damon struggled with who he wanted to be, who Elena wanted him to be and her expectations of him. Though it's hard not to share in Elena and Alaric's disappointment in his selfish willfulness, it's hardly surprising.

In "Disturbing Behavior" Damon lets it be known that his Damonness should not be underestimated: don't tell him what he will or won't do, don't make assumptions about how self-destructive he can be. Acting a little brattier than usual, Damon decides he's sick and tired of being Stefan's stand-in. If he thinks it's a good idea to teach Bill Forbes a lesson, he will. If Alaric's in his way, he'll snap his neck, no hard feelings. Damon's own behavioral modification is his reaction to the pressure of having that Stefan-shaped hole in his life. He's evolved into a funny mix of Old Damon, the one who arrived in Mystic Falls mocking everything and killing at will, and New Damon, protecting those he's grown to care about. He stands up to Bill Forbes for Caroline in a perfectly Damon way: one that mocks Caroline (calling her annoying) and goes against her wishes while still defending her, a person he respects (in his own Damony way). But the elder Salvatore is met with nothing but rejection to his grand-standing: Elena argues with him, Caroline beats him up, and Alaric refuses his make-up morning cocktail. With Katherine arriving at his doorstep looking for a partner in crime, Damon can "take a beat" from Mystic Falls.

Just as Damon is pushing away, Alaric has finally reached his own breaking point — and it's his neck being snapped one time too many. He knows he shouldn't be disregarded and temporarily killed by his best friend, just because Damon can. After moving back to the Gilberts' in "The Hybrid," Alaric takes further steps in establishing who he wants to be: not only guardian of Jeremy and Elena, but to the people of Mystic Falls by forcing his way onto the council. Though Bill Forbes is incredibly misguided in his methods, what he says about the council and the well-being of the residents of Mystic Falls is right on the money, and Alaric understands that. Assuming the role of the Gilbert family representative, Alaric could use his unique position as a supernatural insider without compromised personal interests, in the way that Sheriff Forbes and Mayor Lockwood have. It's a strong move for a character who not very long ago was seemingly satisfied with being an accomplished day-drinker and nothing else.

Caroline also stands up for herself in "Disturbing Behavior," shutting down two men who have pushed her around and hurt her. No matter what the universe throws at Caroline Forbes (and it throws a lot), she manages to stay true to herself, which is never more apparent than in how she handles her father in this episode. He's physically tortured her and judged her in a fundamental

way, and she still loves him; he's still her dad. She doesn't hesitate to come to his rescue, and, in the town square as he's headed out of town, she's brave enough to give him a proper goodbye. Of course, since this is *The Vampire Diaries*, there is no simple, sweet closure of Daddy and daughter reunited; instead Bill Forbes tells Caroline that she'll never be okay again. And while that may be true to a certain extent — the human life she had, the girl she once was is gone — Caroline is denied the understanding she deserves from her dad, the parent who used to get her. As Anna tells Jeremy about their connection between the worlds, a relationship is a two-way street, and Caroline alone can't bridge the distance between her and her father. Just as he couldn't torture the vampire out of her, she can't change what her father believes if he's not open to understanding.

The explanation that Anna provides about the way she's able to communicate with Jeremy from the Other Side provides a great metaphor for all the relationships on the show: it's a push-pull dynamic where both sides need to be engaged in order for it to work. In order to see Anna, Jeremy has to *want* to, and with his unresolved feelings for her, he does; she's constantly in his thoughts. His past relationship is literally haunting him, a situation that's made incredibly complicated with the return of his living, breathing witch girlfriend. It's heartbreaking to see the fear and isolation Anna suffers; she's all alone on the Other Side, at Jeremy's inadvertent beck and call. But Jeremy has to own up to the truth, and in the struggle between the past and present, he chooses Bonnie and honesty.

Though Stefan thinks he's carefully guarding his own secret, and masterfully playing the two Originals, Rebekah's uncanny ability to always know when Stefan's lying outs him as a would-be traitor, a sidekick with a mutinous plot brewing. Klaus may claim not to be angry, just curious about what it is that Stefan is holding on to from his old life, but will our vengeful Original be so calm when he discovers Stefan's secrets? The doppelgänger lives, and, after she tried so desperately to bring Stefan home, Klaus has gone and done that for her. Welcome home, Stefan.

COMPELLING MOMENT Caroline taking charge of the situation where both men are acting foolishly: she beats up Damon, and she rescues her dad and tells him to "grow up." Long live Caroline Forbes.

CIRCLE OF KNOWLEDGE
- No Matt Donovan in this episode.
- This episode has no "cold open": the title card is straight after the "Previously on *The Vampire Diaries*" recap, instead of after the usual three or four minutes.
- *Disturbing Behavior* is a 1998 thriller about teenage Scott (James Marsden), who moves to a new town with his family only to discover that the do-gooder clique at the high school, the Blue Ribbons, are being reprogrammed by a neuropharmacologist intent on "fixing" teens' naughty behavior. As Scott and his bad-girl love interest Rachel (Katie Holmes) discover, the mind-altered teens lose their perfect attitudes when violent or lustful urges come upon them (which happens, like, daily), and the movie climaxes with a faceoff between evil jocks and a kooky janitor.
- Gloria uses a number of herbs to assist her in rooting out Stefan's secret, among them vervain (to cause him pain), witch hazel (long ago thought to have powers of divination), and Diviner's Sage, or *salvia divinorum*, a plant with hallucinogenic properties.
- Damon makes explicit the irony of Bill Forbes — a gay man who not so long ago came out to his wife, daughter, and small-town community — trying to "fix" his daughter's vampirism and out the rest of the vampires to the council.
- There are four coffins in the back of the truck that arrives in Mystic Falls, down one from the five seen in "As I Lay Dying" and "The End of the Affair" (now that Rebekah has been undaggered). Elijah is in one of the coffins; who are in the other three?

THE RULES It is possible to resist vampire compulsion, as Bill Forbes is able to do after decades of honing that skill with "human focus." Instead of using an object to trace a person, Gloria uses a person, Rebekah, to trace an object, the necklace. Later, Gloria puts Stefan under a paralysis spell to keep him still while she extracts the information she needs from him. Using herbs and by drawing Stefan's blood, Gloria is able to access his spirit or essence and find out what she needs to know about the necklace and Elena. The necklace has magic of its own and was a talisman of the Original Witch. On the Other Side, a ghost can see and hear the living world but is otherwise isolated. A medium, like Jeremy or a witch, has to reach out and the ghost has to respond, a push and pull from either side of the living-dead divide.

PREVIOUSLY ON *THE VAMPIRE DIARIES* Stefan tells Katherine he has it "under control," and as we learned in "Under Control," when Stefan says that, he means the opposite. The brief moment of Anna lying in bed next to Jeremy was reminiscent of their quiet goodbye moment in "Blood Brothers." As Gloria tortures Stefan for information, the montage contains Elena moments from "The Turning Point," "Friday Night Bites," "Crying Wolf," "The Last Days," and "The Sacrifice." Alaric also gave Damon a talking-to about the rules of their friendship in "The Dinner Party," demanding respect and honesty.

FOGGY MOMENTS As the mayor's son, and a founding family member, Tyler didn't have to attend the party held at his own house? Lucky.

QUESTIONS
- How does Bill practice resisting vampire compulsion? Does he know a friendly vampire? Has he been compelled before?
- Why is the Gilbert ring taking longer to resurrect Alaric? Does it expire from overuse?
- Now that she has the necklace and Damon in tow, what is Katherine's master plan?
- Is Vicki really a danger, or is that just Anna's feeling from the "darkness" that appears when Jeremy sees her?
- Is it significant that the grimoires lit on fire when Bonnie and Jeremy were investigating the necklace?

*Klaus: The only thing stronger than your craving for blood is
your love for this one girl. Why don't you turn it off?*

3.05 *The Reckoning*

Original air date: October 13, 2011
Written by: Michael Narducci
Directed by: John Behring
Guest cast: Mark Buckland (Chad), Vicki Eng (Nurse), Anna Enger (Dana)
Previously on *The Vampire Diaries*: Zach Roerig

*Klaus hijacks senior prank night at Mystic Falls High, forcing Bonnie and Matt
to find a way to save Tyler and forcing Stefan to turn off his humanity.*

Other TV series take much longer than four episodes of a season to build
up to the kind of no-holds-barred onslaught that "The Reckoning" delivers,
but *TVD* dives right in. In an impressive display of villainy, Klaus is the
perfect puppet master, forcing the seniors to play their parts in the ultimate
prank on Tyler. He demands solutions to his hybrid and ripper problems,
and in doing so brings terror to the high school, a setting that has long
represented the normalcy the seniors are denied outside its walls — made
particularly true this time following Caroline's "let's make memories" plea.
By bringing the action inside the halls of Mystic Falls High School again,
the writers also bring all its history — the other showdowns, the past relationships — adding layers to the current events for the characters and for
the audience at home. "The Reckoning" is a standout episode of the season,
one that manages to display *The Vampire Diaries*' strengths all at once as it
explores the key themes of the series and hits its signature tone (the one that
makes viewers feel *all* the feelings and tweet with capslock on).

The Vampire Diaries is known for its fast pace, and this episode wastes
no time at all: Klaus nabs Elena before the title card. But its speed and the
relentless tick-tock of the gym clock don't mean a reckless plot; the writers
are at their cleverest here, pushing the mythology forward, changing the
relationships between characters, and defying our expectations in ways that,
once twists are revealed, make total sense.

Tragedy and heroism are often intertwined in Mystic Falls, and "The
Reckoning" gives us an unlikely hero in Matt Donovan. The episode begins

with his isolation: he's all alone in the workout room in the seemingly empty school, his quiet fortitude the perfect encapsulation of just how bleak life is for Matt. The spooky noises he hears could be one of the supernatural creatures that he knows haunts his town, it could be the ghost of his dead sister, or (as it turned out to be) it could be his best friends in the world having fun without him. Though Matt idealizes last summer when, as he tells Bonnie, he only had two problems (Elena breaking up with him, and being terrible at CPR), his life has long been challenging and lonely. Then he was living with his wild-child sister, rarely seeing his mom, and had a long AWOL father. His decision to kill himself and have Bonnie bring him back in order to speak to Vicki and save Tyler plays on two important aspects of Matt's character, his deep melancholy and his willingness to help his loved ones, no matter what. His sacrifice is both selfless (to save Tyler) and tragically selfish: he just wants to say goodbye to his sister. The solution Matt comes up with to their ghost-communication problem is, fittingly, incredibly human: you don't need magic to bring someone back to life. But because of his choice and Bonnie's excellent lifeguarding skills, Matt is now linked to the Other Side. He can see Vicki, and the moment he does is intensely emotional. Since its beginning, *The Vampire Diaries* has been a show centered on grief, loss, and family, and this moment between the Donovan siblings encapsulates that.

The climax of the episode brings that mix of tragedy and heroism to new heights in the battle of wills between Stefan and Klaus. Klaus dragged Stefan back to Mystic Falls to take him to task for his betrayal. The Originals live by a code of honor: Klaus has stuck to his promise and not killed Damon, but Stefan has not been true to his word and Klaus seems deeply disappointed in him for that. Because of their past connection, seen in "The End of the Affair," Klaus wanted Stefan to earnestly *want* to be loyal, and Stefan managed to play the part well enough that all summer long Klaus never resorted to compulsion. Everything Klaus asked of Stefan, he did, including murdering countless people, but Klaus catches him in his lie: there was one thing that was holding him back. His love for Elena, the ultimate sign of his humanity. For months, Stefan has fought to hold on to his humanity despite the powerful draw of his ripper side and all the intoxicating blood that comes with it. In a powerful scene, Elena finally gets angry at Stefan. What he owes her, and the strength of their love, is powerful enough for Stefan to resist compulsion. And Stefan tries, the poor guy, physically restraining himself and ready to stake himself. He displays great heroism and fortitude but Klaus is stronger. His wrath and will overpower Stefan; he destroys Stefan's defiant love for Elena, his need to protect her from harm. Now Stefan *will* do whatever Klaus asks of him, and worst of all, he'll enjoy it. As Klaus says to Elena in the gym, "I invited him to the party. He's the one dancing on the table."

In a classic *TVD* twist, Klaus's hypothesis that Elena's survival has been the hitch in his plan turns out to be false; her blood is the key, the missing ingredient to his hybrid experimentation. It's an elegant solution that keeps Elena relevant to the mythology of the show; after all, her role as "the doppelgänger that must be sacrificed" was wrapped up last season. Instead of wanting her dead, Klaus needs Elena alive, and human, in order to create his long-dreamed-of hybrid army. His choice of Stefan as her protector is the finishing touch on an episode's worth of dastardly and smart choices for the villainous Klaus. As much as his rage against Stefan's defiance is heartfelt and his desire for a hybrid army is primarily motivated by a deep sense of loneliness, Klaus is not one to let his emotions rule him. But he cannot resist having a little fun in doling out his punishments for the lies and betrayal perpetrated against him, and it makes for incredibly entertaining television.

Elena has long had the Salvatore brothers as her protectors, but in "The Reckoning" she finds herself abandoned: Damon's out of town and Stefan's only able to restrain himself so long before he becomes her attacker. The relationships between them are once again twisted. In the scene in the Salvatore library, Damon's touching pledge to never leave Elena's side again is nicely undercut by Stefan's arrival. Instead of being hurt by Damon and Elena's closeness, he is amused by it. The brothers are still her protectors, but Stefan no longer cares about her or her feelings.

Damon chose to leave town at end of the previous episode, but his road trip with Katherine is immediately frustrating (and not just sexually frustrating for poor Katherine). She knows that keeping Damon from returning to Elena will require some work, and she tries multiple ways to get him distant enough: with literal distance, by stealing his phone, by coming on to him in the car, and by reasoning with him about the long-term benefit of raising Mikael instead of running back to Mystic Falls. But he turns back. There is no bigger picture if Elena is dead. Just as Klaus sees Stefan's love for Elena as the thing that's wrong with him, that needs "fixing," Katherine sees Damon's devotion to Elena as a weakness that prevents him from successfully eradicating his enemies. Though Damon wants to save his brother by killing Klaus, his immediate motivation is to protect Elena. Their difference of opinion in "Disturbing Behavior" about how he should behave himself matters little to him when her life is in danger, and she feels the same way. Her reaction to his arrival at the hospital reveals just how much she depends on him.

She may not be able to acknowledge a shift in her feelings about Damon, but as Elena refuses the return of the necklace, she confronts her new reality concerning Stefan. After witnessing him murder Dana and Chad and herself being the victim of his attack, Elena knows that Stefan is really gone, and she has to hold on to that memory, however painful. What she's wanted all summer she finally has: Stefan is back but he's a full-on, remorse-free ripper. The switch is flipped. Klaus has forced his true obedience.

COMPELLING MOMENT Paul Wesley's performance, particularly in the final struggle before Klaus overpowers Stefan's will.

CIRCLE OF KNOWLEDGE
* Though he's a target of senior prank night, Mr. Saltzman is a no-show in this episode.
* "The Reckoning" is a popular title choice across various art forms because of the religious connotations (the Day of Reckoning being an alternate name for the Last Judgment) and the weightiness of its intrinsic meaning: past misdeeds are avenged and punished in a reckoning, as Klaus does here to Stefan.
* R.I.P. Dana and Chad. Senior year won't be the same without you.
* Interestingly, if Klaus had only listened to Elijah and used the doppelgänger-resurrecting elixir 500 years ago ("Klaus"), this whole mess could have been avoided, and Klaus could have had his hybrid comrades for centuries now.
* Fittingly, Tyler is in the science classroom when he turns; he is the subject of Klaus's wacky experiment.
* In L.J. Smith's *Dark Reunion*, Klaus pushes Tyler to activate his inner werewolf by tasting the fresh blood of a high school girl, as he does here in forcing him to become a hybrid by drinking Elena's blood.
* Katherine and Jeremy find Mikael entombed in the oldest wing of the largest cemetery, which would be 1855's Elmwood–Pinewood cemetery in the Third Ward of Charlotte, North Carolina. Mikael has been there since the 1990s.

THE RULES There are many ways to communicate from beyond the grave: Ghost Vicki is able to move objects and send a text message. When Matt is temporarily on the Other Side, he sees Vicki and speaks to her. Brought back with good old-fashioned CPR, Matt is now able to see Vicki and hear her on this side. Tyler is successfully made into a hybrid with one key alteration to the method Klaus had tried before: the potential hybrid must drink the blood of the doppelgänger to complete his transition. That detail was the Original Witch's failsafe to keep Klaus from siring his own species; if he broke his curse, the doppelgänger would be dead, and Klaus would therefore be unable to sire any hybrids. As with Bill Forbes's resistance to compulsion in "Disturbing Behavior," Stefan is able to struggle against Klaus's compulsion — but in the end has his will overpowered.

PREVIOUSLY ON *THE VAMPIRE DIARIES* Klaus refers to not being quite himself the last time he met Dana and Chad; in "The Last Dance," he was possessing Alaric's body and he compelled them to do his bidding. The last time Damon and Katherine made out was in "The Return," and he rejected her advances in "The House Guest." When he clears the gym, Klaus tries out his American accent again, after using it in the opening scene of "The Birthday." As in "The Last Dance," there is a chase through the school hallway, a climactic scene in the cafeteria with Klaus, and a makeshift stake made from a janitor's broom handle. Damon carries Elena down the hospital corridor in a moment that echoes his rescue of her in "Bloodlines" and when he brought her back to the witch house in "The Sun Also Rises."

OFF CAMERA *Entertainment Weekly* named "The Reckoning" one of the top 10 TV episodes of 2011. They aren't the only ones who loved it: cast members Zach Roerig, Kat Graham, and Steven R. McQueen also listed it as a favorite of the season. Zach Roerig underwent a week of scuba training in advance of his drowning scene, and, though he was, of course, given oxygen in between takes, he tested his lung capacity, holding his breath for as long as he could so they could get the shot.

FOGGY MOMENTS Just how were they planning to get out of that classroom with the mousetraps set everywhere? If Vicki can send a text message to Matt, why doesn't Matt just hit reply and skip the whole drowning scenario?

QUESTIONS

- "Given the choice, doppelgänger or hybrid, I go hybrid every time." Any significance in Klaus's line about his relationship with the Original Petrova?
- Is Rebekah's bad attitude toward the "doppelgänger bitch" jealousy over Stefan, or does it date back, say, a thousand years?
- What made the Original Witch hate Klaus so very much?
- How will Damon and Elena get any anti-Klaus scheming done with Stefan, now a truly dutiful henchman, watching over them?
- Where has Klaus gone?
- Even if Klaus were killed, would Stefan *want* to re-embrace his humanity? Or is he too far-gone into the bloodbath lifestyle of the Ripper?
- Will being a hybrid be as wonderful as it seems now for Tyler? Or is Caroline right to look so concerned?

Elena: You think that I'm crazy to believe I can protect myself
from a vampire who's flipped the switch on his humanity?
Alaric: I think you found a way to get out of bed this morning, and that makes
you the strongest person I know. I think you can do pretty much anything.

3.06 *Smells Like Teen Spirit*

Original air date: October 20, 2011
Written by: Julie Plec and Caroline Dries
Directed by: Rob Hardy
Guest cast: TJ Hassan (Coach), Taylor Kinney (Mason Lockwood), Onira Tares (Cheerleader)
Previously on *The Vampire Diaries*: Ian Somerhalder

It's the first day of senior year: Elena deals with flipped-switch Stefan, while Vicki convinces her brother that she needs a stronger foothold in the world of the living.

There's a lot of bad behavior on display in "Smells Like Teen Spirit" but there's also a cost for exercising that freedom and willfulness. Anna reminds us that there is a price to pay for upsetting the balance of nature, and as the kids return to school, it's easy to see just how topsy-turvy their world has become as they compare the first day of senior year to this time last year.

High school is a lonely place for a lot of teenagers, and though Matt Donovan is the star of the football team, he's desperately lonely — and his sister is too. In his truck at the beginning of the episode, Matt feels far more isolated now than last year. Though Vicki tells Matt that he was always better at being a part of "this" than she was, she still wants to come back. Stuck on the Other Side and only able to speak to Matt when he thinks of her, Vicki's willing to make a devil's bargain with the Original Witch. She can be made more corporeal if she agrees to kill Elena, thereby cutting off Klaus from his hybrid-making blood supply. It's a high price to pay, but Vicki (who was never a big fan of Elena's and was killed by Stefan as he was protecting Elena from Vicki's attack) chooses her own freedom over Elena's life. Though Matt was desperate enough to drown himself for a chance to talk to his sister in "The Reckoning," his strong sense of morality isn't shaken, and he knows that having Vicki back is "wrong" (his version of "the balance of nature is upset"). With Bonnie's help to cut off the magic that was pushing Vicki through to the living side, Matt has to let his sister go and say a final goodbye.

Matt helped his sister come back in ignorance: he didn't understand the fallout of the magic or know the deal Vicki had made with the Original Witch to kill Elena. Jeremy, on the other hand, knows what he's getting into but can't seem to help himself, turning to Anna for help with the Vicki situation. He thinks of Anna so often that she's constantly popping up, and, in the final moments of the episode, they are able to touch each other. Bonnie's romance with Jeremy is already crowded by the spirits of his dead girlfriends, and with this supernatural twist, it's only going to get more complicated. Bonnie is frustrated by Jeremy's lack of understanding of how this feels for her and by his insistence that he hold on to Anna, instead of letting her go. Bonnie is all business in a crisis, rightfully brushing off Jeremy to deal with the real problem at hand: Matt resurrecting his ghost sister.

Just as the others' problems are supernatural-sized versions of regular high school drama, Caroline finds herself with two major annoyances on day one of senior year. First, her boyfriend's transition is not going smoothly. She's rightfully concerned that Tyler's new status as a hybrid means a regression to the old Tyler: the obnoxious, self-centered, domineering, and aggressive jock from season 1. The return of the pre-werewolf personality is

further complicated by the sire bond to Klaus. Tyler's transition is proving to be *way* more than an exercise in learning self-control. Though Tyler doesn't want to be anyone's "freaky hybrid slave minion," he has no idea how powerful Klaus's hold is over him. He easily gives in to Rebekah's "gift" and feeds on the cheerleader: is that because he's a newbie vampire thirsty for blood, or because Rebekah tells Tyler that Klaus would want him to feed?

Caroline's other problem is Rebekah: in the extreme high school setting of *TVD*, the competition between these two girls is also heightened. Since Rebekah is stuck in Mystic Falls, she may as well have a little fun while she's here, and she's decided to play the part of the usurping new girl who takes Caroline's popularity, her status on the cheerleading squad, and her boyfriend. As an overachiever, so much of Caroline's identity is wrapped up in her accomplishments, and she's easily irked by Rebekah. It could never be a fair fight between Vampire Barbie and Barbie Klaus — with age comes strength and experience — but what Rebekah seems to lack is Caroline's heart and the determination that gives her and the loyalty it breeds in others. Take Tyler, who says that everything he likes about himself is her, a borderline troubling dependence on Caroline, who taught him how to be a better version of himself and lose the closed-off persona he once hid behind.

For now, it's unclear how far Klaus's hold over Tyler goes, but with Stefan, his power is complete. As awful as Stefan is with his humanity turned off (and playing Twister with his breakfast is pretty twisted), it's a ton of fun to watch. Paul Wesley looks to be having a grand old time being the obnoxious Salvatore brother, playing the tormentor, bully, and enforcer. And it's making the love triangle fascinating: Stefan watches Elena watching Damon get his "flirt on" with Rebekah and comments on her jealousy, knowing that Damon would *love* that it bothered her to see them together (even though it was her idea). And though Stefan and Elena share a moment when he catches her, Elena has her share of moments with Damon too — when he shows her the way to a vampire's heart (*hello*) and when he unnecessarily dabs some ointment on her cheek. Both brothers have made oaths where Elena is concerned: both Ripper and Regular Stefan will always protect her, and Damon has sworn to never leave her. In "Smells Like Teen Spirit," he also says he'll do whatever she needs him to. For better or worse, those boys have Elena's back.

As it's been since season 1, Elena's humanity is her strength. Without giving up hope that Stefan will once again find his own humanity, she's determined to be her own bodyguard, to learn to defend herself. Despite living with vampires, werewolves, witches, and Originals for a year now and often being their target, Elena has never felt unsafe in the way she does now: Stefan, the person she loves, attacked and fed on her and would likely have killed her, had Klaus not needed her alive. Just two days later, in "Smells Like Teen Spirit," in the wee hours of the morning a sleepless Elena drags her butt out of bed to train with Alaric, and her resolve to stay strong extends straight through the whole episode despite a terrible first day back at school. Elena suffers an amped-up version of high school drama in the encounters she has with her own violent jerk of an ex-boyfriend, who won't leave her alone.

Elena's singular focus on Stefan since "The Birthday" has not been without its problems: she knows he's murdering people, *many* people, but she doesn't visibly react to the horror of that reality; she just wanted him home so she could draw out his old, moral self. In "The Reckoning," she witnessed him kill firsthand and, in a powerful moment, finally got angry with him, telling him that he owed it to her to fight against Klaus's compulsion. In the wake of Klaus compelling Stefan to "turn it off," Elena has not cowered but stood up to fight, her Petrova fire sparked. She wants to remember him attacking her and she's going to fight to protect herself from being his or Klaus's victim again. The final exchange with Stefan in this episode is classic: despite the cruelty of his closely whispered taunt that she's pathetic, Elena finds strength she didn't have that morning when she was practicing staking the dummy. As she focuses on her physical strength and combat training, Elena is strengthening herself emotionally too, and that moment staking Stefan is an incredibly empowering and satisfying payoff for our "warrior princess."

For Elena to turn to Alaric for training in vampire hunting is a smart move; she can learn a ton from Ric, and not just about the nitty-gritty of fighting. He has experience in having a loved one turn into a ruthless vampire, and uniquely understands the pain Elena is in and the way that pain is fueling her. And it also gives *him* a purpose (beyond teaching a motley monster crew about American history). He continues to watch out for Elena, hovering over her interactions with Damon to make sure those glances don't linger too long. In a decidedly less complicated way than with the Salvatore brothers, Alaric has Elena's back, and not just when it comes to shooting Stefan with a little vervain.

Though Klaus was MIA this episode, he was still very much in control of the characters, a situation that soon may be upset should Mikael prove true to his statement to Katherine that not only can he kill Klaus, but he *will*. But until then, there's a pesky ghost infestation problem in Mystic Falls, and Mason Lockwood seems determined to do more damage to the Salvatore mansion décor than Stefan.

COMPELLING MOMENT Obnoxious Elena! Her half-faked, half-real unhinged on the bleachers act was entertaining, charming, and heartbreaking, and it forced the misbehaving Stefan to turn straight-edge.

CIRCLE OF KNOWLEDGE
- No Klaus in this episode.
- "Smells Like Teen Spirit" is the name of Nirvana's breakthrough song

from their 1991 album *Nevermind*. Vicki is the literal teen spirit of the episode, and with her mission to come back no matter the cost, this teen spirit smells like trouble.

• Stefan says the girls he's compelled are helping him be all that he can be, quoting the U.S. Army's well-known slogan, used from the 1980s until 2001.

• Damon calls Elena "Buffy" . . . and the fandom goes wild. It took three seasons before an explicit *Buffy the Vampire Slayer* reference was made, but this was perfectly timed, coming as it did with this episode's Giles–Buffy-esque training scene in the forest between Alaric and Elena. Never one to be shy with doling out nicknames, Damon also calls Elena "warrior princess," a reference to Xena, the warrior princess whose excellent fighting skills came in handy in the cult fave TV show that aired from 1995 to 2001.

THE RULES When Tyler expresses his staunch Team Klaus support, Damon suggests that it's a result of being sired: a rare phenomenon where a new vampire (or, in this case, vampire-werewolf) feels loyalty to the vampire whose blood created him, his "sire." Mikael reveals that he does not feed on living things; he feeds on vampires.

HISTORY LESSON In Mr. Saltzman's AP American history class, the course begins with the country's original founders, the Native Americans. Rebekah suggests that the Vikings may also have founder status; see page 58 for more on them.

PREVIOUSLY ON *THE VAMPIRE DIARIES* With this first day back at school, there are allusions aplenty to the early days of season 1. Elena covers her neck wound with make-up, which Caroline used to do during her Damon phase ("You're Undead to Me"). Damon is annoyed by Stefan playing with his food, so to speak; the roles were reversed in "A Few Good Men" when Damon brought home sorority girls. Also, in "The Dinner Party" flashback, Damon came home to find Stefan partying with ladies and leaving corpses lying around the house. Just as Elena did with Jeremy in the pilot episode, Caroline pushes Tyler into the boys room to give him a talk about keeping it straight at school. Elena and Stefan's run-in in the hall is a dark version of their original meet-cute in the pilot. Vicki's favorite hangout, the stoner pit, returns as does that decorated van from "The Last Dance." Football and cheerleading practice is very "Friday Night Bites," while Stefan shoving the guy whom Elena bumps into is a callback to "Under Control." After Bonnie set two fires in the parking lot ("You're Undead to Me," "Brave New World"), Vicki has a go at it, exploding Ric's car.

OFF CAMERA It was impossible to keep Taylor Kinney's return to *TVD* a surprise when he brought his headline-grabbing girlfriend, Lady Gaga, along with him to Atlanta for the shoot. Torrey DeVitto (see page 72) named the moment when Stefan catches Elena and they share that look as one of her favorites of season 3. In an interview with *TV Guide*, Malese Jow explained that she feels Anna's relationship with Jeremy is "beautiful and innocent": "[They were] both lost souls, who put a little spark in each other and that hasn't changed with her death."

FOGGY MOMENTS Why hadn't Elena already told Alaric that Stefan was her new bodyguard? Was the bonfire party a school event on MFHS property? There was a keg of beer in plain sight at an event held by the "Spirit Squad" promoted with posters in the school. Maybe in Mystic Falls underage drinking is the least of anyone's problems. When Vicki picked up the joint from the windshield wiper, would it have appeared to be levitating to the partygoers around her?

QUESTIONS

- What happens to a vampire who is fed on and drained of blood? Are they desiccated but still alive?
- Could a regular vampire survive on the blood of other vampires, or is Mikael special in some way?
- Mason made his cliffhanger surprise appearance, beating up Damon for a little revenge-y fun. Which other spirits are now more corporeal in Mystic Falls? Did the Original Witch do that deliberately or is it a side effect to messing with the balance of nature?

Mason: I can't change what happened to me, but maybe I can change what happens to Tyler. I don't need revenge, Damon. I need redemption.

3.07 *Ghost World*

Original air date: October 27, 2011
Written by: Rebecca Sonnenshine
Directed by: David Jackson
Guest cast: Frank Brennan (Tobias Fell), Jasmine Guy (Grams Bennett), Kelly Hu (Pearl), Arielle Kebbel (Lexi), Stephen Martines (Frederick)
Previously on *The Vampire Diaries*: Kat Graham

On the Night of Illumination, the ghosts find they have a foothold in the physical world.

Such a high mortality rate in Mystic Falls means a wealth of ghostly potential to draw on. Bringing back lost fan favorites could have played out like a cheap emotional trick, but instead, "Ghost World" was all treat, tying up loose ends in a way that provided closure and resonated across the storylines. Grams says that spirits with unfinished business have returned: some are back to seek revenge, others redemption.

Anger persists even in the after-afterlife. The tomb vampires who wanted revenge on the founding families for the crimes of 1864 haven't changed course. Tobias Fell, head of the history department and founding family member, bears the gruesome brunt of Frederick and company's anger, but the rest of the spirits in this ghost world seize the day as a way to do right by their loved ones.

At the root of this emotionally complex day is Bonnie Bennett. The mess they are in is a result of Bonnie resurrecting Jeremy; though she tells Grams she had no choice, she did make one, knowing that there would be consequences. She often has to focus on fixing witchcraft-related messes rather than dwell on her feelings, and even before she realizes there's a mess to deal with, she tells Caroline that she simply doesn't know how to handle her boyfriend-ghost drama. In "Ghost World," Bonnie once again puts her own feelings aside in order to step up and handle the problem, destroying the necklace and sending the ghosts back to the Other Side — even though that means losing Grams again. Sheila was more than a grandmother to Bonnie: she was her guide, her role model, her support, and her comfort. Bonnie was devastated when Grams died in "Fool Me Once" and it took a long time for her to recover; to have Grams appear as the "veil" lifts, holding Bonnie's arms — supporting her in her magic and in her life — is a huge moment, and a cathartic one for the audience. Grams tells Bonnie that she's stronger than all of this, and Bonnie demonstrates that strength in her resolve and in her demand for respect from Jeremy. It has to hurt that this "fine mess" all came from Bonnie's desperate act of love, and that the object of her affection has turned away from her into the arms of a ghost of a former love.

Like Bonnie having to deal with the consequences of her choice in "As I Lay Dying," Jeremy will have to face the fallout of his actions. He knew that he shouldn't kiss Anna, both because she's already lost to him and because he should be faithful to Bonnie. But, as he tells his sister, he couldn't help the way he feels, right or wrong. Jer's lost so many people, so suddenly and horribly, that when he got a second chance to be with Anna, he took it. He and Anna seemed to be delighting in their secret relationship, having conversations and moments that no one knew about but the two of them. But as much as it staved off Anna's loneliness, it also turned Jeremy into a liar. That Jeremy and Anna's kiss took place in the Grill's ladies room was a moment of redemption for Jeremy: their last moments together were there, before the police dragged her away in "Founder's Day." That moment was one of inaction for Jeremy; here he seizes the moment — and Anna.

At Anna's core, the very reason she returned to Mystic Falls in the first place, is her bond to her mother. She came to free Pearl from the tomb, and when Pearl was killed, Anna was cut adrift. In her conversations with Jeremy about the Other Side, the one recurring point she makes is how alone she is. When she steals the necklace from Damon's room, it's to prevent a nightmarish eternity of isolation. But she won't suffer that fate. Just as Anna has been roaming the Other Side, so has Pearl, and in one of the most touching scenes in the series, mother and daughter find each other again. Finally, Anna's original quest is complete, and her fear of being alone assuaged.

For Elena, Lexi fills a role akin to Grams' for Bonnie: she gives her the guidance and support she needs in a moment of crisis, not only physically overpowering Stefan and imprisoning him (something that Elena and company failed to do in "Smells Like Teen Spirit") but teaching her the Ripper Detox program. Their attempt to starve the Ripper isn't only about bringing back the Stefan they know and love; it puts the brakes on a rampaging killer. Stefan may have been joking about going on a townsfolk binge during the

Night of Illumination, but there's a dark truth to that statement: he feeds and kills with great regularity. As much as Elena is selfishly motivated — she wants her boyfriend back — her determination to cage the Ripper is for the public good.

As Lexi taught him in the 1860s ("The Dinner Party"), Stefan needs to feel something, *anything*, and she starts with pain. Lexi's presence is a godsend for Elena, but this opportunity is also a moment for closure for Lexi, who's had to stand by powerless on the Other Side, watching her best friend of 150 years descend into full-on ripperdom. And boy does Stefan do a great job of being a grade-A jerk in his attempts to make Lexi and Elena feel pathetic for caring so much and dedicating so much of their lives to him. But neither woman buys into his manipulation. In a powerful moment, Elena leaves the holding cell, unable to watch Lexi torture Stefan any longer, and instead of getting a breath of fresh air, the reprieve she needs, she hears sirens and sees the flashing lights of the chaos in the town square. For Elena Gilbert, when you escape one nightmare, you just walk into another. The divide between the living and dead is there for a reason, and as desperately as Elena wants Lexi's help and solidarity, she accepts that she has to go it alone and let Lexi find some peace.

Before Elena leaves Stefan alone in the cell for the night, she translates the lesson she learned from seeing Jeremy hold on to Anna to her own relationship with Stefan. In season 1, Jeremy and Anna's relationship acted as a foil for Elena and Stefan's, a Gilbert and a vampire, and here it does once again. In a less direct way, Jer's dual affection for Anna and Bonnie acts as a cautionary tale for Elena, who has two Salvatores to juggle. More explicitly, Elena's advice to her brother to stop living in the past by loving someone who's already gone applies to her own situation, and (thankfully) Elena's self-aware enough to realize that. She can't love a ghost forever either. Bolstered by Lexi's resolve that Stefan is still in there somewhere, Elena holds on to hope for Stefan, but he needs to fight. There will be consequences if he doesn't: he'll truly lose her.

Before Damon killed Mason in "Plan B," he recognized his past self in the werewolf — in love with Katherine and made a fool because of it. It's telling that the ghost who chooses to spend his time with Damon (and not with Tyler) is not interested in revenge (though he does have some fun getting pay-back at first), but in redemption. Mason wants to protect Tyler and his agenda dovetails with Damon's need to save his brother from Klaus's control. Nothing

like a common enemy to make former foes friends. In a beautifully written moment, Mason explains what it's like on the Other Side: you just watch and regret, and now he's been given the opportunity for retribution. With that signature chilled-out-surfer laugh, Mason's willing to accept Damon's "crap-ass" apology, and the duo's rapport is back and in fine form. On their adventure through the booby-trapped cave, the mini-exploration of Damon's trust and friendship issues leads to a resolution not only of their dynamic but of Damon's with Alaric. Just as there were consequences to Damon killing Mason — both when the werewolf pack came looking for vengeance, and now with Mason's demand for an apology — Alaric demands that Damon be held accountable for how he treated him. Since "Disturbing Behavior" (which is ages ago in *TVD* time), Alaric has stood his ground and refused to be buddy-buddy; he won't brush off Damon's action as being a "Damon" thing to do and therefore somehow exempt from consequence. Alaric's point that he shouldn't have to forgive a friend for *killing him*, that he should be treated with respect, is an important one. At the same time, these two need each other, and it's seems as though a heartfelt apology, even if it is recycled, is enough for Team Beer and Blood to reunite. Cheers to that.

COMPELLING MOMENT Two heartfelt family moments: Grams appearing with Bonnie, having been right next to her the whole time, and Anna meeting Pearl in the road, realizing she won't be alone any longer and being able to hug her mom.

CIRCLE OF KNOWLEDGE
- No Tyler or Klaus.
- *Ghost World* is a comic book series by Daniel Clowes originally published from 1993 to 1997; in 2001, it was adapted into a film of the same name, starring Thora Birch and Scarlett Johansson as Enid and Rebecca, two clever and disconnected recent high school graduates figuring out what the hell to do with themselves whilst stuck in a mundane existence.
- File this under important details: Grams says to Bonnie about witches talking to each other on the Other Side, "Who do you think makes all the rules?"

THE RULES Normally, ghosts are able to see the living world but not interact with it (save for creepily moving some objects around when they *really* need to make a point). Humans with an open channel, like Jeremy, can communicate with a ghost if both are trying to bridge the divide. However, the situation in "Ghost World" arose when the Original Witch took advantage of Bonnie's spells (raising Jeremy from the dead, and breaking the magic helping Vicki) and used her own talisman (the necklace) to "wedge the door wide open" between this side and the other, allowing ghosts to physically interact with the living world. Bonnie's manifestation spell (which was helpfully pointed out to her by Ghost Grams) made "veiled matter" visible, i.e., the living could see the ghosts. Not everyone who died is on the Other Side: the only ghosts who manifest were supernatural in life and ended up in what Alaric calls "supernatural purgatory." Supernatural spirits without unfinished business go someplace else (the other Other Side?), which seems to be a place of rest or peace.

HISTORY LESSON The original Night of Illumination was celebrated 150 years ago in Mystic Falls to symbolize the safety of the peaceful times after the war (both the Civil War, and the war against the vampires). Anna's snarky commentary to Jeremy suggests that Carol's speech is full of lies perpetrated by the founding families; the period of prosperity after the war was due to the appropriation of the vampires' wealth and land.

PREVIOUSLY ON *THE VAMPIRE DIARIES* In "162 Candles," Grams told Bonnie, "A witch's talisman is a powerful tool," and Emily Bennett used her necklace and Bonnie to sort out some of her unfinished business in the living world. Mason tortures Damon in imitation of how Damon killed Mason in "Plan B." In their pre-ghost relationship, Jeremy and Anna also kept each other secret: Anna didn't tell Pearl she was dating him, and Jeremy kept his knowledge of Anna's vampirism from his sister. Returning from "Founder's Day" is Frederick and his merry band of tomb vampires, keen to seek revenge on the founding families at another town-square event. Caroline ransacks the soap dish looking for the necklace; Katherine famously discovered the moonstone there in "Know Thy Enemy."

OFF CAMERA "Ghost World" was conceived as a nostalgic episode, a treat for longtime fans and one that would give closure to certain characters, most notably Pearl and Anna. Of mother and daughter finding each other, Julie Plec told *Entertainment Weekly*, "Anybody who didn't watch the series until this season wouldn't necessarily have any emotional connection to that moment, but I felt, as a fan of our own show, who had connected to this girl and that relationship, it just had to happen. And then you put up a bunch of beautiful lanterns and a nice long lens and a great song, and it's the saddest moment you've ever seen [laughs]. I've seen that moment 15 times, and I still cry like a baby every time I see it."

QUESTIONS

- Since Jenna didn't show up, does that mean she is without unfinished business and has found peace?
- With head of the history department Tobias Fell out of the picture, is Alaric in for a promotion at Mystic Falls High?
- Who set up the anti-vampire booby-traps protecting the cave? Damon says it's as if he wasn't invited in. Is it an ancient residence or has a witch spelled the entrance to prevent vampires from entering?
- The necklace returns to its original state in the hearth. Does that mean the Original Witch still has a foothold on this side with the necklace as her talisman?
- Did Mason know the Lockwood legend about an Original-killing weapon before he died, or was that something he learned on the Other Side? (And if the latter, from whom did he learn it?)
- What do those cave markings mean? Will they lead to a weapon that can kill Klaus?

Rebekah (to Elena): He's my brother, and I'm immortal.
Should I spend an eternity alone instead?

3.08 *Ordinary People*

Original air date: November 3, 2011
Story by: Nick Wauters
Teleplay by: Julie Plec and Caroline Dries
Directed by: J. Miller Tobin
Guest cast: Maria Howell (Ayana), Karlee Morgan Eldridge (Callie)
Previously on *The Vampire Diaries*: Ian Somerhalder

As Alaric decodes the cave drawings, Elena goes straight to Rebekah for the origin story of the Original family. Damon and Stefan play quarters.

An episode like "Ordinary People" reminds us that, at its heart, this show is not about a love triangle but about family. Across centuries, familial bonds prove to be of the utmost importance, but that doesn't mean those relationships aren't fraught with power struggles, hurt, fear, and betrayal. In magic, so in life: for every strength, there is a weakness.

As in every other exposition-heavy episode, this origin story of a predatory species not only satisfies our burning questions about the Original family (and raises more), but it pushes characters in compelling new directions, provides parallels across storylines and centuries, and sets up the midseason finale. Mystic Falls hasn't just been a vampire town since the 1860s; it's the birthplace of the species. The Original family lived in proto–Mystic Falls, and the hybrid curse was cast there. How mystically fitting that Katherine, the doppelgänger, found her way there and that Elena, doppelgänger the second, was born there.

After spending a thousand years believing Klaus's version of events, Rebekah's belief that she and Klaus are bonded always and forever, that her father is their common and fearsome enemy for killing their mother, is shaken. The drawings tell a different tale entirely, one of matricide. In the first flashback scene, Rebekah calls her brother "traitor" in jest; by episode's end she has reason to believe that he is a traitor of the worst kind.

As when we first saw the Salvatore brothers as humans in "Lost Girls," seeing Rebekah and Klaus (and glimpses of Elijah) when they were ordinary mortals is a treat. In "The Sun Also Rises," Elijah had been resolved to kill his brother to avenge the rest of his family — an act that would sever the oath to be one with Klaus always — but he stopped in the hope of resurrecting his other siblings. Rebekah has been loyal to her brother for a thousand years (minus some daggered time-outs), and there is a stark difference between what she'll put up with from her brother, because he's family, and what kind of treatment she'll accept from the vampire she once loved, Stefan. Family certainly trumps romantic love, but Rebekah has also been privileging one brother over her others, either out of fear or a special sense of loyalty to the brother her parents rejected.

Since her introduction in "The End of the Affair," Claire Holt has been the perfect Rebekah, but this is clearly her episode to shine. Rebekah asserting her dominance but clearly envying what Elena has speaks to how

Sebastian Roché as Mikael

For the role of Mikael, father to the Originals, the producers looked at actors from across the pond and cast Sebastian Roché. The French actor, who studied at the Conservatoire National Superieur d'Art Dramatique of Paris, has been working since the mid-1980s and moved to America in 1992. Among the many shows he's appeared in are *General Hospital*, *The Mentalist*, *24*, *Fringe*, *Criminal Minds*, *Grimm*, as well as film projects such as *The Last of the Mohicans*, *Beowulf*, *The Adventures of Tintin*, and *Safe House*. But regular viewers of The CW know him best as *Supernatural*'s Balthazar.

Sebastian succinctly described Mikael to *TV Fanatic*: "He's calm, but ruthless." He appreciated the extra mile the *TVD* creators went: "One thing I really liked is that, as soon as I got the part, Julie called me and told me about the character, what was going to happen as far as the character development, so I thought that was a really nice touch." Roché also discovered an admiration for Atlanta while filming *TVD*, as he told Wetpaint. "I had imagined Atlanta being sort of a very urban city with towers and being very concrete. But it's actually a really nice city with different, lovely neighborhoods and very mixed towns. I discovered some wonderful restaurants and venues and people. I have to say the people are lovely. Hovering about at Piedmont Park and Virginia Highlands, I really enjoyed it very much. And the cast all hangs out together, being in Atlanta. They're a small family. The cast and crew were amazing to me." The feeling was mutual as Julie Plec related to *Entertainment Weekly*, "He showed up for a costume fitting, and I got an email from the costume designer that all of the women in the costume fitting were flushed and atwitter because he's a very charming, handsome man. He's a classically trained theater actor, he is mysterious, he has an element of danger to him. We liked the idea of bringing an adult into our world that wasn't one of our founding families. He's just got a quality that is really exciting."

fundamentally human this villain's needs are. A home, friends, a life, a bond to her family that she can count on, always and forever. Claire Holt creates a sympathetic portrait that exposes Rebekah's humanity, her weakness, and her ferocious strength. Though she is crumpled and sobbing by the end of the episode, desperate not to be alone for an eternity, Rebekah has not lost any bite as a potential adversary — whether she join sides with Elena or sticks with Klaus. It's completely natural that Elena, queen of empathy, would identify with her. Instead of escalating the mean-girl showdown, she sees similarities between herself and the murderous Original vampire: both are motherless girls with big hearts who love despite the risk, who prize the bonds of family, and who — in their epic stubbornness — don't give up on a person easily, or at all. It leads Elena to the conclusion that Mikael reaches as well: the bond that ultimately matters is that between the brothers. In the calm, sweet moment between Damon and Elena, before she drifts off to sleep, she acknowledges that hers is not the most important relationship with Stefan: "I think you're going to be the one who saves him from himself. It won't be because he loves me; it'll be because he loves you."

Family can be a source of strength or of weakness, and both are represented in Mikael. Back when the Originals were ordinary people, the innate parental instinct to protect one's children drove Esther and Mikael to extremes. But at some point (perhaps after Esther's murder?), Mikael drastically changed course, and he now hunts the monsters he created and feeds on vampire blood. This was a father who frightened his children into submission, who let his pride override the balance of nature and endanger his children's well-being, yet Mikael hasn't forgotten the power of family. He is the one to pinpoint the loophole in Stefan's seemingly unbreakable submission to Klaus: the threat of a permanent hole in his brother's chest. Despite this understanding of familial bonds, both in flashback and in his interaction with the "Salvatore boys," Mikael is harsh and unyielding. Take his intervention in Klaus's jovial overpowering of Elijah. From Mikael's perspective the lesson is necessary: the reality is they are among werewolves; survival is a real concern. Klaus's "foolish and impulsive" nature, as Mikael characterizes him, leads to Henrik's death, when he takes the boy to watch the men turn into wolves. Interestingly, Mikael doesn't direct his anger over his son's death toward Klaus, despite his failure to protect his youngest brother, but instead launches a counterattack. He makes his family superior to the werewolf threat — stronger, faster, heightened in every way. You have to be at least a little bit deranged to come up with this plan and to carry it out, ignoring the strong warnings from Ayana against creating a "plague," and having to kill your own children — all five of them — in the belief that this untested magic will work. It's a huge risk and one that speaks to Mikael's pride and determination — and that was *before* he became a vampire and had his personality amplified. He will not run from his enemies or from a threat, but will turn and fight them, or chase them down for centuries if need be. What was his true purpose in creating vampires — protecting his loved ones or asserting his dominance?

When Rebekah tells Elena that Mikael tore his wife's heart from her chest for breaking his, it's entirely believable — his rage over the shame of incontrovertible evidence that Niklaus is not his son, but his enemy's, drives him to massacre half a village. What drives him now? Innocent of his wife's murder, as the cave drawings suggest, is he seeking vengeance against Klaus? Does he believe that the species he created with Esther is an abomination that should be eradicated? Mikael and Esther fled the Old World to avoid a plague that took the life of their first born, only to create a new plague themselves, perpetrated by their offspring.

Elena makes explicit the connection she sees between herself and Rebekah, and in the family dynamics among the Originals there are further parallels to other relationships. The way Mikael attacks Klaus for his foolishness could have just as easily been words that Giuseppe spat at Damon. Brothers have saved each other or refrained from killing each other time and again, but *The Vampire Diaries* has also shown us a father unhesitatingly kill his sons. In "Blood Brothers," Giuseppe shot his boys dead for siding with the vampires. Mikael once wanted nothing more than to protect his family, no matter the cost, but after creating the most powerful predatory species, his goal is the opposite. The threat Mikael poses to Klaus is unquestionable. The real question is how the bond between the siblings will change in the wake of this life-altering revelation that Klaus killed Esther, not Mikael.

"Ordinary People" reminds us the bonds of family are the source of these characters' greatest strengths and greatest vulnerabilities. The Salvatore brothers feel they owe each other their lives and will fight for each other until the end of time, all the while self-deprecatingly mocking their own humanity. Will that same family unity — together as one, always and forever — play out when the Originals have their homecoming?

COMPELLING MOMENT Rebekah, Klaus, and Elijah standing at their mother's grave, surrounded by the ash of the burnt white oak tree, pledging to be together, always and forever.

CIRCLE OF KNOWLEDGE
- No Matt, Tyler, Caroline, or Jeremy in this episode.
- Robert Redford made his directorial debut with the 1980 film *Ordinary People*, based on a 1976 novel by Judith Guest. The story centers on Conrad (Timothy Hutton) and his parents (Donald Sutherland and Mary Tyler Moore), a middle-class family dealing with the death of Conrad's older brother and Conrad's depression and attempted suicide. It's a remarkably moving story about an ordinary family dealing with grief,

isolation, forgiveness, responsibility and guilt, and the consequences of feeling defined by one life-altering mistake. Its themes resonate with the story revealed in the Originals' flashback — particularly Klaus's part in Henrik's death and his relationship with his mother — as well as with Stefan's current inability to feel anything. Conrad's therapist (played by Judd Hirsch) has some key advice for his patient who's deadened himself to feeling, too scared that opening himself up to positive feelings would unleash a torrent of pain as well: "A little advice about feeling, kiddo: don't expect it always to tickle." Highly recommended.

- In 1000 AD, the humans retreated to the caves for refuge from the were-wolves on a full moon, but in modern-day Mystic Falls, the reverse is true: the Lockwood wolves use an underground cell to confine themselves.

THE RULES The spell that created vampires drew power from the sun, the ancient white oak tree, and blood. In nature's effort to restore balance, these elements became vampires' weaknesses. The sun burns; the white oak tree can kill Originals (and any type of wood can kill the Originals' descendent vampires) and its ash harms them. Vervain gets its anti-vampire properties from growing at the base of the white oak tree, and vampires have an insatiable craving for that which created them: blood. Additionally, the Originals were no longer able to enter their neighbors' homes without invitation, providing humans with a refuge from the otherwise near-indestructible predator. Esther, the witch of the Originals a.k.a. the Original Witch, invented the daylight-ring spell to allow her children to walk in the sun; the Originals all wear matching daylight rings.

HISTORY LESSON While Columbus didn't sail the ocean blue til 1492, the Vikings landed in North America as early as 1000 AD, according to their sagas and evidenced by archaeological remains found in L'Anse aux Meadows in the northern tip of Newfoundland. Vikings — Danes, Svear, Goths, and Norwegians who spoke Old Norse — had a far more complex society than the popular image of cartoonish horn-wearing raiders. Loyalty to family, honor, and propriety were key among their societal values (qualities that the Originals hold dear). Vikings sailed across the North Sea from their lands to Britain and Ireland, to Iceland, to Baffin Island and Newfoundland. Much like the promised land of health and strength for which Esther and Mikael left the Old World, the Viking sagas spoke of "Vinland the Good," the land of grapes and warm winters, a paradise, for which Leif Eriksson, first son of Erik the Red, sailed in 1000 AD. Though there is no evidence that these real-life explorers ventured anywhere so far south as Virginia, with a powerful witch to help them, who knows how far an intrepid couple could go — surely all the way to Mystic Falls. (Though Elijah said his parents were from Eastern Europe in "Klaus," if Esther and Mikael were looking for a ride to North America, they would likely have had to cross with the Vikings.) The markings in the caves are in the runic alphabet (an angular set of characters developed in response to the material into which they were carved). Runes were used to record names, accomplishments, legends, and poems, as well as in magic for spells, divination, and protection.

PREVIOUSLY ON *THE VAMPIRE DIARIES* Damon references "werewolf Pictionary," a game he played with Mason Lockwood in "Memory Lane." Elena theorizes that the cave drawings could be Klaus's fakes; in "Klaus," she learned from Elijah that he and his brother had been faking artifacts about the invented curse of the sun and moon. When he was terrorizing Jenna in her own kitchen in that same episode, AlariKlaus said that werewolves outdated vampires, and Rebekah's story backs up that supernatural timeline. Elena is all judgey when Rebekah reads Stefan's diary, but she was doing that in "The End of the Affair" and "Ghost World" (though she didn't snoop in his underwear drawer). In "History Repeating," Stefan took Damon out for some brother bonding and drinking, with the goal of finding out his true purpose in Mystic Falls; Damon returns the favor here. Damon expects Elena to be mad at him for going rogue and freeing Stefan, but she's not; she understands why he did what he did, just as she did in "The Last Dance" (when she was led to believe Bonnie was dead in order to fool Klaus). Despite both vampires wanting to do her harm, Elena empathized with Anna in "Fool Me Once," realizing that she was just looking for her mother, and she empathizes with Rebekah here.

OFF CAMERA Devon Allowitz plays Henrik (R.I.P.); Devon is the son of first assistant director Michael Allowitz. This episode is named after one of Kevin Williamson's favorite films.

FOGGY MOMENTS In the opening scene, Damon calls Mikael "Poppa Original," having seen his name on the wall along with Niklaus, Elijah, and

Rebekah. But how did he know Mikael is the father and not one of the other Original siblings that Elijah told Elena existed? If Esther had the ju-ju ability required to do the vampire-creation spell herself, why was she begging Ayana to do it? Was this just to trick the audience into thinking that Ayana was the Original Witch, not Esther?

QUESTIONS
- Did witches also create werewolves?
- Notably absent from Rebekah's story is any mention of the original Petrova. Who was she and what role did she play in their story?
- Of Mikael's heart-snatching technique, Stefan says now they know where Klaus and Elijah learned that trick. Are there other tricks the boys learned from their father?
- Rebekah insists that if Mikael is awoken they are *all* doomed. Does Mikael pose a threat to humans?
- Will Rebekah help them take down Klaus?

Katherine: Humanity is a vampire's greatest weakness. No matter how easy it is to turn it off, it just keeps trying to fight its way back in. Sometimes I let it.

3.09 *Homecoming*

Original air date: November 10, 2011
Written by: Evan Bleiweiss
Directed by: Joshua Butler
Guest cast: Kimberly Drummond (Mindy), Matthew Murray (Football Player), Zane Stephens (Tony)
Previously on *The Vampire Diaries*: Joseph Morgan

It's homecoming in Mystic Falls, and the gang has a seemingly perfect plan to kill Klaus.

    With a *kaboom!* the first part of season 3 came to a close. In Mystic Falls, as in real life, trying to protect against any eventuality, to completely control a situation so it plays out in your favor is a fool's errand. Mikael failed in that mission when he recreated his children as vampires, and here he fails again after a millennium of hunting Klaus. The carefully plotted attack on Klaus fails to account for Klaus's own thoroughness or for the seemingly heartless Katherine and Stefan saving Damon's life. Even Klaus's victory turns hollow, when Stefan pulls the rug out from under him in the final moments of the episode, by stealing his coffin family. While the episode's plot was a tad on the unnecessarily convoluted side (anything that requires an explanatory flashback within an explanatory flashback is), what "Homecoming" did elegantly was provide set-piece scenes between our characters that were emotionally complicated, surprising, and beautifully acted.

Though humans are her playthings and her supper, it's Rebekah's humanity that drives her, and the broken bonds of family — with Mikael in turning them into vampires in the first place, and with Klaus for murdering their mother — devastate her. But this girl ain't broken: she does what she must to lure Klaus back, she stands up to her father, and she's all dolled up and ready for her first high school dance. In her conversation with Mikael, their first in a thousand years, she makes it clear that she has no illusion about Niklaus or about her father: both betrayed her trust and their family. That Niklaus ever became a killer — that any of them did — is a sin she lays squarely on her father's shoulders. After being burned by Klaus's lies, Rekebah is betrayed again. Elena uses her new connection to Rebekah and her understanding of what her mother's necklace symbolizes to her to take her out of the equation, to ensure that she won't have a crisis of conscience and prevent them from killing Klaus. It *is* a very Katherine thing to do — smart but ruthless — and Damon pointing that out is a clue to the viewers at home that doppelgänger hijinks will later ensue. Elena's surprise dagger in the back for Rebekah is just the first of many unexpected takedowns in "Homecoming" — the most jaw-dropping of which is on Mikael.

A predator who feeds on predators, the grandpapa of all vampires, the sire of all sires: gone too soon. A fascinating character in the brief glimpses we got of him, his need for vengeance and his disgust with vampires battled his continued love for his family. When confronted by Rebekah, he stands there and takes it, telling her he was never after her, just Niklaus. His quest of a thousand years was to avenge his wife's death, but the self hatred that came from creating the world's greatest predator coupled with an amplified capacity for pride and anger, prevented him from seeking allies among his children. The showdown between Mikael and Klaus was electric, in part because, though the two of them are not blood-related, they are incredibly similar: both sires of a "master race," both essentially acting alone for a millennium, both willing to do whatever it takes to assert their dominance. In a case of nothing being black or white on *The Vampire Diaries*, the villain of the series is shown in an incredibly fraught emotional moment. Klaus stands at the threshold, tears streaming down his face at Mikael's words, but he's no less a threat because of that vulnerability. His intensity of emotion only serves to demonstrate the strength of his conviction to one day become untouchable. With this victory over Mikael, Klaus is freed of the ties that have bound him since he killed his mother. His belief that his remaining family members, once undaggered, will "let bygones be bygones" is bold — but what choice do they have? Klaus has grown accustomed to forcing people's loyalty and he's ready for a family reunion. Of course, sneaky little devil Stefan has wrested absolute control from Klaus; like his adversaries, Klaus failed to protect against every eventuality and has lost that which he values most.

The leader of the hybrids isn't the only one of his species to end the night badly: his minions get wolfsbane-bombed and their hearts torn out, while Tyler gets his heart broken. The relationship between Caroline and Tyler slowly built after Tyler became a werewolf, as the two leaned on each other and saw each other through the worst. But with hybrid Tyler loyal to Klaus — a loyalty that is forced — his choices are counter to what the "real" Tyler would do if he had free will. He vervains Caroline to "protect" her, but by doing that he's taking away *her* free will, her right to risk her life battling Klaus and the sired hybrids to help her friends. While Tyler is right in that he can't change the fact that he's sired, that it is a gift to be free from the pain of changing every full moon, he doesn't seem to realize how significant the cost of that loss of free will is or how fundamentally upsetting it is for Caroline to have her boyfriend lose his sense of right and wrong and side with the bad guy. In a sad moment for a couple who clearly still loves each other, Caroline can't compromise her beliefs for Tyler or accept him taking away her right to self-determination.

No matter how hard you try, you just can't think of everything. While our heroes brainstormed all the possible angles, betrayals, and outcomes in an effort to safeguard the master kill-Klaus plan, Klaus was doing the same — he had his hybrid army, a house safe from Mikael, and insurance that if he was taken out, Damon would be too. Nothing was left to chance. But who can predict what Miss Katherine Pierce will do? In a great evolution from last season's "Masquerade," which featured a diabolical plan to take out Katherine, now *she's* the one who saves both Salvatore brothers, letting her love for them get in the way of murdering her oldest enemy. Humanity may be a vampire's greatest weakness, but it's also what makes their eternity worth living, and for once Katherine lets her love for the boys be her guide. An awesome twist, even for those who anticipated a doppelgänger scheme was in play; after all, there's nothing quite like a Katherine smirk upon the reveal.

Katherine proved to be the deciding player in "Homecoming" and, in pointing Stefan toward taking revenge on Klaus, she may be setting up the next season 3 arc as well. Stefan is now free of compulsion: it's up to him to decide which Stefan he'd like to be, how much of his humanity he'll re-embrace, if any. He's saved his brother yet again, but Damon and Elena have no idea why Stefan betrayed them. Reversing the dynamic from earlier in the season, it is Elena who suggests that they may have to let Stefan go. In an episode consumed with trust issues, at least Damon and Elena find comfort and have trust in each other.

COMPELLING MOMENT To Joseph Morgan and Sebastian Roché for the showdown between Klaus and Mikael: perfection.

CIRCLE OF KNOWLEDGE
- No Alaric or Jeremy.
- After learning in "Ordinary People" that the Originals hailed from Mystic Falls (850 years before there was a Mystic Falls), "homecoming" takes on a literal meaning — Mikael and Klaus are both coming back to their original home. The title also nods to the American tradition of a homecoming football game and dance in late September or early October, which is usually attended by alumni and other former residents. Not usually relocated to a hybrid's mansion.
- Who doesn't want to stay home and overanalyze ancient hieroglyphic thingies with Alaric? The Bonnie-Elena scene was a solid BFF conversation (of which there can never be too many), and it was classic Elena to listen to Bonnie's perspective on the key difference when it comes to fights between siblings, think about what she said, and apply it to another situation in her life, giving her insight into the Klaus-Rebekah dynamic.

- "Here's my RSVP." A quintessentially Damon moment.
- After Elena daggers Rebekah, Damon puts a tarp over her body, but in the last moments of the episode, Rebekah is just thrown on the dirt ground in her homecoming dress. C'mon, guys, at least lay her on Sheriff Forbes's cot or something. Even Klaus has the decency to provide cushy coffins; Originals are used to a certain degree of respect.

THE RULES We are reminded of the rules of daggering (yes, it's a verb in the *TVD* world): a vampire would die if they daggered an Original, but a human or another Original can wield the dagger and survive. Anyone could have used the ancient white oak tree stake. An Original can compel a hybrid (because of its vampire side), but not a werewolf (Klaus couldn't compel Ray in "The Hybrid"). Mikael's body is engulfed in flames in death.

PREVIOUSLY ON *THE VAMPIRE DIARIES* Stefan mentions Elena's "track record with high school dances," referring to the disasters of "Unpleasantville" and "The Last Dance." Damon and Elena establish that they do, in fact, trust each other; how far they've come since "Bloodlines" when Elena was very unsure of the answer to her question, "Can I trust you?" Like Rebekah keen to go to her first high school dance, Anna showed up at the Decade Dance in "Unpleasantville," her first one ever too.

OFF CAMERA My Morning Jacket was kind enough to come to Mystic Falls to play Klaus's wake for Mikael. The Kentucky rock band formed in the late 1990s; the four songs heard in this episode are all from their Grammy-nominated 2011 album, *Circuital*. Said frontman Jim James to *Rolling Stone*, "All of the vampires and werewolves we met on the set of *The Vampire Diaries* were nice regular folks just like most of us — good upstanding citizens, but forced to live with this secret tragic double-life dilemma. They treated us most fairly and with dignity and respect as they sucked our bodily fluids dry and smothered us in sexy kisses. God bless them. God bless them all."

FOGGY MOMENTS How did Klaus so easily find all those werewolves to turn into hybrids? It took him and Stefan two months to track down Ray. Why did Mikael go along with the revised plan, showing up at the Lockwood mansion that he couldn't enter and turning his only Original-killing weapon over to Damon? When you wait a thousand years to take revenge, why not wait one more day? Pounce on Klaus on his way to the coffin truck. From Mikael's perspective, would it have mattered if Klaus killed Stefan and company that night for lying about Mikael's death? Collateral damage!

QUESTIONS

- Since Mikael could compel the hybrids, does that mean a strong, older vampire could mess with a weak, younger hybrid's mind?
- Did Matt know that Katherine, and not Elena, was his date to homecoming?
- Will Momma and Poppa Original be reunited on the Other Side?
- Where did Stefan take the Original coffins? Was it Katherine's idea to steal them? How did they steal them?

Jeremy (to Elena): You get on my case about school and work — who cares? None of us are going to make it out of this town alive.

3.10 *The New Deal*

Original air date: January 5, 2012
Written by: Michael Narducci
Directed by: John Behring
Guest cast: Kimberly Drummond (Mindy), Justine Ezarik (Pretty Bartender), Zach Sale (EMT), Zane Stephens (Tony)
Previously on *The Vampire Diaries*: Steven R. McQueen

Klaus targets Jeremy in an effort to goad Stefan into returning his coffin collection.

Out of the frying pan and into the fire — that is the way things go on a typical Sunday in Mystic Falls, and at the beginning of "The New Deal" it seems to be taking its toll on the gang as they await "Klaus-aggedon." The futility of keeping their chins up against so powerful an enemy weighs heavy and raises the question of what motivates them in these extreme conditions.

A perfect exercise in futility opens the episode: Elena tries to outrun a

hybrid. No matter how hard she trains, hybrids and vampires will always be faster, stronger, and more powerful than her. While Elena struggles on, Jeremy has flat out given up on his "normal" life: he's been fired from the Grill (which he hoped for in "The Birthday") and he doesn't even bother to hide his plagiarism (and on a history paper in Alaric's class!). Alaric and Elena go on high alert, trying to corral Jeremy into talking about his despondency, but Jer has a valid question not easily answered: why should he care? When faced with every indication that he won't even have a future, let alone a normal one, there seems to be no point in trying to build one. Instead, Jeremy resolves himself to a life of daily threats and extreme violence. And, following in Alaric's footsteps, why not add day-drinking and a questionable choice for a friend?

The wait for the next threat doesn't last long: Klaus returns as the prime motivator; once again his demands drive the plot along, terrorize the characters, and give us high stakes scenarios that reveal true motivations. At the same time, the story gets a new layer of villainy with Stefan giving Klaus a taste of his own medicine. Stefan exacts his revenge by targeting Klaus's loved ones, just as Klaus returns to town and attempts to do the same to Stefan. With Mikael dead, Klaus finally has the opportunity to stop running and put down some roots — and where else but in his hometown, Mystic Falls? But Stefan has muddled this happy, anticipated moment by stealing his coffined family. As Stefan explicitly states, his goal is to destroy Klaus and he targets his weakness: family. The parallels between the families on *TVD* continue with Klaus and Damon discussing their common ground and with siblings forced to make difficult choices. Should Stefan have saved Damon's life when he had the choice to take Klaus's and end the insanity? Should Klaus have left Rebekah undaggered and faced the consequences of his past actions? Should Elena have decided for her brother that he deserves a better life, one free from front-porch decapitations? There are no easy decisions to be made, but it wouldn't be *The Vampire Diaries* if things were simple and the right choices were clear.

Despite there being no easy choices, decisions still need to be made, and often without the luxury of time. What motivates these choices? Klaus uses violence to get what he wants (and often he deliberately puts a short deadline on his demands to spur action), and his targets respond by protecting loved ones, honoring family bonds or a sense of duty, giving in to their own selfishness, focusing on their need for revenge, or following that basic instinct for survival. In "The New Deal," characters explore these motivating forces as they act independently from one another, no longer a group with a common goal as in "Homecoming." In this splintering, new alliances are formed, most notably when the dead witches stop (hilariously) torturing Damon and let him in the house. Their shared hatred of Klaus unites them with their former enemy.

"The New Deal" also forces the question of what cost is acceptable in trying to make your loved ones safe. In the past, a character has often been protected against their will — Alaric bound in the witch house during the sacrifice and Caroline vervained by Tyler at homecoming are two recent examples — and Elena's decision to send Jeremy away to Denver is another instance of this muddy choice. By having Damon compel Jeremy, Elena and Alaric take away his free will — but it's for his own good. It's a tough choice for Elena to make: she feels guilt-ridden instantly and anticipates the day he'll find out what she's done. Damon's point is that it's better to have him resent her choice, to be estranged from her brother, than for him to be dead. From an audience standpoint, it's a hard choice to watch her make. As lost as Jeremy is, he is also fierce in this episode: he says what needs to be said, he steps up his game when he realizes he is a pawn, and he wields a crossbow and cleaver like Alaric Junior Edition. But for Elena, watching her baby brother behead a man on the front porch is a breaking point. As it would be for most.

Elena feels responsible for her brother, just as Alaric does for the Gilbert kids — epitomized by his heroic dart in front of the SUV — and just as Stefan and Damon feel responsible for each other. As much as they drive each other crazy, Stefan, no matter how far gone he is, will never stop saving Damon, and Damon will never give up on his brother — no matter what the other wants.

On the other side of the spectrum from those willful Salvatore brothers is Tyler, who starts to understand what his sire bond actually means when Klaus forces him to do something he doesn't want to do. Tyler accuses Alaric and Elena of overthinking his hybrid status, just like Caroline, but his answers to their questions seem to surprise even him. He *would* harm himself if Klaus commanded it; he can dodge arrows but he can't exercise his own will. That situation is nicely paired with Jeremy's, whose sovereignty is taken from him by Elena, Alaric, and Damon for his own good, just as Tyler's release from the werewolf curse is cast by Klaus as something done for his own betterment.

Like Elena, awash in guilt about her brother and what she's done to him, Damon's guilt about his brother is a constant cross to bear — after all, Stefan got into this whole Klaus-Ripper state saving Damon's life — and Damon finds out that Stefan *saved his life again*. The building relationship between

Damon and Elena only further complicates an already muddled situation. She's been leaning on him for comfort, companionship, and as her partner-in-scheming but, in "The New Deal," she carefully draws the line at physical attraction by dodging his "attractive looks" comment. Damon decides to be honest with Elena about Stefan, so she knows the full story before he leans in for a kiss. Damon finally makes it crystal clear what he wants from Elena; she can't deny it. What fun is romance without guilt and complications?

COMPELLING MOMENT That decapitation. Instead of showing the actual beheading — or a giant pool of blood besmirching the sacred Gilbert porch — the spatter on Jeremy's face, the clatter of the cleaver hitting the porch, and Elena's bloody cleanup made it more haunting and real than if the headless hybrid had been shown. Well played, *TVD*.

CIRCLE OF KNOWLEDGE
- No Caroline or Matt.
- On *The Vampire Diaries* characters often treat each other like pawns and playthings, but in this episode there were a number of outright references to games: Damon plays darts, which Klaus bests him at; Jeremy and Tyler play at target practice; and Damon's "olly olly oxen free" reminds us that the whole episode is a game of hide and seek with various targets: both Klaus and Stefan have been in hiding, and the Original hybrid is madly seeking his coffins.
- Perhaps Shakespeare was thinking of the devilish Klaus and the joy he takes in villainy when he wrote in *Julius Caesar*: "And some that smile have in their hearts, I fear / millions of mischiefs."

THE RULES Tyler kindly provides Jeremy with How to Kill a Hybrid 101: rip out the heart or chop off the head. The spirits of the dead witches are able to hide the coffins in plain sight, making them invisible to everyone but those whom they allow to see them. Stefan's comment that Klaus doesn't just get to live forever is in keeping with the established rule of nature: there has to be balance, and the witches are the keepers of that balance.

HISTORY LESSON In 1933, Franklin D. Roosevelt was elected president based on his campaign promise of a "New Deal" for the American people, and during his first 100 days of presidency, a record number of bills were passed to ease the hardship of the Great Depression and help with the economy's recovery. He and his brain trust worked to restore the banking system, alleviate unemployment, establish labor laws, and increase public works projects.

PREVIOUSLY ON *THE VAMPIRE DIARIES* Witchy ghost Emily Bennett gave Bonnie bad dreams that led her to the old cemetery in season 1 and that also gave us our first glimpse of Bonnie's bedroom in "162 Candles" when she woke up from one of those dreams, as she does here. Damon describes Stefan as a "buzzkill," which he first did in "A Few Good Men." Elena slaps Stefan instead of Damon, who was the target of the Gilbert backhand in "Friday Night Bites," "Haunted," "The Sacrifice," and "The Last Dance." Just as Alaric and Elena try to reach out to Jeremy with food, Jenna tried to have family mealtime with Jeremy in "The Night of the Comet," but he bailed. After Damon offered to erase Jeremy's memory again in "Under Control," Elena said she wouldn't do that again to him.

OFF CAMERA "The book fans have, for two and a half years, been screaming at the top of their lungs, 'Where's Meredith? Where's Meredith?'" Julie Plec said to Zap2It.com. "Meredith was in our original pilot draft, but you have to do some editing and some streamlining when you take a project from book to TV, and Meredith was one of the victims of that streamlining." See the "Where's Meredith?" sidebar (opposite) for a longtime book fan's perspective on Dr. Meredith Fell's arrival in Mystic Falls.

FOGGY MOMENTS How did Stefan get the coffins into that house unseen, and into that basement? Not a fun moving job. What was Bonnie's role in veiling the coffins? Did she cast the spell to hide them, drawing on the dead witches' power? If so, then why did it seem like she and Stefan were looking at the coffins together for the first time at the end of the episode? Before Bonnie reveals that she knows where Stefan is, Elena says Bonnie believes her locator spell isn't working. Why wouldn't it be?

QUESTIONS
- Back in "Disturbing Behavior," Damon killed Alaric and it took Alaric longer than usual to come back to life, leading Damon to quip that his ring's going bad. And here Alaric is resurrected but not healed; his ring can't be entirely relied on. Why is it faltering? Does a spell wear out like

"Where's Meredith?"

This was the question heard 'round Vampire Diaries book fandom when the principal cast of the *TVD* pilot was announced in 2009, sans one central character from L.J. Smith's original book series. Meredith Sulez, one of Elena Gilbert's best friends, was cut from the pilot script in the interest of stream-lining an already overwhelming roster of characters, but fans of the books couldn't let go of their cool, practical, witty favorite, and clung tight to Julie Plec's promise that Meredith would make her way to Mystic Falls eventually.

Fans who have made their entry into *Vampire Diaries* via the television series may not understand what all the fuss is about, but imagine the show without, say, Caroline or Bonnie . . . or Elena's right arm. Meredith's absence from our television screens has long been a glaring omission for many a book fan. Her exclusion was the one change in the page-to-screen transla-tion that truly hurt. No matter how different and complicated the show's friendship dynamic between Elena, Caroline, and Bonnie has been, book fans have always wondered, "*What if?*"

So imagine the surprise and excitement when our patience paid off, and Dr. Meredith Fell finally made her TV debut in *The Vampire Diaries* season 3 in a reveal the production managed to keep a secret in spite of Torrey DeVitto's numerous interviews leading up to her character's introduction in "The New Deal."

Whether Meredith will become an integral part of the TV show's ever-evolving plot puzzle remains to be seen, but Plec and writers have not shied away from fan service; Meredith Sulez's backstory plays a huge part in TVD's book universe, and some of that story has been folded into the show's Original mythology. Perhaps we can expect Meredith Fell to play an even bigger role in season 4's events?

—*Vee, co-founder of Vampire-Diaries.net*

a battery? Could Bonnie, who has Emily Bennett's grimoire with the Gilbert ring spell in it, make a new ring for Alaric? Should Alaric be carrying a vial of Damon's blood around, just in case?

- Will Bonnie or Damon tell Elena about Stefan's plan?
- Is there a way for Tyler to break his sire bond to Klaus?
- Is Bonnie's dream giving her a clue as to how to kill Klaus? How will the Original Witch's necklace, which Klaus holds in her dream, fit into the puzzle? Who or what is currently occupying that coffin?
- How is Dr. Meredith Fell related to Logan Fell? Did she grow up in Mystic Falls with Jenna and company?

Torrey DeVitto as Dr. Fell

Third time was the charm for Torrey DeVitto and *The Vampire Diaries*. The actress originally auditioned for role of Elena and then came in again for Courtney Ford's one-episode role in second season. Finally, the stars aligned with Meredith.

Born in New York, on June 8, 1984, Torrey Joel DeVitto balances her busy acting schedule with interests in photography, volunteer work in hospices, and fundraising for charities that are close to her heart. She's also an accomplished musician — like her father, Liberty DeVitto, long-time drummer for Billy Joel — and Torrey can most recently be heard as a featured violinist on Stevie Nicks' 2011 album *In Your Dreams*. Though she has diverse interests, Torrey has known she wanted to act since she was a teen. "I graduated high school early and knew that I wanted to jump right into acting. Even while I was in high school I was always auditioning for anything that came through Orlando, where I lived at the time." She spent a month living in Chicago when she was 16; she was there to work as a model but, she says, she had limited success due to her height. Television roles followed including a bit part on *Dawson's Creek*; single episodes of *Scrubs*, *The King of Queens*, *Jack & Bobby*, *Castle*, and *CSI: Miami*; and a recurring part on *Drake & Josh*. Torrey made her mark in ABC Family's *Beautiful People* (2005–2006) and most infamously as *One Tree Hill*'s Nanny Carrie — a part she's so strongly identified with by viewers that "Nanny Carrie" trended on Twitter during her first episode of *The Vampire Diaries*. Her film roles include *Cheesecake Casserole*, *Evidence*, *The Rite*, and a number of horror flicks, including *I'll Always Know What You Did Last Summer* (2006) and *Killer Movie* (2008), which costarred her future husband Paul Wesley. The two got married in April 2011, and by year's end were working together again when Torrey landed a role on *The Vampire Diaries'* third season. The busy actress had to split her time between Mystic Falls and Rosewood, Pennsylvania, the fictional *Pretty Little Liars* town where her overachieving character Melissa Hastings resides (and torments little sis Spencer).

Torrey is happy to be playing Meredith Fell, describing the character to Starry Constellation Magazine as "smart, sharp, strong and straight forward. I love getting to portray females that have a backbone." She knew how important Meredith was to the books, having read them a few years back. "I actually auditioned for the pilot, and when Paul booked it, I went to Borders and bought the whole series," she told HollywoodLife.com. "It was so long ago that I didn't remember specifics about Meredith, but I did remember her. She's definitely different on the show, and that's why I didn't revisit the books. I didn't want to get conflicted views in my head." Not only was Torrey jumping into a character much anticipated by fans, but she was joining a series well into its groove. "To go into a show that's been going on for three seasons now," explained Torrey to Zap2It, "and to know everybody so well and then to come in, I was like, 'Oh, man, I'm going to be judged so

hard; I'm so nervous. What if I suck? What if they think I suck?' And I was just like, 'Stop. You got hired for a reason.'" Of course, her fears were unfounded, and she's had a great time on set. Most of her scenes are opposite Matt Davis's Alaric, which she's enjoyed. "I think he is a great actor and has a really great sense of humor. He and everyone else on the cast made me feel really comfortable coming into all this."

When Torrey isn't in Mystic Falls or Rosewood, she dedicates her spare time to volunteerism and charitable causes. For years, she's worked directly with patients in a hospice in California and became a hospice ambassador in 2012 for the National Palliative Care Organization. "I think one of the biggest misconceptions is that it's scary to be with the dying, or that it would feel too morbid to be a part of it," she explained. "I have found such a light in being a part of hospice, one I would have never have thought I'd discover. . . . Being a volunteer helps me appreciate things in my own life so much more." Together with Paul Wesley, Torrey has become involved with Global Roots, an organization that works to help improve the lives of needy children, orphaned or abandoned in places of war, famine, or social unrest.

A woman who's both socially conscious and fandom conscious, Torrey DeVitto has proven committed to bringing her best to all aspects of her life and work. As for Meredith Fell, she told *Entertainment Weekly*, "I know there's a lot of book fans that love Meredith, and I know she's a little different on the show, so I just hope I do the book fans justice."

Damon: The only way to call someone's bluff, Stefan, is to be willing to lose everything if you're wrong.

3.11 Our Town

Original air date: January 12, 2012
Written by: Rebecca Sonnenshine
Directed by: Wendey Stanzler
Guest cast: Kimberly Drummond (Mindy), Daniel Newman (Daniel), David Colin Smith (Brian)
Previously on *The Vampire Diaries*: Candice Accola

Caroline's 18th birthday turns into a funeral; Stefan tries to out-villain Klaus.

"We must be willing to let go of the life we have planned, so as to have the life that is waiting for us." On the occasion of Caroline's 18th birthday, Caroline, and then Elena, go through the process of letting go of their old selves and expectations, mourning the girls they no longer are or could ever become again. The episode's reflection on the necessary changes that come as adolescents move into adulthood, letting go of who they once were or thought they might be, was touchingly rendered, particularly in the impromptu funeral rites. Since this is a supernatural drama, this transition to a new phase of life is heightened, and the loss of life and rebirth is literal for Caroline, both in mourning the loss of her human life and in her near-death in this episode. Both Caroline and Elena decide to let go of the past and bravely embrace their future. As much as Matt's right that the girls are "stuck" in this dangerous supernatural life, they both make a choice to live, not to wallow.

Friends don't strip friends of their free will. And yet, on *The Vampire Diaries*, friends do just that with great frequency. Bonnie lets Elena know exactly how she feels about the choice to compel Jeremy, and Elena knows Bonnie is right. But she feels it's a crime worth committing in order to protect her little bro. In a nice scene of BFF disagreement at Caroline's birthday-funeral, Bonnie calls Elena out on her tendency to be a bossypants, wanting to control people's actions. And, as if to prove Bonnie right, shortly thereafter, Elena tries to track down Caroline in the woods to make sure she doesn't get back together with Tyler. Elena is always, in one way or another, trying to get Damon (and now Stefan) to behave as she thinks they ought to.

In another free-will-related storyline, Tyler deals with the ramifications of his sire bond to Klaus. From his initial heartbreaking acceptance of his inability to act independently of Klaus's wishes to his false hope that he *can* stand up to his sire where Caroline is concerned to his devastating realization that he remains under Klaus's power, Tyler battles with what it means to be a hybrid in a way that demonstrates that he is miles away from his cocky, don't-overthink-it attitude of "The New Deal." Against his will, Tyler has traded one curse for another.

And now that Stefan has his free will back, what he's chosen to do is a disappointment to all (save maybe Damon, who seems to be enjoying this dimmer-switch Stefan, most of the time). Klaus is "hurt" that Stefan didn't reignite the friendship they shared, while Elena is stunned that he is so far gone and willing to hurt her in such precisely targeted ways. Does Stefan truly believe that all he has left is destroying Klaus? What will be left for him if he ever succeeds?

Back in season 1, when Damon was Stefan's (and Mystic Falls') biggest problem, Stefan wondered how he could beat the monster without becoming one himself. How much he's changed since then. In "Our Town," Stefan is determined to best Klaus at his own game, to be the better villain, in order to ultimately destroy him. How much Stefan will risk in his quest for his revenge, whether there is any moral boundary left he won't cross, is the question that no one — particularly Damon, Klaus, and Elena — knows the answer to. Was Stefan ready to drive his car off Wickery Bridge to end Elena's human life or would he have backed down if Klaus hadn't? Stefan avoids answering this question, and before he abandons Elena and drives off, Stefan tells her he no longer cares what she thinks of him. Stefan wins this battle against Klaus, who agrees to get his hybrids out of town, but he does so in an exceptionally cruel way — unnecessarily cruel, since there are a multitude of ways to threaten Elena's life, where Klaus would still hear real fear in her cries without it being so personal. As Elena says to Stefan, he knew this was where her parents died, where she nearly died, and he also knows how desperately she doesn't want to become a vampire ("The Last Day"). Is he trying to destroy her along with Klaus?

While it is terrifying for Elena to relive the first worst moment of her life (she has so many worst moments), Bad Stefan unleashed makes for an exciting episode. Stefan's choices are his own, and he proves a formidable villain, from surprise decapitations to the Wickery Bridge incident. Klaus's smirks and cutting remarks, Stefan energized by testing the Original's limits, and Damon proud of his baby bro for outsmarting Klaus: they are three of a kind, really. Both Klaus's strategy of making allies of the town's leaders and Stefan's wild plans are things that Damon has done or would do. Klaus, Stefan, and Damon are talented at scheming and terrorizing, but that humanity dimmer switch is controlled by how much they care about the "collateral damage" in question. In "The New Deal," Klaus used violence to get what he wanted, but here (for the most part) he's changed tack to diplomacy. He builds alliances, and establishes control, with Carol Lockwood, legitimizing his presence in Mystic Falls, and painting Stefan as the one out of control. (Granted, he is.) One pawn who is hurt is Caroline. Though Klaus apologizes to her, telling her it's not personal, it always is, at least for the person who is the collateral damage. Elena, Caroline, and Tyler directly suffer because of the pissing contest the

boys are engaged in. (Not to mention the pile of dead hybrids; they too presumably have loved ones somewhere or other.)

A question just as beguiling as how far gone Stefan is — and what it will take to bring him back — is Klaus's endgame. He's in a new position: his thousand-year run from his father over, it's time to settle down, and he's chosen Mystic Falls. Would he honor his bargain with Mayor Lockwood to protect the citizens of Mystic Falls in exchange for being left alone? That is, in essence, the arrangement the Salvatore brothers had with Carol and Liz; what's so wrong about Klaus giving peace a chance?

As punishment for his hybrid's willfulness, Klaus quite deliberately makes Tyler bite Caroline, an action that results in distancing Caroline and Tyler (Tyler's pledge that he can choose her over Klaus proven empty), in Klaus gaining the cooperation of the town sheriff, and in a budding connection between Klaus and Caroline. Just what is this ruby-lipped millennium-old hybrid up to? Judging by those shining tears in his eyes, his beautiful speech to her about embracing life is made in earnest. Does he have an ulterior motive or does he simply want to connect with Caroline? His birthday gift of a diamond bracelet quite specifically attempts to one up Tyler's charm bracelet by giving her a taste of the "genuine beauty" he promises is out there in the world waiting for her if only she'll take it. What will Caroline make of this strange turn of events?

Though Elena and her friends being there for her and giving her that impromptu funeral helped, Caroline seems to take Klaus's words to heart. On the morning of her birthday, Caroline's future, once so full of promise, seems to her bleak and uncertain; a girl who is optimism epitomized wants to wallow in her realization that she'll forever be 17. But that grief evolves into acceptance, especially after being faced with the alternative — death. Klaus urges Caroline to adjust her perception of her self and her future to her new circumstances. She can't think of time as she did when she was human; she's a vampire now and has, like, a million birthdays ahead of her. Where she saw limits, Klaus asks her to see limitless potential. The scene is emotionally philosophical, a quality that characterizes this whole episode from the major moments, like Elena's two bridge scenes, down to the smallest, like Alaric's "I put a kid on a plane" line to Meredith.

While the romance between Elena and her vampires is not at the center of the episode, it is intrinsically linked to the various elements and themes in play. As Bonnie accepts she must say goodbye to Jeremy, and Caroline is prepared to let go of her hoped-for happy ending with Tyler, Elena is confronted by Stefan who believes she just hasn't admitted to herself what has already been broken between them. Is Stefan right: did he lose her the moment he left Mystic Falls as Klaus's lackey? Is there a way for these two to find their way back to each other? Klaus says that kind of love never dies. But on the other side of the Salvatore coin, Damon believes his romance with Elena is "right but not right now."

Full of daring choices that prove bold storytelling need not go for cheap twists, "Our Town" delivers the unexpected while ruminating on the journey between stages of life. A standout episode of the season.

COMPELLING MOMENT For the sheer unexpectedness coupled with beautiful performances and writing, the Klaus and Caroline scene takes the (birthday) cake. But honorable mention to pretty much every other moment in this episode.

CIRCLE OF KNOWLEDGE

- American playwright Thornton Wilder (1897–1975) won a Pulitzer Prize for *Our Town*, which was first performed in 1938. The play, set in fictional small town Grover's Corners, New Hampshire, in 1901 and 1913, consists of three acts: Daily Life, Love and Marriage, and Death and Eternity. The first act introduces us to the town and its residents — the same families have lived there for centuries, as in Mystic Falls — and Mrs. Gibbs, the doctor's wife, dreams of leaving town just once in her life to visit a place where they don't speak English, to see beyond the confines of her small-town life. ("There's a whole world out there waiting for you . . ." as Klaus tells Caroline.) In the second act, the teenagers have graduated high school, and it's Emily and George's wedding day. Seventeen-year-old Emily's anxieties are akin to Caroline's: she's letting go of her childhood self and with that comes fear of isolation and the desire for someone to love her forever and ever. George struggles with whether to leave his small town to grow or stay in Grover's Corners because there's "nothing better elsewhere." In the third act, Emily has died, and her ghost joins the spirits of those Grover's Corners folks who died before her. She watches the mourners visit her grave, and she wants to go back to revisit her past, now aware of the fleeting and wonderful life she had: "Do any human beings ever realize life every minute they live it?" In the end, she realizes it's impossible to go back. *Our Town* is chock-full of truisms about the cycle of life, family, and community, but one in particular resonates with the key scene between Caroline and Klaus, and her choice to move into this new phase of her existence: "You've got to love life to have life, you've got to have life to love life."

- Thank you, show, for explicitly acknowledging that the humanity switch has more settings than simply "on" and "off."
- Klaus asks Damon to "give peace a chance"; he clearly wasn't in Mystic Falls when Damon told Stefan, in regards to the Mason Lockwood situation, that he wasn't going in for any of that "'Give Peace a Chance' crap" in "Kill or Be Killed" (both referencing the 1969 John Lennon–penned song).
- Damon hopes Liz Forbes won't "drink the Klaus Kool-Aid," a reference to the Jonestown Massacre of 1978, a phrase that's come to mean the danger of blind faith among followers, which will lead to self-destruction.

THE RULES Klaus reminds us that his blood is the cure for a vampire with a hybrid (or werewolf) bite. The hybrids are very easy to kill, the equivalent of baby vamps — not yet as skilled or strong as an older supernatural creature (such as a Salvatore brother).

PREVIOUSLY ON *THE VAMPIRE DIARIES* Klaus is not the first vampire who returns to Mystic Falls looking to settle down again: in season 1, Pearl and the better-tempered tomb vampires wanted to rebuild their lives in the town as well. Elena first learned that it was Stefan who saved her from drowning after the Wickery Bridge accident in "Bloodlines"; in "The Last Day," after Damon force-feeds her his blood, Elena admits how desperately she doesn't want to be a vampire. Lying in her bed, Caroline asks Klaus, "Are you going to kill me?" just as she asked of Damon in "Family Ties."

OFF CAMERA Candice Accola was particularly happy about the scenes between Caroline, Bonnie, and Elena in this episode, depicting how they handle the bumps and hardships in a friendship: "I love those moments, and I think it's a great example that young, teenage women on television can actually be supportive of each other and be honest with each other, without name calling and stabbing each other in the back continuously." On how Elena and Matt's friendship has evolved since season 1, Zach Roerig told the

Huffington Post, "There was always an existing friendship, and there was a love from their childhood, but it's not the same friendship that there was before. All of that is gone. Elena is a different person now, like Matt told her on the bridge, so it's all about moving forward. And he's changed too. His best friends are a witch, a vampire, and a doppelgänger who's fallen in love with two vampires. [Laughs.] He's really had to accept all of this, and it made him become kind of like a new guy. I think that he and Elena are just going to keep getting closer as friends."

QUESTIONS
- Which was the most memorable *TVD* beheading? Elijah taking off Trevor's noggin in "Rose," or Stefan surprise-decapitating Mindy in "Our Town"?
- What were Dr. Fell and Brian Walters fighting about when Alaric interceded? What is Meredith "messing with" that could ruin her career? Who murdered Brian and why did they use a stake?
- What did Caroline wish for when she blew out the candles on her birthday-funeral cake?
- Three sleeping Originals: Elijah and the other two siblings. Who is in the fourth coffin?

Abby: I want to help you.
Bonnie: You can't. You have no magic and I don't trust you.

3.12 *The Ties That Bind*

Original air date: January 19, 2012
Written by: Brian Young
Directed by: John Dahl
Guest cast: Daniel Newman (Daniel)
Previously on *The Vampire Diaries*: Kat Graham

Bonnie tracks down her mother to help open the spelled-shut coffin, Damon plays detective with Meredith, and Tyler tries to break his sire bond.

Family takes all forms in Mystic Falls, and though the ties that bind these characters to each other are often touted as the most valuable and important force, it doesn't mean that they aren't fraught with all kinds of bad ju-ju. In "The Ties That Bind," the relationships between family, friends, and romantic interests are tested, tried, and tentatively repaired.

For a three-season core character, it's been a long time coming for Bonnie Bennett to get this kind of storyline attention, and her family history went a long way in showing how Bonnie got to be so *Bonnie*. Back in the '90s, Abby was not so different from her daughter: a Bennett witch caught up in vampire problems, she risked her life to help her best friend, Miranda Gilbert. In the present, she's as forthcoming as her estranged daughter always is, telling Bonnie the truth even though she knows it will be hard for her to hear. Abby's kindness and loyalty to Jamie, someone she considers her family, are other qualities she shares with Bonnie. (And it shouldn't be a big surprise; after all, both women were raised by the incomparable Grams Bennett.) From Abby's story, we learn that Elijah and Klaus weren't the first Originals to come waltzing through Mystic Falls in search of the doppelgänger: Mikael was there when the girls were only three years old, and it was Abby who put him in the crypt in which Katherine and Jeremy found him. She risked her life to take out an Original and save Elena — sound familiar? — but instead of returning to Mystic Falls, Abby made a different choice, one that put her own needs over her family's.

Bonnie's mom reinvented herself — wanting to be a woman, instead of a witch — and Caroline comes home to find her estranged boyfriend and her absentee daddy on a similar mission of reinvention. From angry jock to suffering werewolf to cocky hybrid, Tyler's been through a *lot* of major life changes in the past year. After he nearly killed Caroline by biting her in "Our Town," Tyler finally understands how powerful the sire bond is, and he is determined to do whatever it takes to free himself and to protect Caroline. A massive first step. Bill Forbes is also trying to atone for his past mistakes — torturing Caroline and all that — and he's game to help Tyler regain his free will. Just as Abby offers to help Bonnie at the end of the episode, Bill accepts the risk of coaching a hybrid to turn. Though he very nearly died from Tyler's attack, Bill doesn't seem to have any intention of abandoning Caroline or Tyler. He's raring to swing that axe at Tyler again!

"The Ties That Bind" was an apology-filled episode: Tyler's apology to Caroline, Bill's veiled apology, Abby's to Bonnie . . . and Stefan's to Elena.

As Tyler and Abby make tentative first steps back to who they used to be — or who they want to be — the badass Ripper can't help having twinges of old Stefan feelings. Though his humanity dimmer switch is set low, Stefan has been feeling *tons* — as evidenced by him saving his brother back in "Homecoming" and his need for revenge against Klaus — and his don't-care attitude has been getting less and less convincing. It all comes back to the Lexi Recovery Plan: get him to feel something, even negative emotions like rage against Klaus, and sooner or later the good stuff sneaks back in too. Stefan's emotional responses are becoming less easily repressed and more varied. It's incredibly subtle what Paul Wesley has done with Stefan in the 12 episodes since last season's finale: through these teeny, tiny gradations of expression, he conveys when Stefan is totally gone into Crazy Ripper territory, when he's just faking it, when he's letting his old self resurface, and how conflicted he is about what he should allow himself to feel, about which

Persia White as Abby Bennett Wilson

Though Abby Bennett is a stranger to her daughter, Florida-born Persia White is no stranger to The CW. Best known for her role as Lynn on *Girlfriends*, which aired from 2000 to 2008, Persia has been performing since she was a little girl. She started acting in films and TV shows in the mid 1990s, and landed her first recurring role on *Breaker High*, playing one of the high school kids on the ship along with Ryan Gosling. She's also an activist and musician.

Her character's relationship with Bonnie is strained, but the two women who portray the Bennetts get along famously. "I got together with Kat Graham before we starting filming and that was great because she really cares a lot about giving her character some history as well," explained Persia to Collider.com. "Fans haven't been able to see that until now. Over the first two seasons, her character was kind of a mystery. So, it was really nice to hear what her backstory is as well, just so I know, and then we have our own combined history. It's a very fun process." It wasn't all serious character study, though; the two shared fun times as well, as Persia told TVFanatic.com. "We both have a musical and dancing background. Sometimes we laugh so much together on set, they have to tell us to be quiet and stop goofing around. I love many of the cast members on *The Vampire Diaries*, it really is the best cast and crew I've ever worked with."

Stefan he should be. And in "The Ties That Bind," the things that Stefan experiences — his villain-parrying with Klaus, Elena trying to dodge him for the day, the change he sees (and admires) in her, and her admission that she kissed Damon — culminate in flashes of his humanity. He's full of hurt and sadness and, perhaps, hopelessness with a side of jealousy, and his actions reveal that. He apologizes to Elena for the traumatizing Wickery Bridge incident; he tells her she's better than either Salvatore brother; and he punches Damon for kissing his one true love. In a show known for its fast pace and plotting, Stefan's journey this season has been delightfully slow. Klaus's observation that a crazy Stefan is a friendless Stefan is just what the Ripper is realizing himself. Will Stefan soon decide that there are more important things in life than destroying Klaus?

As much as there was weighty emotional stuff in "The Ties That Bind" (a must-have in any *TVD* episode), it was balanced by a good lot of fun: enter Detective Damon, the Meddler. His protectiveness over Alaric is incredibly endearing, even as he accuses the mysterious Dr. Fell of murder. And while murder is no laughing matter, the way this Mystic Falls killer intrigue is being handled is nothing but fun. Red flags abound with Meredith — the murdered ex, the "angry drunk" comment, trying to take off Alaric's ring — but on the flip side, she's a literal life saver, willing to put her career at risk by cheating at her job when she can, saving lives with supernatural healing powers. (And, really, what's vampire blood but exceptionally powerful, effective medicine?) While her status as a prime suspect may be up for debate, what's clear is that Torrey DeVitto's Meredith is a welcome addition to the *TVD* world.

In another fun Damon scene, he seizes an opportunity when Klaus manages to get back the coffins (well, three of them). In his conversation with Klaus at the witch house, Damon seems barely able to contain his glee; unbeknownst to us and to Klaus, he has an ace up his sleeve, a surprise move. If Klaus wants his family back so badly, Damon will give him an undaggered big brother. It was a classic *Vampire Diaries* ending: could there be any better cliffhanger than the return of Elijah?

COMPELLING MOMENT Bonnie telling her mother how Grams died; Kat Graham killed it portraying Bonnie's strength and sadness in that moment and the rawness of her emotion.

CIRCLE OF KNOWLEDGE
- No Jeremy or Matt.
- The episode's title comes from the Christian hymn "Blessed Be the Tie That Binds" (which is, incidentally, sung twice in *Our Town*) about the bonds of love that create fellowship and kinship in a community: "Our fears, our hopes, our aims are one / Our comforts and our cares. / We share each other's woes, / Our mutual burdens bear; / And often for each other flows / The sympathizing tear."
- In the opening dream sequence, Bonnie walks past the tombstones of her ancestors: Sheila (a.k.a. Grams), Amelia, and Ernestine — all Bennett women just like Bonnie, her mom, and great-great-granwitch Emily. The long line of women with the Bennett name suggests it's maternal, and every woman kept her own surname (or never married) and passed it along to her children. Perhaps the "Wilson" in "Abby Bennett Wilson" is Bonnie's dad's last name.

- Abby lives in Monroe, North Carolina, which is in the greater metro-politan area of Charlotte (where she entombed Mikael in the '90s).
- A minor moment but a symbolic one: when Stefan comes home to find Klaus chilling in the Salvatore great room, he takes the control . . . and turns down the music.
- Klaus baits Stefan with the same strategy that Mikael used on Klaus in "Homecoming"; he reminds him that being Crazy Stefan will be a lonely existence, just as it is for the king of the hybrids.
- After his run-in with Dr. Fell, Damon looks for a bunny in the pot on Ric's stove. In 1987's *Fatal Attraction*, crazed jilted Alex (Glenn Close) boils the pet bunny belonging to her lover's daughter; a "bunny boiler" has become shorthand for a person, usually a woman, who turns violent.
- Dr. Fell thinks Bill Forbes was actually attacked by an animal, so it looks like she and the general council membership don't know about were-wolves or hybrids, just good old-fashioned vampires.
- "I don't think you realize how bad you've gotten!" Oh Elena, Stefan spent his summer on a serial-killing rampage. Choking and compelling Jamie, instead of immediately decapitating him, is an improvement on Stefan's recent behavior.

THE RULES A hybrid's transition to wolf form is as torturous as it is for a regular werewolf. Bill theorizes that it will get easier with practice, and that when Tyler "owns" the pain he can break his sire bond. Abby uses some herbal, magic-dulling knockout powder on Bonnie. After doing the spell to trap Mikael in the crypt, Abby's powers gradually faded as she stayed away from her family, causing her to wonder if nature punishes witchy mothers who abandon their witchy children.

OFF CAMERA Just as Elena gives her blessing to Alaric, Paul Wesley had a little chat with Matt Davis before he smooched Torrey DeVitto, Paul's wife. As Paul related on *Rachael Ray*, "[Matt] came up to me and he was like, 'Is this okay? Is this going to be okay? Are you sure?' I was like, 'Dude, no, it's okay! Get in there! Get in there, champ! Do what you gotta do!' Perfectly normal, healthy environment." As for Meredith's relationship with Damon, Torrey enjoys their dynamic, as she told *Entertainment Weekly*: "When you have two strong personalities in the room, they kind of go back and forth with each other because neither one of them is gonna back down. She doesn't fall for the lure that is Damon. She's obviously attracted to his friend Alaric. She's not even scared of Damon. She doesn't buy it. I think all his little tricks and things don't work on her like they do other girls."

FOGGY MOMENTS Who did Damon compel to speed up the Abby research? Shouldn't Sheriff Forbes, who presumably knew Abby when she lived in Mystic Falls and who helped the girls locate *all* the Abby Bennetts in America, have been able to produce the same result? Abby launches into the explanation of why she left Mystic Falls — which includes info on witches, doppelgängers, and vampires. How did she know that the girls were in the supernatural loop? Because of Daniel's visit? Would her frankness not have seemed weird to Elena and Bonnie? It is just as painful for hybrid Tyler to turn into a wolf as it was when he was a werewolf, but in "As I Lay Dying," Klaus could turn back and forth at will without pain. Is his Original status making him so resistant to pain, or is this a mythology inconsistency?

QUESTIONS
- Abby says that no one could manage to kill Mikael, making the attempt sound like a group effort. Who else in Mystic Falls was part of this late '90s battle against Mikael? Did Elena's parents know she was the doppelgänger? Was the council involved? Since Abby left back in the '90s, does she know that Miranda and Grayson died?
- Where did Damon hide the locked coffin? What the heck is in there?

Elena: I can't lose any more family.

3.13 *Bringing Out the Dead*

Original air date: February 2, 2012
Written by: Turi Meyer and Al Septien
Directed by: Jeffrey Hunt
Previously on *The Vampire Diaries*: Joseph Morgan

The Mystic Falls Murderer strikes again at Bill Forbes and Alaric. Elijah, Klaus, Stefan, and Damon's dinner party has a few unexpected guests.

"Bringing Out the Dead" was an ode to family in all its messed-up glory. For better or worse, these characters are bound together, across centuries, but the "family above all" credo raises the question: do you punish crimes perpetrated by family against family or do you forgive the unforgivable?

As Klaus said in "Homecoming," he trusts that his siblings will let bygones be bygones, and his honesty with Elijah — after the glorious fight — about his past crimes seems to Klaus to be enough to set the brothers on the path to peaceful reconciliation. Elijah, however, has no such intention. He may have a new haircut, but he is still guided by the same force as in "The Sun Also Rises": to exact revenge on Klaus and to reunite his siblings. Despite Klaus treating them rather poorly, what he cares most about is his family, and the threat of being left alone, abandoned by his siblings, for an eternity, is a nightmare. As far as revenge plots go, Elijah's is a good one: he resurrects his brothers and sister and they all turn against Niklaus. But, of course, the family reunion goes farther than the siblings when the contents of the locked box arrives. Esther is somehow alive again. She returns not to punish Niklaus, but to grant him forgiveness for killing her a thousand years ago.

Caroline finds herself in a similarly fraught situation: her father is on the brink of death — and choosing to end his life rather than be a vampire like she is — and she must come to terms with his past actions and her feelings. Instead of having time and space to get past him torturing her and judging her, Caroline is given only a tiny window for resolution. As she talks it over with Elena on her front porch, she acknowledges that she loves her father despite what he's done to her. Though her dad says that being human is all about the cycle of life, a parent dying before their child, that doesn't take away the hurt, the lifetime of not having her dad there when, as Elena explains, you just need your dad. That loss will be with Caroline for however long she lives, but at least in her final moments with her father, he gave her some peace, telling her that, vampire or not, she is who he and her mother hoped she'd grow up to be — and to an overachieving child like Caroline, there's nothing she'd rather hear.

Elena and Matt and Caroline aren't family, but they are united through thick and thin, supporting each other through the worst despite any messy personal history. They stand by one another through these countless times of crisis, and it's that same bond that has developed between Alaric and Elena, a family forged through the strangest of circumstance and now intrinsically linked. Elena tells Matt she can't bear to lose anyone else, and in the way she clutches Alaric's hand as he returns to life, it's evident how strongly Elena loves those around her.

If that link can be built from nothing, can it be healed once broken? That's the question Bonnie's wondering as she and her mother are forced to work together to open the coffin. The blood-knot spell, requiring two witches of the same bloodline, is more than a little symbolic, especially once the coffin reveals not the destroyer of Klaus, but his creator. Abby has expressed her regret for abandoning Bonnie, but what Bonnie needs from her mother is action, not an apology. In Abby finally making the effort — the spell is successfully broken — it feels like a first step in binding mother and daughter together again.

The centerpiece of "Bringing Out the Dead" is the dinner party attended by the pairs of brothers, whose relationships have endured all manner of tests over the centuries. The similarities between the Damon-Stefan and Klaus-Elijah dynamics have been highlighted before, but in this episode's discussion of the original Petrova, Tatia, the Salvatores learn that they were not the first brothers to come to blows over this remarkable girl. And like a good villain who speaks the truth, Klaus is exactly right about the danger the boys pose to Elena and the delusion they're under that they are the ones to protect her. The life Klaus sketches out for Elena (*"Matt Donovan? Really?"*) is probably closest to what Elena once pictured for herself. But whether or not she still wants a happy Mystic Falls family is not for a group of men to determine at an old-fashioned vampire sit-down, any more than it's up to Caroline to make her father's choice to live or die for him. The love the Salvatore brothers both have for Elena could drive them apart should she one day choose between them, but until then the allure of the Petrova doppelgänger is something they share a weakness for. In a breakthrough moment for Stefan, who's been denying for so long that he has feelings, he actually says out loud what everyone already knows: he loves Elena. And Damon does too. Will these boys come to the same conclusion that Elijah and Klaus seemed to centuries ago — that the bond of brotherhood should trump the love they have for Elena?

COMPELLING MOMENT The Original and Salvatore brothers breaking bread. A dinner party that involves these four winking at each other and trading barbs is an instant classic.

CIRCLE OF KNOWLEDGE

- No Jeremy or Tyler.
- Martin Scorsese brought Joe Connelly's 1998 novel *Bringing Out the Dead* to the silver screen in 1999 with Nicolas Cage as Frank, a paramedic working in New York City in the early 1990s. The film follows Frank over a week of working graveyard shifts with different partners as he tries to get himself fired. In desperate need of a break, Frank can see the ghosts of those he wasn't able to save, and he's haunted by his memories and the horrors of human life and death. One saving grace is the connection he makes with the daughter of a heart-attack victim, Mary (Patricia Arquette).
- Bill Forbes believed it wasn't right to cheat death; with the exception of Liz Forbes, everyone in this episode has done just that, from Matt (through Bonnie's rescue) to Elena (who died in the sacrifice) and Bonnie ("The Last Dance") to the vampires and hybrids.

THE RULES To undo the spell binding the coffin closed, two generations of a bloodline, symbolized by the blood knot, must perform the spell together.

PREVIOUSLY ON *THE VAMPIRE DIARIES* Elena and Stefan discovered her parents' stash of vampire-killing weapons at the lakehouse in "Crying Wolf"; the stake that killed Brian Walters is from that set. The last time Elijah "screwed over" the Salvatore brothers was in "The Sun Also Rises," when he decided not to kill Klaus, in the hopes of being reunited with his family. When Stefan finally begins eating his supper, Klaus says, "That's the spirit," just as he said to Stefan when he made him drink blood bag after blood bag in "As I Lay Dying." In "Bloodlines," Bonnie's magic failed her because she was blocked; it was her fear that was closing her off to her magic, which is perhaps what Abby's problem is too (theories about angry spirits aside). In the flashback in "Klaus," the Original brothers talk of once caring for a Petrova woman, meaning Tatia, and Klaus declares it was "too many lifetimes ago to matter."

OFF CAMERA Daniel Gillies expressed the difficulties of not being much more ahead of the action than the audience, particularly when it came to meeting his final two Original brothers. "You don't know what they're like

until they arrive," he explained. "In one scene, I said, 'You'd better look out or you'll have Kol to deal with.' I hadn't met Nathan [Nathaniel Buzolic] at that point when I was doing those lines. In my mind, Kol was — Nathan's tremendous, but we were describing him as this . . . leviathan, this ogre. So my relationship with [my siblings] is kind of what we guess it is." In an interview with TheTVChick.com, Gillies explained what appeals to him about such scenes as Damon and Elijah's meet-up in the field in this episode: "I've got to say, some of my favorite scenes have [been] between Ian and myself. I really enjoy working with Ian. . . . [Damon's] so snarky and weird and Elijah seems so stoic, but they both have a sense of humor. I think that's what's funny. One's sort of a snarky, bitchy humor, and Elijah's kind of got that weird, monk-like comedy. Like everything in the world is sort of funny, because I could murder it all. It's an interesting combo, those two on the screen together."

FOGGY MOMENTS Why would the Mystic Falls police have Elena's fingerprints on file? From that time she threw a chair through the Sheriff's office window? Alaric was first attacked downstairs and then the fight moved upstairs, but he never saw his attacker? Alaric's ring seemed to resurrect him without the same delay. Are its powers still waning? Will he still require a little Damon blood to heal up properly?

QUESTIONS

- Who is the Mystic Falls Murderer? Are Elena's fingerprints on the murder weapon a clue (she isn't the only one with those fingerprints), or misdirection?
- Esther's resurrection raises a lot of questions: did Klaus know that she could come back to life? Is that why he was so desperate for that coffin back? How is she alive? Has she been preserving herself, like Gloria did, or been in a daggered-like state for the past thousand years? Was she the one directing Bonnie to her coffin? Does she have the ability to kill Klaus?
- In "Ordinary People," Rebekah, Klaus, and Elijah stood over her grave; who dug her up and when? The coffin she was in was definitely modern: was she coffin-transferred over the centuries? When was the coffin sealed with the spell the Bennett witches break? Who sealed the coffin?
- Where has Tyler run off to?

Esther: I love my family, Elena, but they are an abomination. I betrayed nature when I created them; it's my duty to kill them.

3.14 Dangerous Liaisons

Original air date: February 9, 2012
Written by: Caroline Dries
Directed by: Chris Grismer
Previously on *The Vampire Diaries*: Ian Somerhalder

The reunited Mikaelson family hosts a ball.

Centuries of backstory feed into the events at the Mikaelson ball, as well as two-and-a-half seasons of *TVD*'s carefully orchestrated relationships. In this context, a small gesture — like Elena taking the arm of both her suitors — is for dedicated viewers an iconic moment. From Elijah just barely touching Elena's arm to Klaus and Caroline exchanging a *look* on the dance floor to Matt Donovan's simple kindness to Rebekah that saved his life, "Dangerous Liaisons" was full of minor moments that played major, so fraught with feeling as they were. Not only thanks to the handsome cast in their finery, it was a visually stunning episode, with the soundtrack to match. It looks like the perfect fairytale — but this event episode doesn't play out like one. The characters don't do what's expected of them, and as expectations are thwarted, "Dangerous Liaisons" builds in energy and excitement, creating a powder-keg feeling that finally explodes in its clothes-ripping finale.

From romantic intrigue to moral choices, nothing was clear-cut, straightforward, or black and white. The mother of all complicated decisions is Esther's. She has resolved to undo the wrong she did in creating vampires by killing her five children. Just as Stefan plotted his revenge against Klaus by targeting his one weakness, Esther's plan also centers on family: bringing the kids together with a false promise of a new peaceful beginning only to link them together as one with a blood spell. Her children are just as unsuspecting as they sip champagne laced with doppelgänger blood as when they drank the tainted wine a thousand years ago, then taking the first step to becoming vampires and now taking the first step toward death.

A thousand years ago, Esther put her own love for her children above the rules of nature. But now she will kill the abomination that she believes her children to be in order to right her wrong. It's an interesting twist: this show often values the protection of loved ones over the loss of innocent life, passed aside as "collateral damage." Though Esther speaks candidly with Elena, there is that moment when she says, "Will you do it, or shall I?" implying that with or without Elena's consent, the doppelgänger's blood will be used in this spell. She's pleasantly menacing despite her moratorium on violence. Esther didn't want the townsfolk attacked a thousand years ago, and she doesn't want it now. And though she goes through with the spell, there's a moment where Esther considers her moral Elijah, but her hesitation passes. She's willing to lose him for the greater good.

It's the same choice her accomplice, Elena, makes, and it's the same Mikaelson that she feels reluctant about betraying. For the "greater good," Elena feels forced into being someone she doesn't want to be, both in her plot to get Damon out of her way and in helping Esther carry out her bloody champagne toast. Esther describes Elijah as "so moral," and, in "Dangerous Liaisons" alone, he protects Elena from Rebekah, is forthcoming with her about his mother's return, tells her his suspicions, and asks her point-blank whether he has reason to distrust his mother. The way this Original vampire behaves is how Elena used to be, how she wants to be, but she's making more and more "ends justify the means" decisions. At the Grill, Rebekah warns Caroline that Elena is a backstabber (literally, in this case) and at the ball Elena betrays the trust she and Elijah have developed. In an incredibly tense moment, which could have believably gone either way, Elena doesn't warn Elijah; she deceives him. Our heroine, Elena the Good, keeps on her path of thwarting expectations: she makes sketchy choices and says the wrong thing. She pushes away Damon and instantly regrets it, and then reaches out to Stefan, who's hurt her terribly. Elena is often not comfortable with the choices she makes — from compelling Jeremy to signing Elijah's death sentence — but she constantly questions those choices, her judgment, and what kind of a person they make her. For Elena, there is no such thing as acceptable collateral damage.

Though she arrives at the ball alone, Elena has two attentive suitors and would-be protectors — the brother who loves her too much, and the one who doesn't love her enough . . . or at least doesn't show it. Stefan's act that he doesn't care keeps falling away bit by bit, and it's nicely contrasted with

Alice Evans as Esther

Bristol-bred Alice Evans studied languages and then acting in Paris, two skills that came in handy when her first acting jobs were in French- or Italian-language productions. She made her Hollywood debut in her native language in 2000's *102 Dalmatians*, starring alongside Glenn Close, Gérard Depardieu, and Alice's future husband, Ioan Gruffudd. Other credits include BBC's *Best of Both Worlds*, films *The Abduction Club*, *Blackball*, *Four Corners of Suburbia*, and *Liars All*, a thriller set on New Year's Eve in London, co-starring *90210*'s Matt Lanter and Gillian Zinser. Her TV highlights include recurring roles on *The Chris Isaak Show*, *Lost* (she played the young Eloise Hawking), and *Brothers & Sisters*.

Alice hadn't yet watched *The Vampire Diaries* when she got the call about auditioning for the role of Esther; the mum to two-year-old daughter Ella had the first season on iTunes unwatched. But she felt the role was "meant to be" for her: she kept hearing about the show, seeing it on TV, and she ran into Joseph Morgan at an event. But on the day of the audition, as she related to *The VRO*, she had a terrible flu and was stuck in bed. Fortunately for her, none of the other actors who auditioned were the right fit for the part, and when Alice finally got to audition the next week, she landed the role.

While filming in Atlanta, she watched the first two seasons in her hotel room. When she was cast, she hadn't realized the significance of Esther's role — as the mother of all vampires and the Original Witch — and she found out slowly, which she says saved her nerves from the pressure. She loved the opportunity to play in different time periods, and praised the costume and hair department for the fabulous era-appropriate clothes and wigs. Though she studied languages and felt the Latin-esque spells would be a snap, Alice found that repeating the same gibberish words in each take, 20 to 30 times for a spell, to be one of the greatest challenges of her career. (Kat Graham has also mentioned how challenging the recitation scenes are.) And, as she learned from one of the *TVD* writers, she couldn't just improvise: besides needing to match the dialogue from one take to the next, the words in the spell are deliberately chosen, first written in Latin and then mucked with a little to create the *Vampire Diaries* witch language. Alice doesn't think of Esther as some "random villain," but a woman on a crusade who feels she must right the wrong she did a thousand years ago by making a sacrifice of her own children. As she said in her *VRO* interview, Alice believes that Esther's choice is to "do the right thing even though it's the worst thing for herself."

Elena's inability to hide her feelings for him. On the flip side is her ability to mask her emotions with Damon. With him, she's the one putting on a charade, just as Stefan has with her. The brothers once again find themselves switching roles: the one who used to be cavalier and didn't care about risking

Elena's life, the Damon who arrived in Mystic Falls, is *long* gone, and Stefan has picked up that act (somewhat reluctantly). Are Damon's emotions a liability? Or does he just need to stop being a "controlling dick," as Stefan so delicately phrased it? It's a fine balance: Damon loves Elena so much that it borders on possessive. But having been smacked down, physically by Stefan and verbally by Elena, Damon is embracing the sentiment that no one should tell her — or him — what to do, and he hooks up with the Original sister, who's also suffering the sting of rejection from poor crushed-hand Donovan.

Running parallel to the brothers' latest chapter with Elena is Klaus's attempt to woo Caroline. Damon is shot down for letting his emotions rule him, while Klaus is encouraged to be real. Being emotionally open isn't a liability but a way to connect, a way to avoid an eternity of regret and isolation. That's the lesson Caroline has for her immortal prince. Though Klaus imagines himself — and his relationship to his father in particular — complicated, Caroline sees that at his core there's a simple principle at work: if only he'd stop being such a controlling dick, he could find true companionship.

Caroline refuses to play the part assigned to her by Klaus: she won't be Cinderella taken in by the charming prince. She goes to the ball to keep an eye on Matt and Elena and manages to keep her wits about her with Klaus. He may already know that she's Miss Mystic Falls, but she remembers who he is, what he's done, and who he's hurt to obtain the power and privilege he holds. Unlike some of the other characters who play at being who they're not, Caroline isn't interested in letting people tell her what to do or who to be, which is part of why she's such a refreshing character. She says what she thinks, whether it's to Elena at the Grill over her failure to report the Damon smooch or to the big bad Klaus. And Klaus responds to that honesty, seeing in her what her legions of fans in the audience at home do: she's beautiful, strong, full of light, and full of candor. If Caroline Forbes put her mind to it, there's no doubt that she could sort that Niklaus out. Too bad his mother (who is literally heartless, having lost hers when Klaus killed her) has a plan to kill him and his siblings, and that, once revealed, will surely dampen any spark of humanity stirring in Klaus.

COMPELLING MOMENT The waltz scene for its wealth of swoon-worthy couplings — something for every shipper!

CIRCLE OF KNOWLEDGE

- No Alaric, Jeremy, Bonnie, or Tyler.
- Originally an 18th-century French novel, *Liaisons Dangereuses* is the story of rivals who relentlessly toy with others and each other for their own sick enjoyment, and it has been re-imagined many times, most notably in two film adaptations: *Dangerous Liaisons* (1988) and *Cruel Intentions* (1999). *Dangerous Liaisons* (itself based on a play adaptation by Christopher Hampton) pairs the Marquise de Merteuil (Glenn Close) and Vicomte de Valmont (John Malkovich) as competitors in a game of seduction and destruction. The Marquise requests Valmont make his next target Cécile de Volanges (Uma Thurman), the virgin betrothed to the Marquise's former lover, but he has his eye on Madame de Tourvel

(Michelle Pfeiffer), a married woman known for her virtue. Her plot is for revenge; his is to make a woman betray all that she believes in. Valmont inadvertently falls in love with Tourvel's goodness, and filled with jealousy, the Marquise forces Valmont to break off his relationship with Tourvel. He does, repeating the phrase "It is beyond my control" (he says it about 100 times). More machinations ensue, and Valmont declares war on the Marquise. It ends badly for all parties. Fancy costumes, relentless plotting and scheming, betrayals and jealousy — it's no wonder the writers chose this title for this episode. The dynamic between Klaus and Caroline (and to a lesser extent Rebekah and Matt) mirrors that of the master manipulator Valmont and Tourvel, whose goodness and honesty he finds surprisingly appealing. Let's hope the Klaroline dalliance ends less tragically.

- In "Ordinary People," Rebekah called Klaus a tattletale, and here a thousand years later he's still whining to his mother about his siblings.
- In Esther's room, there is a chessboard with only white pieces.
- Esther burns sage as part of a privacy spell. Burning sage has long been used to cleanse or purify a space, to banish evil and provide protection.
- Not all of Klaus's artwork is stolen from the Louvre, as Caroline suggests: one of his landscapes hangs at the State Hermitage Museum in St. Petersburg, Russia, a museum founded in 1764 by Catherine the Great. His painting is likely in the Winter Palace collection, among works from other European masters.

THE RULES Esther uses spelled sage to create an environment where she and Elena can speak freely, protected from vampires' superior hearing. She explains that Ayana, a Bennett ancestor, spelled her corpse to preserve it, and that Esther has spent the last thousand years on the Other Side. She drew power from the Bennett line, all the way down to Abby and Bonnie, to return to life. Esther's spell — step one in a plan to kill all her children — links the Original siblings together: first they consume the essence of the doppelgänger's blood in champagne (akin to them drinking it in wine when they were first turned), and then, using Finn's blood, Esther "completes the link." His spilt blood creates a tree-like shape on the parchment, traveling from one name to the other, before finally igniting in flames when the spell is complete. (*Awesome.*)

PREVIOUSLY ON *THE VAMPIRE DIARIES* Elena takes the arm of both Stefan and Damon as she enters the ball, making literal Isobel's comment from "Isobel": "As long as you have a Salvatore on each arm, you're doomed." Caroline need not inform Klaus that she quite deservedly won the pageant in "Miss Mystic Falls"; he already knows. Damon throws Kol off the balcony just as he did to John Gilbert in "Under Control." As she does with Elijah here, Elena lied to Damon in "Children of the Damned" when he asked her of Stefan, "Is it real? . . . This renewed sense of brotherhood. Can I trust him?" In "Blood Brothers," Stefan explained to Elena that the pain of knowing what he's done is with him always, as is the temptation to just turn off his humanity so he won't have to feel it, a speech he echoes on her porch after the ball.

OFF CAMERA Elena's gown is vintage, while the dress Caroline wears is an Alberto Makali gown. Candice Accola enjoys these "event" episodes, where new character pairings get to interact: "It is an odd thing with these wonderful, wonderful characters developed throughout the show and the series, but because there are so many of us on set at once . . . even Caroline and Elijah have never been in a scene together, ever! There's all these different characters whose paths don't cross."

FOGGY MOMENTS Did Matt and Elena take separate vehicles to the hospital? Weren't they both at the Gilbert house when they took Alaric to the hospital?

QUESTIONS
- Is there more to that Kol/Damon interaction, when Kol professed not to remember Damon? Is there some history there, or was Kol just being a dink?
- What is the next step in Esther's plan?
- What did Klaus know, if anything, about the state of his mother, Ayana's preservation spell, and/or the blood knot spell sealing the coffin shut?

> *Elena: I wish that there was something I could do to help.*
> *Elijah: You know, one thing I've learned in my time*
> *on this earth: be careful what you wish for.*

3.15 All My Children

Original air date: February 16, 2012
Written By: Evan Bleiweiss and Michael Narducci
Directed by: Pascal Verschooris
Previously on *The Vampire Diaries*: Daniel Gillies

Esther tries to kill all her children by reversing the spell that made them vampires; Elijah kidnaps Elena to force the Salvatore brothers into stopping his mum.

Ditching the glitz of the previous episode, "All My Children" takes the weekly battle for survival underground as the Mystic Falls residents pick sides: will Esther's plot right the wrongs of a thousand years and restore peace, or is it an immoral atrocity that would kill five of the most entertaining characters (well, four plus Finn) in one fell swoop?

The Vampire Diaries has made bold choices in the past — with characters killed off and unexpected plot twists — but events rarely unfold as heralded. Though the threat to the Original siblings from their mother, the Salvatores' to the Bennetts, and Rebekah's to Elena is viable within the *TVD* universe, from an audience perspective, the likelihood of any of these characters dying seems remote enough as to be moot. Instead, the episode takes the buildup of the second half of the season and, with little fanfare, lets the air of the proverbial balloon. The Original family so recently reunited scatters, just one episode later. Esther's plan is derailed and her power cut off. And yet, in a too-convenient moment, lo and behold another threat to the Originals pops up in the shape of a white oak tree carved into the wall of the cave centuries after the original burned.

What's become clear over the course of season 3 is that what motivates the Originals is no different from that which motivates the rest of the characters. They may have lived a thousand years, but they struggle with their humanity as much as the next vampire. It's what makes Klaus so easily distracted by Caroline (and so defensive of her honor to Kol). Elena has seen herself in Rebekah before ("Ordinary People") and she understands that

Caspar Zafer as Finn

"He's a hell of a guy," said Joseph Morgan about his onscreen brother Finn, played by fellow Brit Caspar Zafer. Raised in the Middle East, Caspar has been acting for a decade; his first job was on a soap about a British football team called *Dream Team*. He's since appeared in *The Hound of the Baskervilles, La Femme Musketeer, True True Lie, The Maidens' Conspiracy, Two Families,* and *Monsieur Francois*. The actor is also working on his own documentary project about "a day in the life of the world" called *Day One*.

Caspar moved to America about a year before landing the gig on *The Vampire Diaries*. He auditioned once in New York for the part and nabbed it, but he was completely unfamiliar with the series, as he told *The VRO*: "I didn't have a clue. Didn't know what I was getting into." Caspar described his 900-year bedhead wig from his first episode as "Viking rock star meets pirate meets nutcase." Thankfully Finn lost his old-time costume by his next appearance, since, as Caspar noted, the vampires "adapt very quickly to modernity." Among the Original siblings, Finn is "more sedate, serious" and seemingly obsessed with death. When he was preparing for "Dangerous Liaisons," he thought of Finn's attitude toward death as a bit broody until director Chris Grismer refocused him: for Finn, it's time to end it, a happy and conscious decision rather than a brooding tragic end. Caspar describes Joseph Morgan as "great fun" with "so much energy" and Alice Evans as a "generous" actress. *The Vampire Diaries* is exposing the actor to the fandom phenomenon for the first time, and he loves how interested viewers are in the characters. As for Finn, from Caspar's perspective, his character reaches the "right conclusion."

Rebekah's rage against her comes from hurt. Elena befriended her only to betray her, and despite the torment in the caves — the gasoline and matches are particularly inspired — Elena, through her understanding of Rebekah, comes to realize no real harm will befall her. Without her revenge, what will Rebekah have left but the realization that she has no true friends?

In Elijah's interactions with Elena, he speaks of her nature — being compassionate, not being deceitful — but, like Elijah, she's capable of both. She has an "attack of conscience," as Damon phrases it, after each morally shady thing she does — stabbing Rebekah or compelling Jer or letting Elijah drink the champagne. Just as the vampires struggle to discern their true nature — whether they should be uncaring monsters or the best parts of humans — Elena is figuring out who to be in the high-stakes, mortal-peril-at-every-turn world in which she lives. The unfortunate part for Elena is that even when she isn't the one at fault — here with Esther's actions and Damon turning Abby — she still feels she's the cause. Is the darkness in her best friends' lives a result of who she is, the doppelgänger, and who she's let into her life? After Grams died, Bonnie went to Caroline in her grief and shut Elena out, and the same dynamic seems to be in play again, though with more of a window into Bonnie's feelings. Instead of her just leaving town, Bonnie's distress is shown and Caroline's explanation gives us a perspective other than Elena's.

Fair or not, Elena faces the consequences of her past actions and of her status as a perfect kidnap target in "All My Children." Esther, on the other hand, is raring to deal with her regret: she's watched her children make others suffer for a thousand years and wants to make peace with the spirits and find peace for herself. Though Elijah successfully stops his mother's plan, he hears truth in her words, telling Rebekah that their parents didn't make them monsters, their own choices did. With great insight into his own behavior, he realizes that his morality is exercised only when convenient. It's an impressively self-aware moment for Elijah, and, in his apology letter, one that highlights the kinship between Elena and Elijah.

As they did after Esther's death, the Original family once again scatters — Finn and Esther vaporizing as soon as the spell goes south, Kol fleeing, and Elijah saying his farewells via handwritten note — leaving Rebekah at Klaus's side. Her loyalty remains with her brother, as Damon's and Stefan's do with each other. Damon has had his eye on Stefan, seeing his brother going back to his old lifestyle and he makes room for him to be good by being the bad guy, the one who has to do terrible things in the name of keeping Elena safe. Damon selflessly picks up that mantle, whatever the fallout may be, a role Stefan had been playing even up until the last episode. Will both brothers decide to take a step back from Elena? They won't deny their feelings for her — "Pot, kettle, brother." — but they also seem to think that to avoid any more hurt, for any of them, it's time to retreat. These brother moments are the heart of the series, and Damon is there to support Stefan's decision to take the path away from ripper life and back to bunnies. The turning point for Stefan was that night on Wickery Bridge, and Stefan is slowly realizing the truth of what Elena said then: there's more to life than destroying Klaus.

At the very least, there's the new twist in the Mystic Falls Murderer case . . .

COMPELLING MOMENT Elijah taking Elena on a stroll in the woods, and ending their conversation by smashing a hole in the ground.

CIRCLE OF KNOWLEDGE
- No Matt, Jeremy, or Tyler.
- Soap opera *All My Children* ran for 41 years from 1970 to 2011.
- What's visible of Stefan's diary (when he ignores Elena's call) reads, "wallow in self-loathing. Better to close it off, bury it."
- Abby goes to Caroline's house for her transition, not to Bonnie's. Presumably Abby hasn't been staying with her estranged husband at Bonnie's, and, even if she were, Sheriff Forbes knows and understands about vampires, whereas Bonnie's dad has been established as unsupportive of Bonnie's supernatural side.
- Not only does Elijah make the effort of apologizing to Elena for his behavior in a handwritten letter, but he uses the sacred Original "always and forever" phrase that is nearest to his heart, tied as it is to his eternal bonds with his siblings. Carry your compassion with you, girl.

THE RULES Esther requires the mother-daughter Bennett duo of witches in order to maintain the connection to the power of the ancestral line. By Abby turning into a vampire, she loses her witch status — you can't be both — and Esther loses the power of the Bennett line that she was using to reverse her original vampire-making spell. As she explains to Bonnie, the pentagram represents the connection to magic, salt to the earth, and one torch for each child.

HISTORY LESSON We get a Mystic Falls history lesson in this episode, and perhaps an explanation of why that cave is secure from vampires. If the "natives" were recording history and the existence of vampire-killing weapons there, it's like this is another founders' journal: cave edition.

PREVIOUSLY ON *THE VAMPIRE DIARIES* Stefan is off the human blood, which he previously quit cold turkey after "Let the Right One In." In "Bloodlines," Bonnie fell through the ground and Stefan zipped her up and out; here Elijah does the reverse with Elena. Those underground caves always have bad cell phone reception.

OFF CAMERA Daniel Gillies attempted to explain the allure of Elijah's character, as distinct from the younger vampires: "He appeals to the classical ideal of a vampire. . . . He appeals to this older idea, the mythology of what a vampire actually is. [Elijah] does represent something Bram Stoker tried to create originally. Especially with Nina. That's what makes them fun; they have a historic quality to them. Something's resonating between them that looks like the [ancient] vampire and the maiden." But he insisted the Elena-Elijah dynamic is not romantic. "Nina and I like working with each other, and maybe we're too flirty with each other, and that's all it is. I like working with Ian. Not so flirty. But I like that relationship [between Elijah and Elena], I do. She and I think there's some unsaid thing that's happening that I like, but it's like spiritual romance, I think. They aspire to the same qualities. He's enchanted by a nobility she's able to uphold and he aspires to."

FOGGY MOMENTS How is Rebekah's gown in one piece after Damon ripped it off her at the end of "Dangerous Liaisons"? Rebekah tells Elena she is filming her to inspire the brothers to work quickly, but there's no reception in the caves and she had no way to send the video to them. It seems like this was just a slightly illogical way to lead her to the cave drawing of the sapling and to get in some product placement. How is Esther alive (or at least, not dead) if her power source has been cut off? At what point did Damon decide to break the Bennett bloodline despite Stefan having won the coin toss? Why was Stefan creeping up on Bonnie?

QUESTIONS
- Will Abby complete her transition or will she Bill Forbes it?
- What's Meredith's deal? Why did she take Alaric to her apartment if she didn't want him to see her stash of Mystic Falls Murderer stuff? Why can't he see those files?
- If a sapling near the ancient white oak tree is capable of killing an Original, is it possible that any "descendent" tree of that oak is also deadly? How will Rebekah and Klaus locate the killer white oak tree?

> *Damon: I watched you go over the edge, and I didn't do anything to stop you.*
> *Stefan: You couldn't have.*
> *Damon: Sure, I could've. I just didn't want to. But I want*
> *to now. Whenever you go too far, I will be there to pull you*
> *back. Every second, every day, til you don't need me.*

3.16 ~~19-12~~

Original air date: March 15, 2012
Written by: Julie Plec and Elisabeth R. Finch
Directed by: John Behring
Guest cast: Arthur Bridgers (Barker), Hannah Fierman (Marianna Lockwood), Lindsey R. Garrett (Samantha Gilbert), Marcus Hester (Zachariah Salvatore), Lee Spencer (Gerald Forbes), Sarah Wheeler (Woman)
Previously on *The Vampire Diaries*: Paul Wesley

Stefan and Damon spend a little time brother bonding and reminiscing about the last time Mystic Falls had a council-member murder mystery; Elena investigates Meredith.

In a town where history is always repeating, Damon's plan to reopen a century-old unsolved murder is a solid one and it leads the mystery-solving duo to the culprit, while Elena and Alaric simultaneously learn that he is the Mystic Falls Murderer. The Gilbert ring is not just a force for good, protecting its wearer from death at the hand of a supernatural being, but an agent of darkness that somehow causes Alaric (and Samantha Gilbert, a hundred years before him) to become a murderer without consciously knowing it. Just as there was a price when Bonnie resurrected Jeremy, it seems that this magic demands a cost for resurrection too. The end-of-episode reveal draws an uncomfortable conclusion to its exploration of how we judge character and whether we can truly know someone or ourselves. Just how far away is that edge before the darkness?

Meredith's conversation with Elena in the parking lot sets up this question: how well does Elena know the man living in her house, and is she actually as good a judge of character as she thinks she is? Meredith quite rightly points out that the girl dates vampires — vampires who have racked up a heavy body count, and recently. But how to trust others when even the self can betray, as Alaric discovers? Locked in his cell, he is puzzling over the holes in his memory, and, with the pattern established between him and Samantha Gilbert's psycho phase, as recorded in her journal, it seems Alaric *has* been secretly living a double life, his split personality a secret even to himself. But before that incontrovertible evidence surfaces, Elena is willing to do whatever it takes to clear Alaric's name. She'll protect her loved ones (with Matt's help) even if it means a little B&E and a trip to the Sheriff's office.

And protecting the person he cares the most for is precisely what Damon is doing by steering his brother onto the Road to Recovery. Damon has been keeping a close eye on his little brother and doesn't need to hear the incessant tapping of Stefan's ring to know that he's about to freak the frak out. Estranged from Elena as they both are right now, it's up to Damon to help keep Stefan from repeating the same mistake of winding himself up so tightly that when he loses it, he *loses* it. It's a task that Damon is keen to take on, unlike when they were in a similar predicament a century ago. Though Damon sasses Elena (hilariously telling her that he's mean, she hates him, and the earth is back on its axis), he's actually grasping for moderation in his existence too. In 1912, Damon was a vampire who waited, "spoken for" and alone for 50 years before discovering the pleasure of being a monster with Sage's (creepy) guidance. He's also been the kind of vampire who could fully devote himself to Elena, put himself at the mercy of her affection, and never quite be good enough. In "1912," Damon is no longer waiting on someone else; in the way *he* thinks is best, he chooses to step up and help the one person he is bound to eternally, for better or worse. It's great to see them together, snarking and teasing each other but at each other's side. Team Salvatore forever.

With Sage in the 1912 picture, it's apparent how open to suggestion the Salvatores are. Damon had spent his vampire-lifetime feeding to sate his hunger only; with a little pep talk from Sage, boom — he's a Lothario. As with 1912 Stefan: it takes very little for Damon to convince him to have a drink of human blood after Lexi's (probable) decades of convincing him to respect human life. Either the Salvatores are easily swayed (and an argument could be made that they are very susceptible, in particular, to the influence of strong women), or it is the innate desire of a vampire to be a *predator* — to hunt, to seduce, to destroy. For a show starring vampires (and with "vampire" in its title), the depictions of the intersection of pleasure and violence have been few and far between. Beyond the storytelling difficulty of portraying such vampires as the romantic interests for a teenage girl without being entirely repulsive, inside the world of *TVD*, the brothers themselves have never really spent time together, enjoying themselves, as vampires. Unlike Stefan and Klaus in the 1920s, Damon's and Stefan's eras of indulgence have never overlapped. In the present day, Damon attempts to bring Stefan to the territory he occupies: no accidental decapitations, but no bunnies either. A space with a nice view of the dark side but a safe distance from its edge.

Instead of encouraging Stefan in his human-blood abstinence program, like Elena might, Damon encourages his brother to control the blood lust — responsible drinking (so to speak), Damon-style. To control it, rather than be controlled by it, as he explained to Elena back in "Miss Mystic Falls." However, Damon's idea of what is acceptable behavior — snatch, eat, erase — goes much further than Elena's, who is rightfully horrified to see her two love interests feeding on a stranger in a dark alley. She expects these vampires to fight their predatory nature, not indulge it; that's the only way she can love them and be okay with what that says about who *she* is.

The pairing of Matt and Elena in this episode — their history and their re-blossoming friendship in season 3 — allows for a nice conversation about why Elena loves these two Salvatores, despite their dark sides. The scene at the Gilberts' home after they stumble upon bloody-mouthed Stefan and Damon up to no good in the alley was pitch perfect, with Matt finally asking what draws her to them. Beautifully, this moment circles back to the beginning of season 1: her loss and grief have changed her, made her accept certain dark realities, and led her to fall in love with vampires. Elena knows her feelings for Stefan and Damon don't make much sense, and in a strange way her estimation of Alaric mirrors it. Earlier in the episode, she tells Matt that she *knows* Alaric, knows that he's innocent. But she's wrong: he's guilty. Just as with Stefan and Damon, there is goodness and humanity, a side that is completely loveable, but there is a dark side. A side that could lose all sense of humanity and rip a woman's head off or stab a council member or take away a person's will in order to drain their blood. What balances that violence, the darkness of their reality, is the safety and solidity these vampire brothers provide her. No doubt, Elena will stay right by Ric's side, despite his murderous alter ego. As much as she needs support, love, and a community, she knows firsthand how devastating it is to lose those things, and though it's often irrational, it's what makes Elena Gilbert so unflinchingly loyal to those she loves. For everyone in Mystic Falls, moderation is elusive, but the best way to stay this side of crazy is by standing by one another when the darkness comes calling.

Cassidy Freeman as Sage

Born in 1982 in Chicago and holding a degree in theater, Cassidy Freeman is best known to audiences of The CW as *Smallville*'s Tess Mercer, her first major role after parts in short films, TV movies, and a pilot for The CW that wasn't picked up but did put her in the minds of the producers. "[*Smallville*] was only the second or third TV show that I'd ever done, so I was a little nervous," said Cassidy. "I came onto the set to do my first scene and there were dozens and dozens of people there to watch. All the producers, every single crewmember, you name it. They were all thrilled that the show was starting up again for the season, and meanwhile I was thinking, 'Could there be more people here to watch me?'" Her nervousness abated with experience, which she gained during her years on *Smallville*, as well as on *Cold Case*, *CSI*, *CSI: NY*, *The Playboy Club*, and in the film *YellowBrickRoad*. In addition to appearing on *TVD*, she was on TV sets in 2012 in *CSI: Miami* and the A&E drama *Longmire*, in which she's a series regular.

Being cast on *The Vampire Diaries* came with its own special reaction from Cassidy's inner circle. "I can't actually tell you how many of my absolutely grown-women friends squealed like teenagers when they heard that I was gonna be in this show," Cassidy told *Entertainment Weekly*. "So I don't doubt that [Damon's] bathroom, and more importantly his shower, is a place of interest. So I felt very fortunate." Asked about Sage's attitude toward each of the Salvatore brothers, Cassidy theorized, "Sage's idea is that of pleasure and that of embracing being a vampire. So anytime that Stefan comes in with his do-all-good attitude, it just doesn't click. I don't think she's necessarily anti-Stefan or tries to push him too hard. I think she just sees a lot of future in Damon, especially back in 1912, where he could be the kind of vampire that she is and she can be a mentor to him. So she focuses more on being able to craft the Damon that we all know out of who he was in 1912, rather than worrying about Stefan too much."

Filming the show was a treat for the actress, thanks to her familiarity with some key players, both in front of and behind the camera. "I actually had met the majority of the cast when they shot *The Vampire Diaries* pilot in Vancouver. And I had met Julie Plec, and I had met Pascal [Verschooris], and a couple of the writers who are on the show are from *Smallville*," she told KSiteTV. "It actually kind of felt like a strange little homecoming."

COMPELLING MOMENT "You're insane." "No, but I think you are." Meredith, for the win

CIRCLE OF KNOWLEDGE
- No Bonnie, Caroline, Jeremy, or Tyler.

- The Wonder Twins, Zan and Jayna, members of the DC Universe's Super Friends, are alien humanoids who have the ability to transform, which they do after fist-bumping and saying, "Wonder Twin powers activate!"
- The prize for beating Sage in the boxing ring is $100, which in today's dollars is approximately $2,300.
- A vampire basking in the pleasure of their power — Sage saying women are not just for food but for pleasure, that if a target won't give in to seduction, then take what you want anyway — works to create a creepy evil vampire character like Sage, but it was unrealistic and borderline offensive for the women in the episode to behave as if what Sage says is true. Women are not secretly burning with desire to be forcibly unbuttoned by random strangers. The woman Damon pounces on in the alley responds to him — a stranger getting all up in her personal space at

night in a secluded place — as if she is *so* flattered that this handsome weirdo calls her pretty. And that's before he compels her. Not cool, show.

THE RULES The magic Gilbert ring has a dark side, giving its wearer a second homicidal maniac personality — the how and why yet to be revealed.

PREVIOUSLY ON *THE VAMPIRE DIARIES* The deliberate brother-bonding drinking night is becoming a Salvatore tradition, first seen in "History Repeating" and reprised in "Ordinary People." The original Uncle Zach is actually the brothers' nephew Zachariah; like his modern-day counterpart did in "You're Undead to Me," he meets a bad end in Mystic Falls. Before Damon makes his appearance at Zachariah's funeral, Stefan sees a crow perched on a tombstone, like in the pilot when Elena was harassed by Damon's creepy bird. Elena guesses that Meredith, as a Fell, will have a secret panel in her closet; she and Stefan discovered her parents' closet stash of vampire-hunting paraphernalia and Gilbert journals at the lakehouse in "Crying Wolf." Elena hid in a closet earlier this season, when Klaus and Stefan dropped by his old apartment in "The End of the Affair." Damon suggests that his brother follow the method he tried to teach Vicki Donovan in "Haunted": "Snatch. Eat. Erase." Elena stumbling upon Stefan with blood dripping from his mouth is very "Miss Mystic Falls," when she saw him attacking Amber. The drinking-to-decapitation incident of 1912 led Stefan to go on a binge that lasted into his "Ripper of Monterey" days, which Klaus mentioned in "As I Lay Dying."

HISTORY LESSON While it was certainly uncommon to see women boxing in 1912, the first recorded female boxing match took place in 1876 in New York City, and at the 1902 Olympics it was a demonstration sport.

OFF CAMERA At PaleyFest, Julie Plec said of Damon and Stefan in this episode and in the second half of season 3 that, love triangle aside, "The brothers are trying to be heroes to each other." Commenting on working on *The Vampire Diaries* and this episode in particular, editor Nancy Forner said, "The most satisfying aspect of editing *The Vampire Diaries* is that I love cutting stylistically like this. It's very creative. I'm never bored, and the producers love it when we push the envelope, they love it when we try new things. They want us to be creative and not do what we did last time. They want something new, something beautiful. Something that is awesome. The photography on *TVD* is also incredible. I can't believe how visually gorgeous this show is. The episode '1912' has the look of a movie. Because of the nature of the story in '1912,' I had the opportunity to do some really cool and unusual sound design for some of the flashbacks."

FOGGY MOMENTS Who decided that Giuseppe Salvatore's bastard son would receive the family name and inheritance? In 1864, that would have been a very odd turn of events. Were there no other living Salvatores to protest this?

Damon's comment that Meredith isn't the killer because she's a woman is completely out of character. She's been his number-one suspect (which is why he calls her psycho), she took him down easily with the surprise vervain attack, and women murder grown men all the time.

Meredith risked killing Alaric by shooting him, just so she could elaborately clear his name — even though he *is* the killer? Why wouldn't she have confided in Elena to either team up with her or at least to stop Elena from meddling in the situation?

In "A Few Good Men," Damon had Sheriff Forbes run a background check on Alaric, and the only thing she came up with was the sad story of Isobel's disappearance. Where did Meredith get her dirt on Alaric? (If he had two restraining orders filed against him by Isobel before they married, wouldn't the cops have suspected him of foul play in her disappearance?)

Sheriff Forbes says she'll release Alaric after verifying that the coroner's letter is authentic. Later, Meredith tells Alaric that she forged the letter. Couldn't Liz just call the coroner and ask about the veracity of the letter? How else did she authenticate it?

QUESTIONS

- Is there some part of Alaric that is choosing his victims, or does the magic ring makes its wearer target council members?
- What made Samantha Gilbert stop her killing streak? Or did she stop? Seems like the councilmen killings didn't continue unabated for an entire decade between her 1912 murders and her confession that landed her in an insane asylum. Did she remove her ring? Get some witchy assistance?
- Will Alaric ditch the ring? Will Elena bring Jeremy home or just tell him to take off his ring? How many times does one have to die before the ring starts empowering the wearer's inner psychopath?
- What's Klaus up to? When will Stefan or Damon clue into the weirdness of Rebekah asking questions about old trees in Mystic Falls?

*Alaric (to Meredith): Everybody needs to find a way
to deal with their dark side.*

3.17 *Break on Through*

Original air date: March 22, 2012
Written by: Rebecca Sonnenshine
Directed by: Lance Anderson
Guest cast: John Paul Marston (Piano Player)
Previously on *The Vampire Diaries*: Kat Graham

Alaric faces his dark side, while Damon and Sage seduce Rebekah for information.
As Alaric tells Meredith, everybody has a dark side that has to be controlled, but what happens when that dark side breaks free and takes on a life
of its own? In "Break on Through," Alaric is engaged in a battle against himself, undergoing medical testing, denying himself sleep, taking precautions,
and opening up about his past violent behavior, as he struggles to understand
that some part of himself was actually capable of murder. In the very cool
cold open, the split in Alaric's conflicting selves is shown in his reflection.
As the frame narrows in on his face, he panics under the confinement before
his reflection no longer represents the Alaric he knows. That moment fore-
shadows the dramatic and scary turning point later in the episode, when he
nonchalantly gets up from the sofa and empties Meredith's syringes before
"Break on Through" moves right into a harrowing chase scene through the
house. (Why must that washroom have three doors?! It's nothing but trouble.)
The violence Alaric exhibited in his younger days provides a window
into his split personality's motivations. Like his fights then, where he felt his
victims "deserved" it or had it coming, when Psycho Alaric takes over, he feels
justified in playing punisher. While it is undeniably true that the council has
failed to protect the citizens of Mystic Falls from vampires, Psycho Alaric's
eye-for-an-eye tactics, like beating the pulp out of a jerk at a bar, aren't the
solution either. It will only turn him into the thing he hates. When Alaric
made the choice to become a vampire hunter in the wake of Isobel's disappearance, he was trying to focus his darkness on what he thought was a

Nathaniel Buzolic as Kol

Born in 1983, Nathaniel Buzolic transforms his natural Australian accent (he's from Sydney) into something more Original for Kol. Like many of his costars, the part he ended up with on *The Vampire Diaries* wasn't the first one he auditioned for, having tried out for the pilot episode back in 2009. Though he's a new face in America, Nathaniel's been acting since he was a kid: "I remember the first time I got up onstage and was able to make people laugh. From that day on, I was hooked." The talented youngster won a scholarship from Australian Theatre for Young People, and soon had a gig as a television presenter on *The Mint* and *Studio Disney*. His other credits include Australian productions *Far and Away*, *All Saints*, *Offing David*, *Out of the Blue*, *Cops LAC*, and *Crownies*.

On playing the youngest brother of the Originals, Nathaniel said, "Kol is obviously cheeky and brings his own dynamic to the show, and I think he's quite different to the other characters that they have got on there. It's a nice touch that the writers have added to the show, and I'm lucky enough to play that. It's been an absolute blast so far." And he's just as fond of his onscreen big bro, Joseph Morgan. "I think he's a fantastic actor and what he brings to the character of Klaus is incredible. And I don't think anybody else could've done what he does."

clear target — nothing wrong with killing evil murderous monsters. But, as Meredith's question about killing Damon raises, nothing is that black and white when considered by a sane, moral person.

While there is hope that Alaric's dark side could be successfully repressed with Bonnie's herbal remedy, for Stefan, there is no magic trick to get rid of the Ripper. It's a self-control issue. Damon's advice is to embrace who he is, a vampire, and behave like one. Drink and be merry, but learn how to stop (before taking the victim's head off). After Elena caught him in the alley, Stefan has been, for the most part, isolating himself and feeling ashamed and angry. In their incredibly awkward conversation at the Salvatore house, Stefan pushes Elena away, and at Alaric's apartment he questions the futility of the qualities at her very core — her hopefulness and her sense of responsibility for others. But Stefan *does* need her dogged insistence that everything will be okay. Her faith in him and his shame when he disappoints her are powerful motivators for Stefan. Despite everything, she hasn't given up on him and won't, and the strength of her conviction helps him control himself in the presence of the bloodied Meredith. It was a bite-sized flash of old

Stefan, the guy he thought he couldn't be again. Damon may tell Sage that hope's a bitch, and she should give up on Finn, but for Elena, hope dies last. Even in the face of overwhelming evidence to the contrary, Elena denies that Alaric is in mortal peril (refusing his just-in-case documents), that he's the one who wrote that continue-the-murdering-legacy note to Jeremy and collected souvenirs of his kills, that she could find herself without him and soon. Her belief that everything will work out in the end is as much the source of her strength as it is a coping mechanism.

As Meredith and Elena help the psychos in their lives, Caroline and

Bonnie are on a parallel journey. Like Meredith's instinct to protect Alaric because what he's become isn't his fault, Caroline convinces Jamie that Abby's vampirism wasn't her choice and that she needs his support. Bonnie and Caroline both try to instill hope and perseverance in Abby: being a vampire, being disconnected from her former life, as well as from her connection to the earth that she had as a witch, is a daily battle, but the fight to reconnect with her humanity *is* possible, as Caroline's shining example shows. But Abby gives in to her weakness and fear, which were heightened in her vampire transition. Despite Caroline's wise and impassioned speech, Abby is unable to reconcile the fragments of the self she knew and her new identity, and she runs, abandoning Jamie and Bonnie again. In that moment, Caroline feels the hurt this will cause her best friend and the painful echo of when her dad made a parallel choice, choosing death rather than becoming what she is. Unbeknownst to Bonnie, as that connection to her mother breaks, she is reaching out to Elena and reestablishing their bond. In a beautiful moment, Bonnie acknowledges that the situation was well out of Elena's control, that it wasn't her choice, and the friends embrace. Friendships help assuage Elena's otherwise lonely existence, heartbreakingly shown in the shot of her all alone in the big Gilbert house. Her call to her little brother demonstrates just how hard it is for her to stay strong and firm in her belief that everything will somehow be okay.

If Meredith, Bonnie, Caroline, and Elena are moved to help a friend out when they see their weaknesses, Sage does the opposite, using a vulnerability as an opportunity for exploitation. Continuing her annoying anti-female talk from "1912," Sage manipulates Damon and Rebekah in a seduction game, but in the end, all three have more information about the others' secret plots than before the "sex sandwich." Sage is painted as the ruthless vampire secretly a fool for love, pining for Finn for 900 years. Instead of being a character that fascinates — like season 1 Isobel who loved compulsion, sex, and violence but whose torch still burned for Alaric — Sage falls flat, saddled with improbable storylines, abilities that defy the established mythological rules, and inconsistent characterization. It's a shame, as a badass boxer from the early 20th century who taught Damon how to delight in vampirism sounds so promising on paper, but the realization of that character (through no fault of Cassidy Freeman) prevents Sage from being a villain one can delight in watching or feel a touch of sympathy for because of her undying love for Finn.

However unlikely that Damon would choose the right milling ledger from a century of options on his first pick, that the oak tree was used to construct the very bridge under revitalization, and that he knew about a secret stash of oak that Rebekah didn't get her paws on, the result is promising. The game is back on. Watch out, Originals.

COMPELLING MOMENT Evil Alaric terrorizing Meredith — a perfect horror-movie sequence.

CIRCLE OF KNOWLEDGE
- No Klaus, Tyler, or Matt.
- "Break on Through (To the Other Side)" is the name of a 1967 song by The Doors from their self-titled debut album.
- Sunshiny Caroline Forbes's favorite type of blood also doubles as her motto: B positive!
- Perhaps even more surprising than Alaric having not one but two bank accounts (with one uncrackable password, *vampslayer*): he has parents! Ed and Dianne Saltzman are alive and well and living in North Truro, Massachusetts, on Cape Cod.
- Damon says he's watching over Alaric to ensure that he doesn't turn into a frog (a reference to the fairytale of the Frog Prince) or a block of salt. In the Book of Genesis, Lot's wife was turned into a pillar of salt for looking back while fleeing the city of Sodom, a punishment for directly disobeying the angels' command.

THE RULES Sage displays a unique skill: she can draw the precise information she's looking for from another vampire's mind, provided that that vampire is "comfortable" (sleeping or sexually sated or smooching in the shower). In previous episodes, witches have extracted information (Bonnie from Mason and Luka, Gloria from Stefan) with great difficulty and with the help of magic, but never vampires, whose abilities seemed limited to mind control (e.g., manipulating dreams) rather than fishing for secrets.

According to Abby, Alaric's psyche was fractured because of his frequent death and resurrection, allowing the darkness inside him to easily take control, something that also happens to dark-magic obsessed witches. Even if he's not wearing the ring, the psycho personality can still take over (as it does before he attacks Meredith and as Samantha Gilbert's did when she was in the asylum). Bonnie's spell, which uses herbs as its binding element, may give Alaric control of his dark side again.

PREVIOUSLY ON *THE VAMPIRE DIARIES* Those Fells have a bad rep: Meredith mocks her own family, referring to the Fells as "notorious busybodies" and in "Children of the Damned," Jenna said of Logan, "He's a Fell. They're all snooty."

OFF CAMERA In an interview with TVGuide.com, Julie Plec provided insight into Elena's character and what keeps her holding out hope: "The one thing Elena understands fundamentally about Stefan is that there's the Stefan who's a monster being led by his own demons — the basic nature of vampirism — and then there's the Stefan that fought like hell to hold onto whatever part of his humanity he could hold onto — and that Stefan is worth saving."

FOGGY MOMENTS How did Sage know about Klaus's habit of daggering his siblings and putting them in coffins? She may have known Klaus "killed" Finn, but keeping family members in coffins was a big secret, which Elijah himself was not aware of ("The Sun Also Rises," "As I Lay Dying"). Since Psycho Alaric has a clear plan and purpose — to cleanse the council — why did he stab himself long before his work is done? How does he choose which council members to target? The medical examiner was discouraging Meredith from using vampire blood; does that not make him a "good" council member in Evil Alaric's estimation? Bill Forbes was also critical of the council, but he was another of Alaric's targets. Samantha Gilbert was on suicide watch at the asylum, with no personal effects, nary a magic ring, and she managed to kill a nurse and a guard. Then the geniuses in charge gave her a knitting needle and left her alone with it. Did they want her to kill herself? What stopped Sage from killing Damon when he threatened to kill Finn?

QUESTIONS
* With Abby gone, will Bonnie come back to Mystic Falls?
* Will the spell and magic herbs help Alaric?

Klaus (to Stefan): Do you really have no appreciation for me? I have given you someone to hate, someone to loathe, a target for all of your anger, so you don't have to turn it on yourself. . . . I really think you should be thanking me.

3.18 *The Murder of One*

Original air date: March 29, 2012
Written by: Caroline Dries
Directed by: J. Miller Tobin
Guest cast: Linds Edwards (Troy)
Previously on *The Vampire Diaries*: Paul Wesley

With white oak stakes at the ready, the gang plots to kill an Original, but Klaus and Rebekah have plans of their own.

The Salvatore brothers have made self-destructive moves in the past, but in "The Murder of One," the poor guys have no idea that their diabolical master plan is akin to staking themselves. In an extension of the series' emphasis on family ties, the bloodlines that run all the way back to the creation of vampires matter. The death of an Original means the death of every vampire sired by that Original. What a shocker for our Mystic Falls friends, who have tried to kill Klaus and his family so many times. If they had succeeded, all vampires, friend or foe, would be dead. It's the perfect twist to raise the stakes as the season heads into the final four episodes.

The white oak stakes make literal the proverbial double-edged sword: what will save them from their enemy will also kill them. In less literal ways, "The Murder of One" reflects on how double-edged swords play a key role for the characters; often what keeps them going is also their greatest source of pain. Alaric's ring has resurrected him time and again, but it's also turned him into a killer. He can't trust himself, he can't be left alone (even with Bonnie's herbal psycho-suppressant), and the weight of the murder, which he can't even remember committing, is heavy on his conscience. Bonnie's magic is a source of great strength, and she's used it to save her loved ones many times over, but it's also a weapon of destruction. As Klaus does to her in this episode, Bonnie is repeatedly called upon to do something that she believes is wrong, something in the service of evil to prevent an immediate threat. And the example of this double-edged sword idea that never abates is in the very existence of a vampire. Their immortality and strengths have a high price: a thirst for blood, an

appetite for the kill, an innate monstrousness that battles their humanity. As Caroline explains to Alaric, when she was first turned, she killed a stranger and she *liked* it. Sunshiny Caroline Forbes has the instincts of a killer. Relationships, too, have their dark sides: where there is love and connection, there is also the opportunity for pain, loss, and exploited vulnerability.

With all that uncertainty and ambiguity, each character chooses what to believe in and lets that guide their actions. Will they seek retribution, or grant pardon? Elena is a staunch believer in standing by her loved ones when their dark side (inevitably) takes control; she explains to Caroline why she withholds judgment, and her bestie follows suit. With Alaric, Caroline is very aware of the choice she is making, to follow the Elena Gilbert Handbook rather than demand punishment for her father's death. Rebekah does the opposite with Damon, punishing him for mistreating her. The gang as a whole is demanding retribution for the crimes Klaus has committed, hoping to take out the lot of the Originals with one fatal blow that allows for no distinctions between individual siblings and their particular actions. (Even Elena sets aside her usual empathy for Elijah, despite his handwritten apology note.)

Questions of right and wrong are brushed aside by Klaus, who answers to his will alone. He sees Bonnie's emotional response as something he can use as leverage to get what he·wants — to be unlinked from his siblings — and he uses Finn's love for Sage as a way to engender his cooperation. Klaus knows the role he plays: he's the villain, and he relishes it. In Stefan's confrontation with him, Klaus reveals just how clearly he understands his function: he's the target for Stefan's anger, the big bad who helps redirect attention from the multitude of lesser evils committed by the "good guys." He has given Stefan purpose. And Stefan knows his enemy is right: since "Homecoming" Stefan has had a single pursuit and has done horrible things on his path to vengeance. But now, with the revelation that the Originals are tied to the vampires they sired, his goal of killing Klaus is plainly self-destructive. He has been wasting his time in seeking revenge and, as he tells Elena, must begin to face his own actions. It's a turning point, a move along the spectrum away from Ripper and closer to Well-Adjusted Stefan.

For Stefan, an examination of what he's lost begins with Elena and a difficult question: how does she feel about Damon? Elena is not prepared to answer, her feelings for him still muddled and undefined. Elena likes to make her choices with care, and this is one dilemma that has no easy way out. Of course, if the secret psycho killer in Alaric decides to go after whichever Original happened to have sired the Salvatores' bloodline, the whole thing will be a moot point anyway. Where would Evil Alaric hide the only remaining white oak stake?

COMPELLING MOMENT The sibling banter between Klaus and Rebekah, arguing over her torturing technique.

CIRCLE OF KNOWLEDGE
*   No Tyler in this episode.

- Aside from the literal murder of one Original (in the hopes of killing them all), the title of this episode may be a reference to the Counting Crows song "A Murder of One" from their 1993 album *August and Everything After.*
- Did the guys keep all those wood shavings and bits from their whittling and sawing? They could MacGyver another stake!
- It's really too bad "Vampire Almanac" Slater is dead. He would be *really* helpful in sorting out these bloodlines.

THE RULES Bonnie unlinks the Original kids with a spell that requires their blood. The death of Finn reveals that the vampire bloodline of an Original is linked: if an Original is killed, every vampire they sired will die shortly thereafter.

PREVIOUSLY ON *THE VAMPIRE DIARIES* Jeremy encountered the difficulty of whittling in "Brave New World," as Damon does here. Alaric asks Damon if he learned nothing from the moonstone incident: in "Know Thy Enemy," Katherine found the bar-of-soap-shaped moonstone hidden in the soap dish; here Damon goes for the obvious hiding spot again with the wooden stake in the woodpile. Damon calls Caroline "Barbie" again; he first called her "Vampire Barbie" after she turned in "By the Light of the Moon." Caroline tells Alaric about the man she killed in "Brave New World"; Carter worked at the carnival, had a flirty moment with Bonnie, and was compelled by Damon to fight Tyler Lockwood. Rebekah's not the first vampire to torture a Salvatore with an Elena dream: in "Memory Lane," Katherine messed with Stefan's mind, showing him how it feels to be rejected. Damon actually fed on Elena in "As I Lay Dying," when he was hallucinating from his werewolf bite and bit her in the town square, thinking it was 1864 and she was Katherine.

OFF CAMERA In an interview with *The VRO*, Caspar Zafer described how Finn's death scene was put together: first, they filmed Caspar lying there dead, then the stunt man stepped in and was set on fire — a "very brave chap," said Caspar — then, for the visual effect of him on fire, Caspar was filmed with black dots on his face for the FX team to use as guides. It was a total of three to four hours of work for a three- to four-second sequence. The set of Klaus's mansion is actually that of former Undisputed World Champion boxer

Director J. Miller Tobin and Ian Somerhalder film "The Murder of One"
(photos courtesy J. Miller Tobin).

Evander Holyfield; Ian Somerhalder was particularly impressed getting to go to work and see the legendary fighter there in his 54,000-square-foot house.

FOGGY MOMENTS In "Break on Through," Elena calls Abby's house and speaks to Caroline, looking for Bonnie's help with Alaric's split personality problem. Did Elena or Bonnie not tell Caroline that Alaric was responsible for the council murders then? It seems like information she would have already known (i.e., before Elena's talk with her in the woods). Klaus seems surprised that Rebekah has a soft spot for the Salvatore boys, but she was madly in love with Stefan a short time ago (from her perspective), so her affection there would be natural. Why did Caroline let Alaric go home alone? Wasn't her duty to watch him to make sure he stayed Alaric?

QUESTIONS
- Who sired Rose? Which Original is the head of the Salvatores and friends' bloodline?
- If it's not Klaus, would the gang still kill him, knowing that Tyler would also die?
- Despite Finn being estranged from his siblings, he was still family. Will there be fallout from the Originals for killing him? Is Matt in trouble for wielding the final blow?

Alaric: He's me. I'm not compelled. I'm not possessed.
There's no humanity switch. What drives him is me.
Stefan: No, no, he's not you. He's the darkest parts of you. Parts we all have.
Klaus: Well, this is depressing, isn't it?

3.19 *Heart of Darkness*

Original air date: April 19, 2012
Written by: Brian Young and Evan Bleiweiss
Directed by: Chris Grismer
Guest cast: Lauren Cohan (Rose)
Previously on *The Vampire Diaries*: Nina Dobrev

Damon and Elena go to Denver, and Stefan draws out Alaric's dark side by tapping into his own.

"Don't back down now": "Heart of Darkness" takes that one sentiment and beautifully explores it in the two main storylines, creating a resonance between the narrative threads despite their differences. Alaric and Stefan battle their repressed evil alter egos in the Salvatore dungeon while Elena and Damon tussle with her repressed feelings. And outside those two passionate struggles — one violent, the other romantic — Tyler returned from his self-imposed exile in the Appalachian Mountains, having pushed himself past the breaking point (literally and metaphorically). By finding something that matters to him (his relationship with Caroline) and holding on to it as a kind of life raft in a sea of darkness, Tyler feels he may have gained control of his own Mr. Hyde and freed himself from Klaus's control. Instead of denying their dark sides (or in Elena's case, the feelings she's afraid of embracing), the characters dive right in in "Heart of Darkness," and the result is an episode pulsing with energy thanks to raw performances, powerful song choices, and well-crafted and layered writing.

Just as Tyler won't know if his sire bond to Klaus is broken until he tests it, Stefan felt that while he had regained control over his bloodlust by helping Meredith without killing her in "Break on Through," it still held power over him. He hadn't exorcised his demonic side, just repressed it. As both Alaric and Stefan realize, the darkness within isn't a separate, alien force that can be denied or blamed, but as much a part of who they are as their goodness. Their violent acts are driven by their own hidden desires and frustrations. Neither is compelled or possessed, and they feel the only way to overcome their darkness is to first embrace it, a method that's reminiscent of Jung's suggestion that one must incorporate the "shadow self" (see *Love You to Death — Season 2*, page 232). In "Ordinary People," Damon told his brother, "I happen to like the edge, Stefan. Your problem is your inability to resist falling over it. You're all or nothing, man, you can't just . . . be." That inner balance is what Stefan seems able to find within himself by facing his darkness. At Alaric's insistence, Stefan taps into his ripper instincts, which lurk just beneath the surface of "good" Stefan, in order to unleash Evil Alaric. While the immediate goal of discovering the location of the stake is met, how, or if, Alaric will overcome his other self remains to be seen. The cost of that information could be dire.

For Stefan, though, the exercise in intentionally calling upon and then

The Strange Case of Dr Jekyll and Mr Hyde

Meredith: Mr. Saltzman, what is your secret?
Guardian angel, or did you sell your soul to the devil?
Alaric: A little of both.

That smart aleck Damon slips a copy of Robert Louis Stevenson's 1886 novella *Strange Case of Dr Jekyll and Mr Hyde* into Elena's care package for Alaric in "Heart of Darkness," and it's an apt choice for both the voluntary prisoner and for his guard and torturer, Stefan. A story so well known that its characters have become cultural shorthand for one's good side and bad, *Dr Jekyll and Mr Hyde* has a deeper resonance with season 3's arc for the semi-retired vampire hunter.

Stevenson's story begins from the outside, being told from the perspective of Utterson, a dear friend of the good and respected doctor Jekyll, and slowly works its way into the first-hand revelations of how the strange circumstances came to pass. At first, there is simply unusual behavior from Dr. Jekyll and seemingly unconnected violent events around London; as with Alaric. There is no reason to consider him a suspect in the murder of Brian Walters, but clues build: the weapon used to kill the M.E. comes from Alaric's stash, and he tells Elena that he has holes in his memory, something they both brush off as the result of too much whiskey ("Bringing Out the Dead"). As Jekyll's condition advances, his other side takes over once he falls asleep, just as Alaric's does. Both men struggle with how to talk about their other side, despising that part of their self and feeling detached from it. Just as Alaric and Elena struggle with the right pronoun in "Heart of Darkness" — "where I . . . or he," "you . . . the other you" — so struggles Jekyll when he writes of the madman who's taken over his existence: "He, I say — I cannot say, I. That child of Hell had nothing human; nothing lived in him but fear and hatred." Fittingly, when Stefan finally beats the bad guy out of Alaric in "Heart of Darkness," his identity is established with the briefest of identity-focused exchanges: "You." "Me."

Though they have no way to predict the ultimate consequences of their actions, Jekyll and Alaric are both unwittingly responsible for their dark sides taking dominance: Jekyll intentionally creates a potion that will transform his physical self, his dark immoral side made manifest, while Alaric opts to wear a ring that magically allows him to cheat death. As both men's dark sides gain a stronger foothold, Hyde and Alaric-Hyde work to destroy their alter ego, endangering their better halves by committing violent crimes: in the case of Hyde, destroying Jekyll's research and laboratory, and, with Alaric-Hyde, hiding the incredibly valuable white oak stake.

When the good side is in control, he tries to remove himself from harming others. Jekyll shuts his door even to his dearest of friends, Mr. Utterson, telling him, "You must suffer me to go my own dark way. I have brought on myself a punishment and a danger that I cannot name." Similarly, Alaric becomes a prisoner, first in his apartment and then in the Salvatore cell. Jekyll's analysis of the split within his personality provides nice insight into that of Alaric, as well as those other *TVD* characters who struggle with the desire to be good and their instincts to act selfishly and immorally. Says Jekyll of how truly each self belonged to him — the dastardly Mr. Hyde or the do-good doctor: "Though so profound a double-dealer, I was in no sense a hypocrite, both sides of me were in dead earnest; I was no more myself when I laid aside restraint and plunged in shame, than when I laboured, in the eye of the day, at the furtherance of knowledge or the relief of sorrow and suffering." Meredith's investigation into Alaric's past reveals a proclivity to react violently to those who were "asking for it" by being violent jerks themselves; as Alaric grew up, he channeled his violent tendencies into vampire hunting, a hobby that quickly morphed into fighting alongside vampires. With no real outlet for his dark side, Alaric shares Jekyll's revelation that "My devil had been long caged, he came out roaring."

Alaric is forced to acknowledge that this side of him exists, that it's a *part* of him, just as Stefan has to face the Ripper. Jekyll "chose the better part and was found wanting in the strength to keep it"; while Alaric seems not to have any control of his evil alter ego, Stefan does. And in "Heart of Darkness," he has a breakthrough when he's able to use his Ripper, attacking Alaric with the intent to kill, and then cage him. Alaric, like the poor Dr. Jekyll of Stevenson's Victorian tale, seems fated to lose the person he chose to be to the darkest parts of himself.

vanquishing his ripper self results in a better sense of self-control. Emerging from the cellar with a deeper understanding of himself, Stefan calls Klaus out on *his* behavior, and the result is a strangely sad conversation. Klaus admits he has no intention of killing Stefan: he's been holding out hope that the friend he once had will return. While there are centuries of untold backstory with Klaus, it would seem that Stefan is the only person with whom Klaus has had an earnest relationship, one where the bonds of family don't dictate closeness or where Klaus himself didn't have to compel the connection into existence. The fraternal bond they shared in the '20s was real, and Klaus deeply values it (which brings to mind Damon cherishing his real moments with Elena in season 1). Klaus's hopefulness is very akin to Elena's, who wouldn't give up on Stefan, choosing to believe the version of him she knew would one day return to her. And (for the time being at least) it is the Stefan that Elena loves who is in control. In an act that signals his independence both from Klaus and his own need for revenge, he orders Klaus out of his house.

Like her big brother wanting a bestie again, Rebekah desires to be part of the (relatively) ordinary teenage life in Mystic Falls. She's an incredibly powerful Original vampire who can do whatever she'd like, and what she chooses to do is organize the Mystic Falls High Decade Dance. Despite her lifespan of a thousand years, Rebekah feels that she's not yet lived. Claire Holt continues to do a magnificent job of making Rebekah sympathetic and vulnerable without losing her bite. The Caroline-Rebekah scene was classic — in particular, their in-unison "No" to Matt's suggestion of doing both decades — and the similarities between the two help establish Rebekah as sympathetic. That humanity makes tragic each earnest emotional moment Rebekah has with someone that quickly turns for the worse: with Elena, she was daggered ("Homecoming"); with Matt, she's rightly suspicious of his kindness but made to feel paranoid; and most significantly for a girl who cried herself to sleep, calling for her mother, she's possessed by Esther, in another of her mother's schemes to kill her, her brothers, and consequently every last vampire. The final reveal of Esther's possession cleverly tied together the various threats developed over the second half of season 3: Esther and Evil Alaric are hell-bent on destroying all vampires and have a weapon in hand.

Exploring the "don't back down now" sentiment in a *very* different way in Denver, Elena takes Stefan's suggestion that she figure out her feelings for Damon and manages to tackle both the physical and emotional dynamics between them. Again in this episode, Elena is reminded that Damon is a very sexual being (his history with Rose, his hookup with Scary Mary), and after initially putting up the barrier again — leaving the motel room after the proximity of Damon and their touching hands overwhelmed her — she finally gives in and stops fighting against herself. Despite a chaste kiss here and there in the past, this make-out was an expectation-filled moment both for the audience at home, and for Damon and Elena themselves, and it was decidedly epic. Beyond the perfectly tense, passionate, fraught physicality of that scene was the frankness with which Damon and Elena (and Rose) discussed their relationship. Lying beside Elena, Damon admits to an essential truth about himself: he doesn't let people see the good in him, because he doesn't want to feel the burden of living up to anyone's expectations — notably Elena's. It's something he's struggled with in the past; last season, Elena urged him to "be the better man" again and again, while he felt he couldn't live up to her expectations, telling the woman in the road in "The Descent" (before he killed her), "I can't be who she wants me to be." But when Elena pulls away from him at Scary Mary's house, Damon realizes that there's a negative flip side to hiding his good behavior: she has expectations of him, they're just lower than he'd like. Elena has come to expect and rely upon a pattern from Damon, where he torpedoes any budding connection at the first obstacle. It's been a convenient way for her not to confront her complicated feelings for him, and what those feelings say about her deepest desires, who she is, and what she wants. Finally understanding that, Damon decides to thwart these expectations, to force her to face whatever she's repressing and figure it out; he puts the ball in her court just as Stefan did in suggesting she go on this explore-your-feelings trip.

Providing some heavy-handed commentary is Rose, a longtime Damon-Elena shipper. Rose's character has always been used as a mouthpiece for the writers, whether for exposition or, as in this episode, as a way to make explicit the pros and cons of each Salvatore as suitor. But as forced as it played out, Rose is nevertheless right about the difference between the way Elena feels for Stefan and for Damon. Love is never easy in Mystic Falls, and, as both Caroline and Elena can attest to in "Heart of Darkness," even the epic moments are soon sullied by complications.

COMPELLING MOMENT The Elena-Damon motel sequence, from start to finish. That's the kind of scene that makes real-life romance pale in comparison.

CIRCLE OF KNOWLEDGE
* No Bonnie in this episode.
* Joseph Conrad's *Heart of Darkness* (serialized in 1899 and published in 1902) tells the story of a British man, Marlow, who takes a job as a boat captain for a Belgian company in the Congo. Through Marlow's description of what he encounters on his journey (most notably, the legendary Kurtz), a strong conflict is established between the European men's concept of themselves as "civilized" and what their violent and cruel behavior reveals about who they actually are. The "darkness" is said to be at the heart of all men, an evil that allures as it repels: "And it has a fascination, too, that goes to work on him. The fascination of the abomination — you know, imagine the growing regrets, the longing to

Moby-Dick and the Quest for Revenge

"How can the prisoner reach outside except by thrusting through the wall? To me, the white whale is that wall, shoved near to me. Sometimes I think there's naught beyond. But 'tis enough. He tasks me; he heaps me; I see in him him outrageous strength, with an inscrutable malice sinewing it. That inscrutable thing is chiefly what I hate; and be the white whale agent, or be the white whale principal, I will wreak that hate upon him." — Captain Ahab, Moby-Dick

In the Salvatore holding cell, Stefan picks up Ric's copy of *Moby-Dick* to pass the time while the imprisoned Alaric is dead. With his vampire speed-reading abilities, by the time Ric wakes up, Stefan has almost finished Herman Melville's 600-odd-page novel. First published in 1851 and now considered one of the greats of American literature, *Moby-Dick; or, The Whale* has at its core a story of an impossible quest for vengeance. Captain Ahab lost his leg to a great white whale and takes his whaling vessel, the *Pequod* (with narrator Ishmael aboard), on a journey to kill the beast. Ahab's single-minded, unwavering determination eschews reason or consideration of the well-being of those in his care; his need to settle the score is destructive, not redemptive. Sound familiar? Stefan's reading material was no haphazard selection by the writers.

Revenge has been a motivating force in stories ever since there was storytelling, and *The Vampire Diaries* is no exemption to that tradition. In season 1, the main story arc was fueled by the desire for revenge. In "History Repeating," Damon's diabolical master plan was revealed: he would open the tomb and release Katherine and the other tomb vampires. Stefan said to Damon, "This can't be about love; this is about revenge," to which Damon replied, "The two aren't mutually exclusive." Damon wanted vengeance on Mystic Falls, on the descendants of the founding families who he believed had imprisoned Katherine. That same spirit drove Stefan 150 years earlier when he hunted the founding families in the first days of his vampirism: he killed Honoria and Thomas Fell and Johnathan Gilbert (temporarily) as acts of retribution for what they did to Katherine ("The Dinner Party").

That same motivating force drove the cranky tomb vampires, led by Frederick. While Pearl tried to reason with Frederick — telling him in "Let the Right One In," "We cannot live our lives about revenge, we need to have better control of our emotions" — the tomb vampires were unflinching in their mission. Even after Frederick was killed, the remaining ones regrouped to destroy the founding families in "Founder's Day." Just as Damon was thwarted in his quest for revenge — his dedication to it faltering when he realized Katherine had fooled him — the tomb vampires are repeatedly unsuccessful. Even when they get one last shot, as ghosts made temporarily corporeal in "Ghost World," the tomb vampires fail to satisfy their need for revenge (though, R.I.P. Tobias Fell, disemboweled and hung up in the town square).

Season 2 was not without its own revenge quests: Brady wanted vengeance for Mason's death in "Daddy Issues" but he ultimately ended up dead, along with his werewolf posse. More significantly, we learned that it was Klaus's taste for vengeance that drove Katherine's ruthless decision-making over the past 500 years. In "Katerina," after she turns herself into a vampire to escape sacrifice, she finds her family butchered, Klaus's punishment for her "betrayal." Katherine warns Elena in that episode, "Whatever you do to escape Klaus — he will get his vengeance. On your friends, your family, on anyone you've ever loved." That threat in turn motivates Elena, causing her to submit to the sacrifice — a choice that has its own snowball effect.

One of its main side effects is on Stefan: to save his brother (bitten by werewolf Tyler in an effort to derail the sacrifice), Stefan gives himself over to Klaus, agreeing to play the dutiful ripper henchman in "As I Lay Dying." Once freed from Klaus's control in "Homecoming," Stefan immediately embarks on a mission of revenge (in part goaded on by Katherine). He seems to believe, as Elijah said in "The Sun Also Rises," that "sometimes there's honor in revenge." But Stefan's mission for revenge — like Ahab's in *Moby-Dick* — has collateral damage: most notably, Elena. In "Our Town," the situation came to a head: Stefan believed he had nothing left but vengeance and was willing to call Klaus's bluff even if that meant an incredibly personal trauma inflicted on Elena.

Like the white whale, Klaus is undefeatable: not only is he an Original and a hybrid, but his very existence could be linked to Stefan's. If Klaus dies, his entire bloodline of sired vampires goes with him. Stefan's revenge on Klaus could be literally self-destructive. And the clever Klaus knows he's the behemoth to Stefan's Ahab; he said as much in "The Murder of One," that he has given Stefan purpose by being the target of his hatred. Back in "Let the Right One In," Harper explained to the imprisoned Stefan that Frederick and the other tomb vampires needed someone to blame, someone to punish, for their century-and-a-half of suffering — and the parties at hand were the Salvatore brothers. The same is true of Stefan: to avoid dealing with his recent spate of murders and his psychological torture of Elena, Stefan has focused himself on Klaus, on "monomaniacal revenge" (to borrow Melville's phrase) in which he excuses himself of any other responsibility or priority. Like Ahab and his enemy whale sharing the spirit of destruction, Klaus keeps Stefan company with his own appetite for revenge. Of the whale, Melville wrote, "Retribution, swift vengeance, eternal malice were in his whole aspect, and spite of all that mortal man could do," words that resound in consideration of Klaus's character.

In "Heart of Darkness," perhaps in part thanks to Melville's weighty tome itself, Stefan comes to realize the fruitlessness of pursuing vengeance: it can never be won but the price of waging that fool's battle is everything he once held dear.

escape, the powerless disgust, the surrender, the hate." Like Stefan and Alaric unleashing their cruelest instincts, *Heart of Darkness* asks whether any person would be resolved enough to "face the darkness" without giving over to it.

- Shame on Caroline for trying to shame Rebekah about her *one* hookup. She's no more promiscuous than the rest of them, and so what if she was.

- Damon calls Jeremy "Whoopi" and asks if he needs a pottery wheel in order to communicate with the spirit world, referencing the 1990 movie *Ghost*, which starred Whoopi Goldberg as the medium who helped Patrick Swayze's character, a ghost, communicate with his still-living potter wife, played by Demi Moore.

- In the scene between Rebekah and Esther, Degas' *The Rehearsal of the Ballet Onstage* (1874) is visible above the fireplace; the original painting — unless Klaus has lifted it and brought it to Mystic Falls — resides in the Metropolitan Museum of Art in New York.

- It would have taken Damon, Elena, and Jeremy just over three hours to drive from Denver into Kansas, assuming Scary Mary lived close to the state line.

- Kol has a funny definition of "getting even." Damon snapped his neck, killed his brother, and humiliated him; as payback, Kol gives Damon a beating that he'll recover from in about five minutes.

- "Heart of Darkness" is the first episode in which Rose appeared and didn't cry.

- Tyler's season 3 arc follows the same pattern of his season 2 journey: he teamed up with the wrong crowd (werewolves then, Klaus now), grateful for a path that freed him from his curse (the promise of breaking the Sun and the Moon curse, his hybrid status); he did wrong by Caroline ("Crying Wolf," "Our Town") and then left town to sort himself out, only to return home after a few episodes' absence with a stronger sense of his identity and better self-control.

THE RULES Alaric's dark half can take control of him not only when Alaric loses consciousness, but when Evil Alaric wills it, as he does to protect himself from Stefan killing him. Esther takes possession of Rebekah's body, and the transfer happens a little differently from what we've seen before. A séance helped open up a channel for Emily Bennett to take over Bonnie ("History Repeating") and a witch cast a spell, fueled by blood, for Klaus to possess

Alaric ("Know Thy Enemy"). Here, Esther simply grips her daughter's arms, and she's able to take over Rebekah's body. Esther-as-Rebekah walks into the no-vampires-allowed cave, implying that it is the soul inside the body rather than the body itself that determines which magical rules apply. But in the case of AlariKlaus in "The Last Dance," he entered the Salvatore house (then invitation-only for vampires, under Elena's ownership) because Alaric, the body, was human. Are Esther's magical skills coming into play here? Or have the rules of possession changed?

FOGGY MOMENTS Why hadn't Elena already warned Jeremy that Klaus knew where he was? Is Tyler so high on the Originals' priority list that his return warranted such subterfuge? How would staying at Caroline's be any safer than staying at his own house? He's traversing the streets of Mystic Falls to get to the Forbes's, and he could just as easily be seen if he was headed to his own house. Another nitpick: when they arrive at the motel, for whose benefit did Damon clarify that it was Elena's idea to stay there? The audience's? Jeremy was in the car with them and would've heard whatever conversation they had about it.

PREVIOUSLY ON *THE VAMPIRE DIARIES* Damon and Elena went on a bonding road trip in "Bloodlines" and, less successfully, in "Bad Moon Rising" with Alaric. In "The New Deal," Klaus had Tyler hang out with Jeremy, befriending him to get him off vervain; Kol fake-friends him too. Caroline and Matt's fake fight works better than Stefan and Elena's did in "Memory Lane," when Katherine was wise to them. In "Ghost World," Elena wanted Jeremy to try to contact Lexi, so she could learn how to de-ripperfy Stefan; as with Rose here, he wasn't sure he'd be able to since he didn't know Lexi. Damon told Jeremy that "hot trumps weird" in "Children of the Damned"; long true to that sentiment, Damon tells Elena he slept with Mary, who was "creepy, not ugly." In "The Return," Elena outlined Damon's usual behavioral pattern, as she does again to him at Mary Porter's: "You don't admit that you get hurt. You get angry and cover it up and then you do something stupid."

OFF CAMERA Director Chris Grismer revealed on Twitter that the scene at Mary Porter's was lit solely by the cell phone flashlight Elena holds. In an interview with EW.com, Julie Plec described what they hoped the

Damon-Elena motel room moment would capture: "I can't speak for every-body else in this world, but when we were talking about what the scene needed to be in the writers room, we've all had those moments where you end up lying in bed in high school with a guy or a girl that you like, and you don't know what's gonna happen, you don't know what it means, but all you know is that you're *infinitely* aware of their proximity to you and every single move that they're making and every single breath that's being breathed between the two of you. We wanted that moment to be that experience. When we talked to Chris Grismer, we just said, 'Milk every single beat out of this that you can. It's so much about what's not being said. It's so much about them just lying next to each other, the beauty and intimacy and sexual chemistry of just being near each other is what needs to be telling the story here. So take as long as you want, and shoot it as much as you want, and we'll put it together from there.' They definitely gave us everything we needed."

QUESTIONS

* Has Tyler actually broken his sire bond?
* Will Scary Mary Porter be on the Other Side with Rose? Is it possible for Rose to track her down in Ghostville?
* Will Esther honor Rebekah's wishes and head to the Decade Dance?
* Is there an uneasy alliance in Stefan's and Klaus's futures now that Esther's plot to kill all the Originals — and consequently all vampires — is back in play?

Alaric (to Elena): Taking care of you and Jeremy has been the closest I've ever come to the life I've always wanted.

3.20 *Do Not Go Gentle*

Original air date: April 26, 2012
Written by: Michael Narducci
Directed by: Joshua Butler
Previously on *The Vampire Diaries*: Matt Davis

The Mystic Falls High Decade Dances continue their tradition of being living nightmares, and the gang says goodbye to the Alaric they knew and loved.

As in the *TVD* universe, where nature demands a balance, so demands good episodic television. While the emotional moments in "Do Not Go Gentle" rang true, the story logic faltered, resulting in an uneven episode that's most enjoyable when one doesn't think too hard about the plot or its context in the wider *Vampire Diaries* mythology. A television show like this one, with its foundation in the supernatural, demands that viewers suspend their disbelief and accept that vampires, witches, werewolves, ghosts, and magic objects exist. What makes *The Vampire Diaries* such a success is that its supernatural world makes enough sense that the human stories told within that world resonate; they are believable. It's incredibly difficult to create a world and stick to its rules, while constantly telling new stories, pushing characters into new places, and expanding the mythology. *The Vampire Diaries* has had a knack for giving us the unexpected in a way that made past events click together. Pieces of the puzzle were always fitting together in a way we didn't predict, but which made a world of sense once revealed.

But when the supernatural world feels manipulated, governed by storytelling convenience rather than internal logic, the emotional consequences of those plot points have to work harder to elicit the desired reaction from the audience. Luckily, in "Do Not Go Gentle," despite the over-reliance on magic, twisting of rules, and convenience of Esther (see "Foggy Moments" below), the story managed to deliver a heartfelt punch, thanks to seasons' worth of established relationships, callbacks to past moments, and the usual outstanding performances and production that *The Vampire Diaries* cast and crew unfailingly deliver.

In this penultimate chapter of a beloved character, Alaric Saltzman — history teacher, day-drinker, father figure, dreamboat, and co-captain of Team Beer and Blood — breathes his last breath as a human, and with him goes the good side of Ric. Though Alaric chooses to die instead of turn into a hate-filled vampire hunter, the choice is not his own: Esther continues meddling in others' lives, a tradition she started a thousand years ago when she and Mikael turned their children.

In his relationships with the Gilbert kids, and with Damon, Alaric had found a family, one that is devastating for him to say goodbye to. Whether blood-related or not, the importance of loved ones is paramount. Usually death is swift and unexpected on *The Vampire Diaries*, but the gang is able to gather, in a candlelight vigil outside the Salvatore crypt, to honor Ric's life and his sacrifice in ending it to protect them. As Bonnie says to Jamie, her friends are the most important things in the world, and it's heartbreaking to watch them say goodbye to another person they love. Matt Davis shows his underused range in this episode, playing the hate-filled psycho with a kind of stillness and quiet purpose, and then showing us Alaric's stoic tears at the end. His last moments with Elena, Jeremy, and Damon capture the strength of those characters' bonds to one another, and the torment of forced goodbyes.

Outside the crypt, Meredith tells Damon that Alaric doesn't really want to be alone, what he wants is to be with his best friend. It's an insight into another *TVD* keystone: isolation is sometimes more terrifying than the monsters of Mystic Falls. And it's true across the board: Jeremy can barely stand his farewell with Alaric, having lost so many people he's loved in such short order, and he realizes how empty his home will be without Ric. The toast to Alaric at the closed Grill bar, awash in an otherworldly blue light, is a fitting and beautiful moment: besides being at Ric's home away from home, Jeremy is with Matt, who's been supporting him all season long — so much so that it earned them a bromance label from Caroline — and the two boys, who know grief too well, find solace together.

In "Bringing Out the Dead," as Ric lay dead in the upstairs hallway of the Gilbert house, Elena told Matt that she couldn't bear to lose any more family. Here she is again. Her dogged insistence that everything will be okay, her determination to stop Esther's plan somehow — by reasoning with Ric, by refusing her blood — is for naught. In her end-of-episode scene at the school with Stefan, another tragic end to a promising date, Elena can barely contain her grief, and Stefan asks her not to. Just as she's asked of him as he battled his demons this season, Stefan encourages Elena to feel; he reminds her that her grief is part of her humanity. Elena has now lost the last of her guardians; there's no one else to help her parent Jeremy, no grown-up to turn to. Though she is loved, she feels desperately alone.

It's a *Vampire Diaries* tradition for "normal" high school moments — heck, for any happy moment at all — to be scuppered by supernatural violence, but (assuming she makes it out of the crypt alive) Bonnie manages to keep her romance intact, and the ordinary Jamie may continue to help Bonnie feel less of a witch-for-hire and more of a person valued for herself, rather than her powers. Bonnie's life is also one of isolation: she comes home

to an empty house, her dad out of town, Grams dead, and mother AWOL. In another step toward enriching her character, we see her vulnerability, her need for comfort (as we're so used to seeing Elena's) . . . and her house! Three seasons in, and we finally get a glimpse of her living room. Who knows what wonders season 4 will hold.

While the rest of the characters turn to their loved ones for support in this time of grief, Klaus finds himself utterly alone. Rejected by Caroline, who loves Tyler and doesn't even entertain the idea of running away with Klaus, he is further rebuffed by Stefan when he attempts to turn the dance's 1920s theme into a nostalgic "strange bedfellows" moment. But neither of the Salvatore brothers is having any of that. Targeted and tricked by his mother once again, Klaus's hurt boils over into rage. In a powerful moment, Klaus vows to thwart any scheme his mother cooks up from beyond the grave. His purpose rediscovered, Elena, as doppelgänger blood source, is back in the crosshairs.

With Klaus as the cautionary example of a life lived willfully and vindictively, "Do Not Go Gentle" reminds us of the unshakable bonds that exist between siblings, friends, lovers, and family in the widest sense of the word. It's what makes that exchange between Stefan and Elena in the gym resonate: none of them is alone, not even in the darkest, most despairing moment.

Robert Ri'chard as Jamie

Best known as the star of *One on One*, Los Angeles–native Robert Ri'chard is an accomplished film and TV actor with a long list of credits dating from the mid-1990s when his career took off. Over the years, Robert has appeared in *Touched by an Angel*, *Cousin Skeeter*, *Coach Carter*, *House of Wax*, *CSI: Miami*, *Veronica Mars*, *The Comebacks*, *Meet the Browns*, and upcoming *A Beautiful Soul*, *Kungfused*, *Bolden!*, and *Silent Voice*. There was a two-month wait for Robert between auditioning for Jamie and learning that he had the part, but then he was off to Atlanta. As he told HollywoodLife.com, "It was a really well-run set, and at first, I was intimidated by the size of the show. Going onto a show that already has such a big following, every mom, every daughter, everyone I talked to was like, 'Wow, you're on a really big show.' So I just decided I was going to go in and work hard and put out a really good performance. I think I felt more pressure on this than when I guest starred on, like, *CSI: Miami*." In an interview with CleverTV.com, he said the role allowed him to do his two favorite things: "falling in love with a woman" and "holding a rifle." Of Kat Graham, Robert gushes, "She's beautiful, a sweetheart [and] so into what she does." Keen to stick around *The Vampire Diaries*, Robert Ri'chard hopes he can bring some "normal girl lifestyle" into Bonnie Bennett's crazy, witchy life.

And perhaps, since peace has proven so elusive, that is really all that anyone can hope for.

COMPELLING MOMENT Alaric and Damon's final conversation, and that cork going in the empty bourbon bottle.

CIRCLE OF KNOWLEDGE

- "Do Not Go Gentle" takes its title from the most well-known work of Welsh poet Dylan Thomas (1914–1953), which concludes, "Do not go gentle into that good night. / Rage, rage against the dying of the light." Written when Thomas's father was dying, the poem suggests that though death be inevitable, nevertheless we all struggle against it. The "fierce tears" of Thomas's poem are made manifest in Matt Davis's portrayal of the dying Alaric.
- Embroidered in the lid of the coffin where Esther lies is a tree, symbolizing the white oak tree that was used to create vampires and which can be used to destroy them all.
- In *The Strange Case of Dr Jekyll and Mr Hyde*, Jekyll, knowing that his dark

side is about to take complete control of him, writes in his final moments as himself, "This is my true hour of death, and what is to follow concerns another than myself." A fitting epitaph for the Alaric who dies in the crypt.

THE RULES As with when she took possession of Rebekah, Esther returns to her own body with none of the usual trappings of magic. It is possible to move magic from one object to another: Esther transfers the protection spell in the Gilbert ring onto the white oak stake to make it indestructible. Using a ton of salt (maybe a literal ton), Esther places a binding circle around the school to trap the vampires inside. Bonnie may have also been trapped inside (otherwise, why didn't she go to the old cemetery to rescue Elena and Alaric?). When Bonnie tries to do a locator spell to find Elena, Esther is somehow able to "fight" Bonnie, preventing her from succeeding, perhaps a side benefit of the circle. Mimicking the spell she used a thousand years ago to create the Originals, Esther turns Alaric into the "ultimate hunter," a process that requires Esther to draw on dark magic. He drinks the doppelgänger's blood (which Esther magically forces from Elena), Esther kills him, and he finishes his transition when Bonnie force-feeds him her blood. Some as-yet unrevealed restriction on Alaric means he will at some point run out of the power Esther bestowed upon him and permanently die.

HISTORY LESSON On the wall next to the history classroom door is the seal celebrating the Jamestown Exposition, a world's fair held in Norfolk, Virginia, the oldest English settlement in the United States, in 1907 to celebrate the 300th anniversary of the town's founding. It was on April 26, 1607, that Christopher Newport and the crew of the *Susan Constant* landed in Virginia. On the blackboard in Alaric's classroom are notes on the chronology of Jamestown's Newport, Captain John Smith, Pocahontas, and her husband, Captain John Rolfe.

PREVIOUSLY ON *THE VAMPIRE DIARIES* Stefan makes a crack about the "pretty tragic" track record Elena has with high school dances, as he did in "Homecoming." Elena once again wants Stefan to teach her some decade appropriate moves as she did in "Unpleasantville." Elena had to watch her guardian be turned into a vampire in "The Sun Also Rises," when Jenna was used in Klaus's sacrifice, and she's forced to witness another transition here. Elena and Stefan echo their earlier conversation in the gym at the end ("Who gave you that horrible advice?" "Just this girl I used to date."), just as they did when they were first falling in love in "The Night of the Comet." When Damon was dying of the werewolf bite in "As I Lay Dying," Alaric came to visit him in his cell in the Salvatore basement, bottle of booze in hand; Damon returns the favor. In "Ghost World," Damon "recycles that same crap-ass apology" to Ric that he gave Mason for killing him, and in his last moments Alaric says it takes him *actually* dying to get a real apology.

FOGGY MOMENTS No one seems concerned about conversations being overheard by Klaus's super vamp hearing: Esther and Alaric talk freely in the coffin room, and Caroline and Tyler discuss breaking the sire bond in the gym. Though Klaus seems to leave the white oak ash out in the coffin room, where did Esther get the dagger that she had Alaric use on Rebekah?

How did Damon spend the time between popping by the hospital and arriving at the dance? Why didn't he alert the gang about Alaric earlier? Why would Damon assume that the magic cure for Alaric (Bonnie's herbs) wasn't working, when earlier he'd discovered that Ric wasn't taking them (and showed the full bottle to Meredith)?

How was Esther still alive? It was established that she was relying on the Bennett witch bloodline, which was severed when Abby became a vampire, and yet she is still able to both live in her own body and perform numerous complicated spells, all at once, without weakening. Esther says the location where Klaus killed her is a magical hot spot, but wouldn't the witch house (a place where 100 witches died violently, not just one) still be more powerful than outside the crypt?

How (and when) did Esther put the ring of salt around the entire high school, unnoticed? When did Esther decide to target Alaric for her kill-the-Originals project? As far back as his first death in "A Few Good Men"? The way she explained it to Elena, it seemed like she was muttering in Ric's ear *every* time he died. Her plan to turn him into a "vampire hunter" with the strength of an Original must be recent, because in "Smells Like Teen Spirit" she made a deal with Ghost Vicki to kill Elena (to prevent Klaus from making a hybrid army), and Esther required Elena's doppelgänger blood to turn Alaric into more than just a regular vampire. With Esther's strict no-killing-the-locals rule with her children, what did Esther think of Alaric killing council members? Was it just a big coincidence that in 1912 Samantha Gilbert also targeted council members when she gave in to her dark side?

Some unrealistic moments: despite going to such lengths in the past to supervise him, the gang leaves Alaric unsupervised when they know he's in his Evil Alaric state. Esther has shown no sign of having any powers of persuasion and Alaric has spent the past year befriending vampires, as well as the better part of his lifetime making sane, nonviolent choices, but Esther was capable of convincing Alaric in the briefest amount of time that *all* vampires are evil and deserve to be eradicated and that he should unleash his violent side. Klaus shows up at the old cemetery and whisks away his mother's body, and completely trusts that his enemies, who have been trying to kill him all season, are telling him the truth about what went down with Alaric. He doesn't even pop in to take a peek at Ric. Jamie wakes up when Bonnie has a little nightmare, but slept through her getting out of bed and leaving the house.

Finally, Stefan says they were in the gym the night Klaus compelled him but, though the evening's festivities kicked off in the gym, they were all in the cafeteria when Klaus compelled him and Stefan bit Elena ("The Reckoning").

OFF CAMERA Caroline's "I watch *The Bachelor*" line was a nod to Candice Accola's own love for the show; she and her aunt would watch it every Monday night. Of Matt Davis's turn as Evil Alaric, Alice Evans told *The VRO* she was "so excited for him as an actor," happy that he has an opportunity to shake up his performance. "He's so complex . . . sparkly, and [we get to] see some of it onscreen." The rifle that Matt is holding (and is forced to point at Jeremy) is actually Zach Roerig's own, as he proudly told *TV Guide*. In a Zap2It interview, Julie Plec commented on Klaus's rage toward his mother's corpse, explaining a key difference between the Original hybrid and Damon: "Klaus isn't ruled by love the way that Damon, even in his darkest moments, is ruled by love. Love is Damon's Achilles heel. For Klaus, his Achilles heel is his fury, his rage at having been unloved or not properly loved. Every time he gets a moment where we can see his vulnerability, the very act of him feeling vulnerable triggers that rage. His response, his fight-or-flight response, is to get angry and to act out and to be hostile and manipulative and evil. With one comes the other."

QUESTIONS
- Is there a way for Klaus to truly render his witch-ghost mother powerless?
- Where are the other two Original siblings?
- If Vampire Alaric hates both vampires and vampire sympathizers, and his hatred is "pure," is anyone safe? Where will he begin his murderous rampage? With Damon, who's conveniently outside the crypt?
- When Bonnie went to the cemetery, was she possessed by Esther, or was her dream-state consciousness making the choice for her? As she said to

Damon earlier in the episode, there's always a choice — so did she make one in feeding Alaric? How badly was she hurt by his attack?

Klaus (to Elena): Consider this me doing you a favor. Once you're dead, you won't have to choose. No broken hearts, their family stays intact. But, just between us girls, who would you have picked?

3.21 Before Sunset

Original air date: May 3, 2012
Story by: Charlie Charbonneau and Daphne Miles
Teleplay by: Caroline Dries
Directed by: Chris Grismer
Guest cast: Hillary Anne Harley (Nurse)
Previously on The Vampire Diaries: Joseph Morgan

Alaric's resurrection as an immortal vampire hunter forces the gang to work with their enemy, Klaus.

Its balance between the supernatural and human elements of the story re-established, the penultimate episode of season 3 of *The Vampire Diaries* puts on a display of all its strengths. With that inimitable *TVD* tone, "Before Sunset" managed to be horrifying but funny, fast-paced without losing us in the twists and turns, and full of attitude. Right from the Civil War imagery in the opening sequence through the rest of the masterful cold open — the disturbing image of Alaric, smoke billowing from his sizzling body, dragging the limp Caroline across the parking lot will be hard to forget — it was crystal clear that this was top-notch *Vampire Diaries*.

The Rebekah-Caroline scene gave a nice preview of what the episode held in store for the clean-up committee of two: enemies becoming allies. The two girls have been at each other's throats all season, competing for position in the school hierarchy, on the cheerleading squad, and bickering over boys, but here Caroline extends her sympathy for Rebekah, and Rebekah returns the sentiment. That peaceful moment is short-lived when Alaric attacks, and the two are made allies, fighting shoulder to shoulder against him.

The lynchpin of these switching allegiances is Elena's supernatural significance: Klaus wants her blood to create more hybrids, and Alaric needs her alive long enough for him to complete his mission of killing the Originals, a plan that is in danger once Klaus knows how to kill his otherwise indestructible enemy. The reveal that Alaric's and Elena's lives are tied together is the kind of mythological twist this show does best: it resonates emotionally *and* it makes sense from a witchy ju-ju perspective. The Salvatore brothers want to protect Elena from all-comers, and the rest of the gang is right there with them in a valiant display of the devotion they have for each other. To save Elena and Caroline, Bonnie reaches out to her absentee mother and dips into the foreboding and unknown territory of dark magic; Jeremy lets a witch stop his heart, despite knowing the risk of letting the Gilbert ring resurrect him; and Stefan and Damon, with Klaus at their side, walk into certain death by entering that high school of horrors.

As Tyler says, there's a difference between real love and fake loyalty, and that contrast has been a recurring theme of the season, which comes to an emblematic moment in the victory party at the Gilberts'. At the beginning of the episode, Elena and Jeremy are re-painting the master bedroom — going "darker," naturally — a room they both hate, because of all the loved ones who no longer rest there. Grayson and Miranda, Jenna, and now Alaric have left that room empty. Elena and Jeremy have lost so many people, and yet still they have a full "backup" family, as witnessed by the friends who surround them to celebrate. A loyal family that would go to all lengths to protect him is what Klaus has tried to force for himself through the sire bond with his hybrids, his relationship with Stefan, his manipulation of his blood relatives, and his courtship of Caroline. But he demands loyalty, instead of earning it. He can't force people to care for him, and he doesn't know how to engender true devotion. The delightfully over-the-top Siege of the Gilbert Homestead is a perfect symbol of that: Klaus wants in and resorts to violence to get his way, but he's ultimately unsuccessful. He's also stymied by Tyler's commitment to his freedom from the sire bond (and to help his friend Elena) and by Stefan once again choosing to reject his ripper-era connection to Klaus. As the father of the vampire bloodline, Klaus finds himself very much in the position of the person he hated most: Mikael. He's been desiccated and imprisoned, rejected by both his blood siblings and his descendent creations, the "one big happy family" that reviles him.

The villainous, diabolical Klaus is, at his core, no different than any of

By Any Other Name . . .

Rebekah hasn't been around *The Vampire Diaries* long, but she's racked up an impressive number of nicknames that go far beyond Bekah and Bex — some nicer than others . . .

- She-devil
- Barbie Klaus
- Evil Blood Slut
- Blondie Bex
- Lushy Pants
- Buffy the Vampire
- Sexy Bex
- The Original Sister
- Goldilocks

the other characters. He wants his family surrounding him, but he makes choices that do nothing but drive them away. If he'd been content to leave town with Rebekah, he'd be alive and well, but instead he ends up desiccated. Klaus still hopes that his siblings will let bygones be bygones after a thousand years of him throwing temper tantrums against those who dare to defy him, and he wishfully tells Elena that he and his siblings are closer than ever, parroting Stefan's earlier statement that he and Damon have become closer in the wake of Klaus's machinations. Klaus's stubbornness, his need to have his way, his obsessive need to protect himself from threats, has driven away his siblings, those who would have stood by him. He demands that Stefan, Elena, and Tyler be grateful to him for the supposed gifts he's given them; instead, Elena expresses her gratitude to Tyler for saving her, and the Salvatore brothers thank each other. It is only Caroline who, unbidden, thanks Klaus, responding to his kind action of helping her escape Alaric. Like the other moments of gratitude in "Before Sunset," selfless actions are rewarded with acknowledgment in Mystic Falls.

Nothing like a villain who takes the truth and twists it, and in this episode that's something both Alaric and Klaus do to Elena. But there is a great deal of truth in how they characterize her actions: she knows that she could break apart the Salvatore brothers by making a choice between one or the other. She knows that she's made choices that her parents, whose mission was to rid Mystic Falls of vampires, would not approve of. She fraternizes

with murderers, she helps them get away with it. Has Elena lost her sense of right and wrong? Violence, compulsion, murder, biweekly torture . . . it's all become a part of her life, and it's changed her. But what remains at her core, solid, is her fierce determination to protect the ones she loves, whatever kind of creature they are or may become. In her speech to Jeremy at the end of the night, Elena accepts that her actions may make her "the bad guy" now, but she'll make the same choices again to save the people she loves.

Alaric knows Elena — her strengths, her weaknesses, who she'd die for, what she values — and he uses that insight to torment her. His single-mindedness and strength of conviction make him a compelling villain, one whom Elena can't talk into showing mercy. He is without humanity and his vitriol is fueled by Alaric's insider knowledge. In a cruel moment, he turns part of the relationship Elena had with Alaric — training her to fight vampires — into a demand that she kill one, her best friend. Of course, Elena (warrior princess that she is) can take it: she proves he did teach her well and frees Caroline, using that old chestnut of the element of surprise. Elena is the kind of girl who will slice her own neck to find out vital information (how Alaric can die) and to save her *other* mortal enemy from being killed (to protect the vampires she loves). Her decisiveness only extends so far, though, and she explains her reluctance at making a choice between Stefan and Damon: she doesn't want to lose anyone else. And, judging from their conversation in the car, the brothers don't want that either. They are closer than perhaps they've ever been, and the idea that one would leave town to allow the other to live happily ever after with Elena is more than bittersweet; it's tragic.

With Alaric still on the loose, the council in the know, and Elena collapsed and bleeding, the stage for the finale is set.

COMPELLING MOMENT The long, wordless goodbye between Klaus and Stefan stands out as an important turning point in their fraught relationship and power struggle.

CIRCLE OF KNOWLEDGE
- The sequel to 1995's *Before Sunrise*, *Before Sunset* is a 2004 Richard Linklater film starring Ethan Hawke and Julie Delpy as an American man and French woman who meet again nine years after they spent one night together in Vienna.
- With the montage in the cold open kicking it off, "Before Sunset" uses a

lot of war imagery and language: Klaus wants to build an army to ward off his enemy's assaults, Alaric is the ultimate soldier in Esther's war, the Gilbert house comes under siege, Damon makes a peace offer to Abby (which is refused), and Alaric creates a mutiny in the council by revealing the enemy within (Carol and Liz).

• In "Homecoming," Mikael called Klaus the "Big Bad Wolf" and in his huffing and puffing and attempt to blow the Gilbert house down, he lives up to the nickname.

• Damon's explanation of why the Salvatore house is open to vampires raises the question of the Gilbert house. The invitation rule has two parts: a living human owner or a resident means vamps are invite-only. When Elena died in the sacrifice, the living-owner rule was voided for the Salvatore house and it didn't re-establish itself once she came back to life (even though, in the human world, she's still the legal owner). With no human actually living there, the place is a vampire free-for-all. The Gilbert house, however, has two living residents. Jer and Elena may have both been briefly dead, but they are currently alive and residing there, meaning the rule is in full effect. (And Elena is, presumably, also the legal owner of the house.) The ownership rule on the Salvatore house is a bit of a gray area, granted, but the spirit of the invite-only rule is to protect humans in their homes, and, in my opinion, that spirit is upheld. As for why Klaus couldn't get in: Klaus-as-Alaric was in the Gilbert house in "Klaus," but in that incarnation of the possession spell, that was because Alaric was allowed in. The vampire version of Klaus still requires an invitation, which is why he resorts to found-object projectiles.

• The average person has five liters of blood in their body, a figure Klaus seems to take into account when he asks Tyler to get three more bags for the slender Elena.

• "Once more, with feeling," says Damon, and the *Buffy the Vampire Slayer* fans in the audience squeal with delight, taking it as a reference to the 2001 musical episode of the series, a favorite of fans (which include Ms. Julie Plec).

THE RULES Like the Originals, Alaric has weaknesses: he burns in the sun (which is why he is confined to the school until sunset), and he's vulnerable to vervain. But not even a white oak stake to the heart will kill him. There is only one way: Esther bound Elena's life to Alaric's, making him temporarily invulnerable but not truly immortal. When Elena dies, Alaric dies.

Bonnie uses the same spell on Klaus that her mother used on Mikael. By drinking Bonnie's blood, Klaus, Stefan, and Damon are bound to her, and she is able to remotely desiccate a vampire when one of them makes contact with his bloodstream, stopping his heart as she simultaneously stops a human's. The spell doesn't require the human to permanently die, which seems fair (in a "balance of nature" way) as the spell doesn't permanently kill the vampire either. This spell taps into "dark" magic, which carries "temptations" with it, and (in a very cool effect) dark veins crawl up Bonnie's arms and onto her face, like she's being affected more directly by the spell she's performing than when she draws power from nature. Klaus is rendered inert by the spell, in a state resembling a daggered Original or the tomb vampires from season 1.

HISTORY LESSON The opening Civil War imagery focuses on the bloody battle at Gettysburg, a turning point in the war, fought July 1863 in Pennsylvania.

FOGGY MOMENTS Why did Alaric wait until Caroline arrived at the school to begin his anti-vampire crusade? Rebekah was alone in the caf, and his super vamp hearing would have alerted him to her presence, as it did when Caroline arrived. Perhaps Rebekah started her clean-up duties, from 8:00 to 8:02, by cleaning up the salt ring around the school, since there was no salt in sight. Who fixed the Gilbert house front door? It was torn off its hinges when Klaus hurled the soccer ball at it, but it's looking good as new when the boys walk Elena to the door. Double fail for Former Lifeguard Bonnie Bennett: she didn't go into CPR-mode with Jeremy, and she didn't blink when Elena — drained of blood and suffering from a head injury — did a tequila shot instead of seeking medical attention (or at least taking a shot of vampire blood).

PREVIOUSLY ON *THE VAMPIRE DIARIES* In "The Sun Also Rises," Damon carried Elena's body away while Stefan stayed behind to watch Klaus die; the same dynamic plays out here when Damon helps Elena while Stefan makes sure Klaus is rendered lifeless. Vampire Alaric tries to call Elena's bluff as she holds the knife to her neck; clearly, he doesn't remember how she stabbed herself in "The Dinner Party." Elijah didn't believe she would do it either.

OFF CAMERA In an interview with AfterElton.com, Joseph Morgan shared his belief that Klaus's complexity isn't necessarily a sign of softening: "He's not good or bad. He's layered. So, the more we learn about him the more maybe we'll empathize or sympathize with him, but he's always going to have done the things he's done. . . . I personally hope that he doesn't just suddenly miraculously become good. I feel like there should be a chance of redemption for everyone, but he's still going to carry that stuff with him." One of Michael Trevino's favorite scenes to film in season 3 was the gang cheering their victory in Elena's kitchen. "That took us back to the pilot," explained Zach Roerig to *TV Guide*. "The pilot was like summer camp, and it's very rare that we're all in a scene together." While the brothers worry that Elena's eventual choice will tear them apart, Paul Wesley suggested at PaleyFest that there is a kind of camaraderie to being in love with the same girl, which brings the brothers together.

QUESTIONS
* Back in the '90s, who helped Abby take down Mikael with the desiccation spell? Whose heart did she stop? Was she able to re-start it as Bonnie does with Jeremy?
* What happened to the liters of Elena's blood?
* What does the future hold for Bonnie and dark magic?
* What will the council make of Alaric's revelations and his own supernatural status?

Alaric (to Jeremy): You'll never be alone.

3.22 *The Departed*

Original air date: May 10, 2012
Story by: Brett Matthews and Elisabeth R. Finch
Teleplay by: Julie Plec
Directed by: John Behring
Guest cast: Erin Beute (Miranda Gilbert), Sara Canning (Jenna Sommers), Jason MacDonald (Grayson Gilbert)

Previously on *The Vampire Diaries*: Nina Dobrev

Elena remembers her last day with her parents, as Alaric's relentless hunt of the Originals leads to his final battle and another deadly car crash on Wickery Bridge.

The Vampire Diaries has long explored the importance of choice, and its season 3 finale brought that theme back to the forefront. Just like its characters, the series is brave enough to make controversial choices, despite knowing that some viewers (particularly those deeply invested in one romantic relationship or another) will be just as frustrated as Damon was on speaker phone, unable to change the course of events but needing their dissent heard loud and clear. With a deliberately different tone from past finales — it wasn't a surprise-around-every-corner frenzy — the episode brought us back to the beginning, to the formative moment of our heroine. "The Departed" gives us the two days in which Elena's life tragically changed.

In the flashbacks, we get a glimpse of the life that was "supposed to be," which Elena lost before we met her in the pilot episode. A girl then untouched by real tragedy, her main worry was that she'd hurt her boyfriend's feelings by being honest about her own; she was someone who could say, without a trace of irony, "It's Mystic Falls. Nothing bad ever happens here." In a particularly well-crafted story structure that intertwines past and present, Elena drifts in and out of consciousness over the course of the episode, back and forth in time to reveal the stark contrast in her situations but also the emotional parallels. That first fateful day, she woke up smiling but was transformed by the accident into someone unsure of how to live, or if she wanted to, as she admits to Matt. Her near drowning was the emotional death of the old Elena Gilbert, the one she let go of with the impromptu funeral on Wickery Bridge, Matt at her side, in "Our Town." And in the present, Elena's final choice — that Stefan save Matt before her — and her watery death put her at another crossroads. Her human life is over and, if she chooses, her life as a vampire is about to begin.

Back in "The Dinner Party," when Stefan realized Elena planned to sacrifice herself to protect her loved ones, he told her that choosing to die like that, "It's not heroic. It's tragic." But "The Departed," and arguably season 3 as a whole, presents a different perspective: heroism and tragedy are inextricably linked. Elena's decision is both a heroic sacrifice and tragic death, as was her father's death before her. Quite deliberately, we are shown Elena imitating Grayson's actions in his final moments, motion-for-motion; Elena is very much carrying on her family legacy when she refuses to be rescued until she sees Matt to safety, using her last reserves of fight and life. And Elena's not alone: Mystic Falls is full of those whose heroic choices lead to tragic consequences. Take Stefan: he has often made decisions that put himself in physical or emotional peril; rescuing Matt instead of Elena is no exception to that. Or Damon who, for the protection of his brother and their friends, stays the course with Klaus instead of hurrying back to Elena in Mystic Falls. In their desperation to protect Elena, Matt and Jeremy choose a course of action that leads to her death. Whether the result of choices large or small, heroic acts on *The Vampire Diaries* are rarely untouched by tragedy.

There's another layer of complication for our characters when it comes to decision-making: what's the right thing to do? Alaric lays it on thick with Jeremy, telling him to "be on the right side" of the battle against the vampires, to protect his sister against her will. It's a call to action that Jeremy and Matt respond to in their own way by drugging her to spirit her out of town. Alaric also judges Meredith's actions, and her choice to use vampire blood as medicine has twice in recent history triggered a transition, first in Bill Forbes and now in Elena. Is she doing the right thing, or is Alaric right to judge? Outside of the life and death struggles, Elena wrestles with the morality of her dual romances, feeling it was "wrong" to string along Matt in sophomore year just as it is now to have both Damon and Stefan in relationship limbo.

Bonnie Bennett's journey runs parallel to Elena's, both girls repeatedly thrust into horrible situations where they feel they have no real choice; it's always a lose-lose situation. But in "The Departed," the two of them assert their independence, deciding not to be pushed around or coddled, that it's time to do what they want to do, regardless of what other people think of their plans. Bonnie doesn't participate in the gang's scheme to capture Alaric and turn over Klaus's body to Elijah, nor does she let them know what she's up to with the body-swapping spell. Bonnie lets her best friends in the world fear for their lives and say their goodbyes, because she's actually saving the day. In defiance of the witch spirits' wishes, she chooses to protect her loved ones by securing Klaus and his bloodline from Alaric's attack, but to do so means protecting the person responsible for so much tragedy in her life. At Bonnie's core is her commitment to safeguard those she considers family, and she proves willing to dismiss old allegiances and form new ones in order to protect her own in "The Departed."

Elena understands that instinct, and it takes just one simple statement from Elijah to convince her to make a deal with him: "He's my brother." Like

Liz and Carol trying to protect their kids, or Matt and Jeremy's plan to get Elena out of Mystic Falls, or the Salvatore brothers' unwavering determination to save each other, the Original siblings are bonded — family always and forever. The moment in the woods between Rebekah and Elijah is a nicely human breakdown: no matter how much of a bastard Niklaus can be, they love their brother dearly. Rebekah's decision to break the deal Elijah made with Elena and the Salvatores is driven by her grief and by her fear. She's lost her one companion, the brother she ran with for a thousand years; between flight and fight, Rebekah chooses fight and destroys her mother's soldier by killing Elena. Very much like Bonnie Bennett, Rebekah opts to make her own decision, instead of continuing to be led by forces around her.

There are those who accept Elena's choices, valuing her right to free will over their own opinion, and those who do what they believe will best protect Elena, her own opinion be damned — like Matt and Jeremy, drugging her, and

Temporary Funerals

Who hasn't been dead at least once in Mystic Falls? Here's a rundown of the various fleeting deaths that have plagued our main characters.

- **Stefan and Damon:** killed by their father ("Blood Brothers")
- **Caroline:** killed by Katherine ("The Return")
- **Bonnie:** self-inflicted death by magic ("The Last Dance")
- **Jeremy:** neck snapped by Damon ("The Return"); shot by Sheriff Forbes ("As I Lay Dying"); heart stopped by Bonnie to desiccate Klaus ("Before Sunset")
- **Tyler:** killed by Klaus ("The Reckoning")
- **Matt:** drowned himself ("The Reckoning")
- **Klaus:** killed by Mikael ("Ordinary People"); desiccated by Stefan and Bonnie ("Before Sunset")
- **Elena:** killed by Klaus ("The Sun Also Rises"); drowned in car crash caused by Rebekah ("The Departed")
- **Alaric:** staked by Damon ("A Few Good Men"); killed by Stevie ("Crying Wolf"); neck snapped by Damon ("Disturbing Behavior"); run over by hybrid-driven SUV ("The New Deal"); stabbed by Elena ("Bringing Out the Dead"); staked by Esther ("Do Not Go Gentle"); and finally killed forever when Elena dies ("The Departed")

most notoriously Damon, who says he'd rather stick Elena in a well than trust Elijah as she opts to. It's the eternal difference between the Salvatore brothers, as Damon points out, and one that has brought the boys to blows in the past. In "Dangerous Liaisons," Elena told Stefan, "When we were together, you used to let me make my own decisions. You trusted me. After all this, at least that hasn't changed." Honoring someone's wishes when their life is in danger is no easy choice, as Elena herself has experienced. In "The Murder of One," Elena and Stefan disagreed about whether or not to give up their plot to kill an Original in order to save Damon. Sounding very much like Damon speaking of her, Elena told Stefan, "What he would want and what we should do are two different things." But in that situation, she chose to honor Damon's wish, instead of doing what her instincts told her; she stayed with Stefan to kill Finn. Stefan makes a parallel choice in "The Departed," by honoring Elena's wish that Matt be saved before her. But by doing that, what the boys have been protecting her from for three seasons has come to pass: Elena has died.

Damon has made it very clear that he will *always* choose Elena's life over another's and, had he been in the situation Stefan was faced with, he would have rescued Elena, kicking and screaming. How will he react to Stefan's choice? And how will Stefan deal with his role in Elena's change? The guilt-prone Stefan knows, better than anyone, that Elena never wanted to become a vampire. He stood with her on the top of that mountain in "The Last Day" and heard her speech about the imagined future she would lose if she turned. For Elena, becoming a vampire was a fate worse than death. In several moments in "The Departed," we are reminded of that imagined future: Elijah makes reference to Elena's children, Alaric and Jeremy make mention of the long human life she can lead; those references subtly remind us of what she is sacrificing at the end of the episode. When Stefan sits in front of Elena's corpse, he mourns not only the end of Elena's human life but her lost future, and we see a glimpse of the future struggle he'll have with his role in her death. These last moments make their "just in case there is no later" embrace (their only kiss of the season) even more poignant upon re-watch.

Despite Elena's choice of Stefan for "right now," not for "always," there will be no tidy resolution to the relationships between Elena and the Salvatore brothers, maybe not even in the series finale; there's no easy answer. With Elena's death, she will change: she is no longer a human who needs to be saved on a weekly basis. As a vampire, her doppelgänger blood is no longer valuable. She'll be stronger and faster and full of impulses previously foreign and repulsive to her. Who Elena will be as a vampire is the next fascinating chapter in her story. As it changes her entire life, it's necessarily going to have ramifications on this love triangle.

In the lead-up to the finale, the hype was around Elena making a choice between brothers, and the poor girl finally does, sort of, in the strangest of circumstances. Throughout the episode, Elena explains her dilemma to Matt and how the decision weighs on her: she's terrified of losing either one of them, having lost so many loved ones already. Ultimately, Elena is guided by remembered advice from her dearly departed mother — that she wouldn't lose Matt if she broke up with him — which is proven true by Matt: ever-steady, he's still by her side and there for her. Elena understands the difference between letting someone go and losing him.

From that deceptively peaceful shot of the water under Wickery Bridge through to Elena's awakening, "The Departed" ended with a masterful sequence that displayed all the strengths of this series. Everything comes together: the scenes underwater, past and present intercut, as Stefan saves Elena at her father's insistence and Matt at Elena's; as Alaric dies in the arms

The Season of the Originals

Heralded as the "Season of the Originals," this season delivered on its promise: we met the family, learned about the creation of vampires, saw the siblings reunited with their mother . . . and witnessed her attempts to kill them all. In true *TVD* tradition, for every answered question, another mystery arises. Below are some of the key facts and big questions concerning the Original mythology as we head into season 4.

- **The Cave:** Who carved the story in the cave? That it is protected from vampires entering (and was booby-trapped with vervain-coated wood) suggests the involvement of witches and an anti-vampire agenda. But the details of the story included — notably that it was Klaus, not Mikael, who murdered Esther — suggest insider knowledge of the Original family history.
- **Poppa Original:** Rebekah tells Elena that Mikael killed her and her brothers, after they'd been tricked into drinking blood-laced wine. So, who killed Mikael? Was it Esther, or did he kill himself? In "Do Not Go Gentle," Esther refers to Mikael as a "true hunter": was he in some way different from his children, or was he an Original vampire like them who at some point decided to feed on other vampires? Could *any* vampire sustain themselves on the blood of other vampires?
- **The (First) Murder of Esther:** For nearly a thousand years, Klaus led his siblings to believe that their father had killed Esther, while Klaus watched. The truth, as revealed by the cave drawings in "Ordinary People," is that Klaus killed Esther, in a rage after she rejected him and put the hybrid curse on him. Did Mikael witness Klaus killing Esther? Did someone else? How did Ayana manage her magic preservation of Esther's body? When did she cast that spell?
- **Witches:** After some misdirection early in the season (Klaus and Rebekah referred to the "Original Witch" rather than to "Mother" even when alone), in "Ordinary People," we learn that Esther is the witch of the Original family, the mother whose story Elijah recounted to Elena in "Klaus." She is a witch but not the *first* witch, and in the village with her lived another powerful witch, Ayana. Who was the first witch? Are Esther and Ayana part of a first generation of witches or does magic date much further back? What became of Ayana? As part of the Bennett bloodline, at some point her descendents must have left the Mystic Falls area and migrated to Salem, only to return in the late 1600s.
- **Vampires' Weaknesses:** In the origin story Rebekah relates, it's clear how the vampires discovered most of their weaknesses: they burned in direct sunlight, they were unable to enter a neighbor's home uninvited, and they sizzled when in contact with vervain. But how did they figure out that the great white oak could kill them? Why were the

daggers forged and ash collected? Who initiated the development of a weapon against the Originals: Ayana, another witch, or perhaps Klaus?

- **The Wolfman Cometh:** We've known since "Klaus" that werewolves predate vampires, but details on their origin are otherwise scant. Are they also the result of a witch dabbling in dark magic? Are they a New World or Old World creation?
- **The Original Petrova:** In "Bringing Out the Dead," Elijah and Klaus reveal that the Original Petrova was named Tatia; that, like Katherine, she bore a child out of wedlock; that the two brothers were in love with her and feuded over her; and that Esther "took" the girl. It was Tatia's blood that Esther used to create vampires (and Esther requires Elena's doppelgänger blood to transform Alaric into an Original-style vampire in "Do Not Go Gentle"). But what became of Tatia? Was there a specific spell cast on her — or on her child — to create the doppelgänger and tie her to Klaus's hybrid curse? How and when did Tatia die ... or is she somehow still alive?

of his best friend, Damon grieves for him and for Elena, realizing she must be dead; and as Alaric appears in the Gilbert hallway, not only do we get an incredibly touching and necessary farewell to the Alaric we all loved so dearly, but we see that moment for Jeremy too — the realization that his sister, the one family member he still had left, is gone too.

The end of Elena's human life is tragic and heroic; she has fought her way into this martyr role for three seasons, always putting her loved ones ahead of herself. Her last act is to see Matt safe, and it's just the briefest of moments before she's gone, no more life left in her. It's a bold choice for the series but one perfectly timed: Elena's growth this season has led her here and, while there will be major fallout for season 4, this sort of fundamental shift in our heroine will breathe new life into *The Vampire Diaries*.

COMPELLING MOMENT The breathtaking and cinematic last four minutes of the season.

CIRCLE OF KNOWLEDGE
- The second Martin Scorsese picture to lend its title to a *Vampire Diaries* episode this season, *The Departed* is a 2006 Oscar-winning film starring Leonardo DiCaprio, Matt Damon, Jack Nicholson, and a slew of

other tough-looking guys playing Boston mobsters and law enforcement agents caught in a vicious battle. At the center of the story are two men, each working undercover for the other side. Both Sullivan (Damon) — the rat in the Massachusetts state police — and Costigan (DiCaprio) — the rat in the Irish mob — must maintain their two separate personas, and as the surrounding violence pushes them to extremes, the film explores questions of identity, purpose, and emotional connection.

- The episode's first glimpse of Elena is a clue that the scene is a flashback; she's shown in the reflection of her mirror, a "through the looking glass" moment.

- On Elena's nightstand in 2009 is *Our Love Is Here to Stay* by Tony and Lois Evans, a daily devotional for married couples. Um, hopefully *not* a present from Matt Donovan.

- Elijah warned Klaus that he would become what he most hated, and Elijah honors his biblical namesake's role as a prophet when this comes to pass. Desiccated and wrapped in chains in a coffin, seemingly abandoned by his family, Klaus finds himself in the same position as Mikael when he was entombed in the Charlotte cemetery for nearly 20 years.

- In "Bringing Out the Dead," Stefan declared that there was "nothing smart about trusting Elijah," but here he does trust him in order to honor Elena's choice. A small moment, but one that signals the character's progress on the journey from Ripper Stefan to Well-Adjusted Stefan.

- The Wickery Bridge accident that killed Elena's parents took place on May 23, 2009; the events of the pilot episode in September. In "The Departed," when Damon is lying in the road, he's hunting in his usual manner; it's not the same moment seen in the pilot. With this flashback, we learn that Stefan wasn't the only Salvatore creeping around Mystic Falls watching Elena from May to September. Damon was there too.

- The end sequence is so moving in a large part thanks to the layers of story to which it harkens back. Explicitly, the first car accident, previously unseen, is intercut with the current one, but more subtly, we feel echoes of Matt's drowning from "The Reckoning," the near crash with Stefan at the wheel and Elena terrified to die and become a vampire from "Our Town," and the impromptu funeral rites that Matt and Elena carried out on that very bridge. For readers of L.J. Smith's book series, the Wickery Bridge crash resonates even more profoundly. At the end of *The Struggle* (book 2), Elena races Matt's car across Wickery Bridge, trying to escape a dark power that wants to kill her, and she crashes into the icy river. Elena calls for Stefan's help and struggles to survive before she succumbs and dies — unaware that she will return as a vampire.

OFF CAMERA The Sigur Rós song "Dauðalogn" (which means "death of calm" in Icelandic) debuted on *The Vampire Diaries* from then-unreleased album *Valtari*; music supervisor Chris Mollere said he was "so very honored and ecstatic to premiere the new gorgeous and amazing Sigur Rós song." In preparation for the drowning sequence, both Paul Wesley and Nina Dobrev became scuba certified, as Zach Roerig had before "The Reckoning." At PaleyFest, perhaps anticipating his character's death, Matt Davis spoke of what is so meaningful to him in being a part of *The Vampire Diaries*: "The joy for me is imagining where everyone's going to go next . . . because I think everyone's so tremendous, so talented, and it's been such a joy working with everyone." Julie Plec told TVGuide.com, "The moment in the end of the finale when [Alaric] shows up broke every rule in the [writing] book, but I didn't care. It was more important for us to give Matt Davis and Alaric that last goodbye; to say, 'Yes, he was the bad guy for the last few episodes, but here he is in that Obi-Wan kind of way.'" In the wake of the finale, Julie Plec did a series of interviews, many of which are incredibly insightful and revealing; check out *The VRO*'s May 11, 2012, interview with the showrunner for her thoughts on the finale and the season as a whole.

FOGGY MOMENTS How did Elijah know that Klaus had been desiccated? How far was it from the storage lockers to Mystic Falls? Some characters were able to get there quickly (Bonnie, Alaric, Rebekah) but Damon couldn't return to Mystic Falls within an hour of Klaus being staked — though it's unclear how long he was knocked out by Alaric's first attack. The timeline and distance were just sketchy enough to confuse viewers. In the grand tradition of television, the doors won't open and seatbelts won't unbuckle once a vehicle is submerged, and the same goes for the manually opening windows in Matt's old truck.

PREVIOUSLY ON *THE VAMPIRE DIARIES* In "The New Deal," Bonnie dreams of opening a casket and looking down at Klaus in it; here she does. The favorite board game of Mystic Falls returns! In the flashback, Jenna references Pictionary, which she played in "Memory Lane." While the

Salvatore brothers' lives may be a proverbial coin toss, there was a literal one in "All My Children," to decide who would kill a Bennett witch. In "1912," Matt made Elena tea (that wasn't "over-honeyed") and they talked about what draws her to the Salvatores, as they do here. Damon quotes Elena's "It's always going to be Stefan" heartbreaker of a line from "The Return." In "Klaus," Elijah told Elena that taking possession of someone's body is one of Klaus's "favorite tricks"; with the help of Bonnie Bennett, he gets to play it again. Stefan has before respected Elena's choices in major moments like those in "The Departed" (much to Damon's chagrin): in "The Last Day," he accepted her choice to rely on Elijah's elixir to bring her back to life after the sacrifice. As Elena told Damon in that episode, "It's my life, Damon, my choice." In all three season finales, Damon's life has been in danger: he was trapped in the burning building in "Founder's Day," dying from a werewolf bite in "As I Lay Dying," and nearly beaten in a fight against Alaric in "The Departed."

QUESTIONS
• What was the significance of 1020, the storage locker number where Damon stashed Klaus?

- How did Bonnie perform the Klaus/Tyler possession spell? Tyler called Bonnie after he and Caroline made their plan to leave town. Was he a willing participant?
- Is it safe to assume that Matt was resuscitated?
- Does Damon have the indestructible white oak stake?
- How long before Elijah clues into the fact that Klaus is not dead?
- Has Rebekah made herself a prime target by killing Elena?
- What measures will the council enact now that it's actually doing its job? What will become of Sheriff Forbes and Mayor Lockwood?
- Since Klaus's body was not entirely destroyed (just a little charred before the coffin lid was shut), how long before he leaves Tyler's body and returns to his own?
- Elena will remember the first conversation she had with Damon, seen in the flashback; she'll also remember the moment of compulsion in "Rose." How will that affect her perception of Damon or her relationship to him?
- Which vampire's blood did Meredith use to heal Elena? Is Elena part of Klaus's bloodline, or another one? Did Elena know that she had vampire blood in her system?
- Whose blood will she use to complete her transition, assuming she does? Her personality will change and be heightened post-transition: what will Elena be like as a vampire?

Music in Season 3

Songs by Scene

3.01 "The Birthday"

1. "Are We There Yet," Ingrid Michaelson: *Elena lies in bed awake on the morning of her birthday.*
2. "What You Know," Two Door Cinema Club: *In the storage room at the Grill, Jeremy video-chats with Bonnie.*
3. "Barton Hallow," The Civil Wars: *Ray sidles up to the bar for a beer, and Klaus sidles up to him.*
4. "Means to an End," Trent Dabbs: *At the bar, Stefan tortures Ray while Klaus looks on.*
5. "Make It Without You," Andrew Belle: *In Stefan's room, Damon gives Elena her necklace back.*
6. "Hello," Martin Solveig and Dragonette: *Damon and Elena enter her birthday party, which is in full swing.*
7. "Shooting the Moon," Mona: *Caroline and Elena walk into the "stoner den" and talk to Matt.*
8. "Hawk Eyes," The Kicks: *The party rages on; Tyler and Sophie dance, Caroline and Matt bicker.*
9. "Anna Sun," Walk the Moon: *Elena calls Damon, who pretends to still be at the party.*

10. "Starpusher," Location Location: *Outside the party, Jeremy finds Matt looking for his truck.*
11. "You Make Me Feel . . . ," Cobra Starship ft. Sabi: *Caroline and Tyler finally kiss.*
12. "A Drop in the Ocean," Ron Pope: *Alaric leaves the Gilberts', Tyler and Caroline hook up, and Damon destroys Stefan's room.*

3.02 "The Hybrid"

1. "Parade," Delta Spirit: *Jeremy walks into the staff locker room, catching Matt changing into his Mystic Grill tee.*
2. "Got It All (This Can't Be Living Now)," Portugal. The Man: *At the Grill, Tyler gives Elena a lead on where a werewolf pack would gather in Tennessee.*
3. "Still New," Smith Westerns: *Elena asks Alaric to join her on a werewolf-tracking hike in the Smoky Mountains.*
4. "A Heavy Abacus," The Joy Formidable: *Tyler plays pool and Matt serves him some funky-tasting coffee.*
5. "Echo," Jason Walker: *Stefan drinks Klaus's blood; Damon tells Elena that he'll help her bring back Stefan.*

3.03 "The End of the Affair"

1. "St. James Infirmary," Gloria's 1920s band: *Stefan arrives at the speakeasy; Rebekah licks his face.*
2. "Distance," Christina Perri: *Elena wakes up to find Damon lying next to her.*
3. "Run Wild," Ume: *Caroline screams in agony; Damon and Elena banter on their road trip.*
4. "My Sweet Hunk o' Trash," Gloria's 1920s band: *Rebekah tells Stefan to stick a sock in it so she can hear Gloria sing.*
5. "You Should Know," Pink Frost: *Damon talks to Gloria, looking for Stefan.*
6. "We Come Out at Night," Snake! Snake! Snakes!: *Stefan and Klaus drink at the bar, talking about why it is Klaus keeps him around.*
7. "Blood Call," The Elliots: *Still at the bar, Klaus tells Stefan that good things must come to an end.*
8. "Kale," Nerves Junior: *Damon sits down at the bar next to Klaus.*
9. "Shelter," Birdy (The xx cover): *Damon and Elena begin their trip home; Liz cares for Caroline.*

3.04 "Disturbing Behavior"

1. "Ready 2 Go," Martin Solveig ft. Kele: *Rebekah describes this song, which plays in the clothing store, as sounding like a cable car accident.*
2. "Go Outside," Cults: *The girls talk Salvatore-swapping at the Lockwood picnic.*
3. "Floating (Time Isn't Working My Side)," Portugal. The Man: *Alaric tells Damon he needs to "take a beat."*
4. "Phenomena," Yeah Yeah Yeahs: *Rebekah, Klaus, and Stefan enjoy their liquid lunches.*
5. "Wanna Be Sure," Aidan Hawken: *Tyler comes home from practice to find Caroline in his room.*
6. "Human," Civil Twilight: *Caroline talks to Elena in the town square, and then says goodbye to her dad.*

3.05 "The Reckoning"

1. "Will Do," TV on the Radio: *In the car, Katherine tells Damon it's "not possible" for her to stop being cute.*
2. "Please Ask for Help," Telekinesis: *Klaus clears the gym of seniors, save for Elena, Chad, and Dana.*
3. "10,000 Lovers," Ida Maria: *Damon pulls the car over to a rest stop.*
4. "Torch Song," Shady Bard: *Damon carries Elena out of the hospital.*

3.06 "Smells Like Teen Spirit"

1. "This Too Shall Pass," OK Go: *Caroline, Bonnie, and Elena face their first day as seniors.*
2. "Black Iron Lung," The Gods of Macho: *Stefan plays a Twister drinking game at the Salvatore house.*
3. "My Body," Young the Giant: *It's time for football and cheerleading practice, supernatural style.*
4. "Brick by Brick," Arctic Monkeys: *The Spirit Squad's bonfire kicks off.*
5. "Rave On," Cults: *Elena gets her drink on, while Stefan watches.*
6. "Satellite," The Kills: *At the bonfire, Rebekah discovers the joy of smores with Damon.*
7. "Take Your Time," Cary Brothers: *Damon applies some first aid to Elena; Caroline and Tyler have a post-coital chat.*

3.07 "Ghost Town"

1. "Changing," The Airborne Toxic Event: *Carol and Tobias Fell give speeches at the Night of Illumination kickoff.*
2. "Hitchhiker," Empires: *Jeremy and Anna go into the restroom at the Grill.*
3. "Come On Come On," Michael Johns & The Ontic: *Lexi surprises Elena at the Grill.*
4. "Fever Dreams," Nurses: *Jeremy looks for Anna among the Night of Illumination crowd, bumping into Frederick.*
5. "This Woman's Work," Greg Laswell (Kate Bush cover): *Bonnie and Grams work the spell, and the ghosts around Mystic Falls vanish.*
6. "In Front of You," The Quiet Kind: *In the old jail cell, Elena explains to Stefan that she still has hope.*

3.08 "Ordinary People"

1. "Don't Stop (Color on the Walls)," Foster the People: *Alaric photographs the cave drawings; Damon and Elena spar while Ric studies the drawings.*
2. "Put Your Hands Up," Nadine Coyle: *Rebekah makes Elena help her pick out her homecoming dress.*
3. "I'm Rockin," The Cadillac Black: *Damon and Stefan arrive at the bar.*
4. "Get Your Buzz On," The Cadillac Black: *The brothers play quarters and talk about the bunny diet.*
5. "Turn It On," The Cadillac Black: *Damon dances on the bar with a couple of randoms, and Stefan feeds on Callie.*
6. "Losing Ground," Trent Dabbs: *Mikael interrogates Stefan at the bar.*
7. "Shake It Loose," The Kicks: *On the way to the car, Stefan and Damon bicker.*
8. "We Don't Eat," James Vincent McMorrow: *Rebekah sobs by the fireplace; Elena and Damon talk in her bedroom.*

3.09 "Homecoming"

1. "Don't Stop (Bit Funk Remix)," Only Children: *Tyler and Caroline decorate for homecoming.*
2. "Free Like You Make Me," Cary Brothers: *Rebekah and Elena talk as Rebekah gets ready for her first high school dance.*
3. "You Wanna Freak Out," My Morning Jacket: *Homecoming at the Lockwoods' kicks off.*
4. "First Light," My Morning Jacket: *Klaus tells Stefan his plan to reunite his family now that Mikael's daggered.*

5. "Holdin' on to Black Metal," My Morning Jacket: *Klaus lets Tyler know that there is an army of hybrids at the party.*
6. "The Day Is Coming," My Morning Jacket: *Klaus warns "Elena" that their plan will ultimately fail.*

3.10 "The New Deal"

1. "Shook Down," Yuck: *Elena goes on a run.*
2. "Teenage Blood," Apex Manor: *Bonnie and Elena talk at the Grill.*
3. "Come on Let's Do It OK!," The Trigger Code: *Elena worries about Jeremy while Damon plays darts at the Grill.*
4. "Holding on and Letting Go," Ross Copperman: *Damon compels Jeremy; Elena and Damon kiss on the porch.*

3.11 "Our Town"

1. "Punching in a Dream," The Naked and Famous: *Damon takes a shower; Elena takes out her frustrations on the punching bag.*
2. "Up in Flames," Coldplay: *Tyler and Caroline talk outside of school.*
3. "You Are," The Daylights: *Damon and Alaric talk outside the Founders' Hall.*
4. "False Alarm," Trent Dabbs: *At the fundraiser, Alaric chats with Damon then Meredith by the model Wickery Bridge.*
5. "Goodbye Horses," The Airborne Toxic Event: *Damon and Sheriff Forbes discuss the Klaus/Stefan situation.*
6. "Keep Running," Gemma Hayes: *Stefan stalks hybrid Daniel through the party with a butcher knife.*
7. "Between," Courrier: *Jeremy leaves; Caroline wakes up to a birthday present from Klaus; Matt and Elena meet on Wickery Bridge.*

3.12 "The Ties That Bind"

1. "Code Red," The Boxer Rebellion: *Meredith and Alaric wrap up their lunch at the Grill.*
2. "Lonely Boy," The Black Keys: *Stefan comes home to find Klaus lounging on the sofa, having a drink and listening to some rock 'n' roll.*
3. "Money Saves," Delta Spirit: *Damon drops by Alaric's apartment, while Alaric works out.*
4. "Rewind (Acoustic)," Diane Birch: *Stefan tells Elena she's better than both the Salvatore brothers, and Abby and Bonnie talk.*

3.13 "Bringing Out the Dead"

1. "Lullaby," Sia: *Caroline and Elena sit on her porch and talk.*
2. "With Wings," Amy Stroup: *Caroline tries to convince her father to change his mind.*
3. "Hate & Love," Jack Savoretti ft. Sienna Miller: *Caroline's father dies; Elena waits for Alaric to wake up.*

3.14 "Dangerous Liaisons"

1. "Short Change Hero," The Heavy: *The Original siblings groom and bicker.*
2. "At Least I Have You," Mates of State: *Caroline and Elena talk kissing Damon and Rebekah's evil plan for Matt at the Grill.*
3. "Devotion," Hurts: *Elena enters the ball.*
4. "Wrap My Mind Around You," Trent Dabbs: *Caroline decides to wear the dress, and Klaus sees her arrive.*
5. "Give Me Love," Ed Sheeran: *The guests take to the dance floor for a centuries-old waltz.*
6. "Stubborn Lover," Sugar & The Hi Lows: *Rebekah asks Kol to help her kill Matt.*
7. "Weapons," The Daylights: *Elena and Elijah talk before she meets with Esther.*
8. "Brand New," Mathclub: *Kol is itching to kill; Rebekah calls him an idiot.*
9. "Up in Flames," She Wants Revenge: *At the Grill, Matt rejects Rebekah; Rebekah and Damon hook up.*

3.15 "All My Children"

1. "Poison & Wine," The Civil Wars: *Elena calls Stefan, then Damon.*
2. "Fire Escape," Civil Twilight: *Kol sasses Rebekah about being out all night and asks Klaus to have some fun with him.*
3. "Medicine," We Were Promised Jetpacks: *Alaric and Meredith talk at the Grill.*
4. "Teardrops on My Pillow," Dum Dum Girls: *At the bar with Kol, Klaus asks Caroline to have a drink with him.*
5. "Rubicon," Ume: *Meredith shuts down Kol at the pool table; Alaric daggers him.*
6. "Guarded," Kevin Daniel: *Bonnie sits with her mother; Caroline talks to Elena at the door.*

3.16 "1912"

1. "Don't Owe You a Thang," Gary Clark Jr.: *Rebekah quizzes Carol at the Grill.*
2. "Let's Dance," The Gods of Macho: *Damon explains that his father knocked up a maid.*
3. "Snakeskin Heart," Black Daniel: *Damon and Stefan ditch Rebekah.*
4. "Black Magic," Magic Wands: *Rebekah interrupts Damon's game of darts.*
5. "How It Starts," The Features: *Stefan admits he's ready to eat the entire waitstaff.*
6. "The Argument," Aidan Hawken: *At the Gilberts', Matt asks Elena why she loves those vampires.*
7. "Be the Song," Foy Vance: *Elena and Alaric pledge to take care of each other.*

3.17 "Break on Through"

1. "Country Lane," Telekinesis: *Meredith, Alaric, and Damon arrive at the Wickery Bridge restoration kickoff.*
2. "Guilty Filthy Soul," AWOLNATION: *Damon invites Rebekah to join him and Sage for a drink at the Salvatore mansion.*
3. "Future Starts Slow," The Kills: *Sage and Damon dance.*
4. "Can't Go Back," Rosi Golan: *Caroline tries to convince Abby to stay; Elena calls Jeremy.*

3.18 "The Murder of One"

1. "Demons," Sleigh Bells: *Alaric, Damon, and Stefan play with power tools and whittle themselves some Original-slaying weapons.*
2. "Shame and Fortune," Yeah Yeah Yeahs: *Rebekah chains up Damon and bleeds him.*
3. "On Your Way," Alabama Shakes: *Sage gives Finn his first (and last) tequila shot at the Grill.*

3.19 "Heart of Darkness"

1. "Starting Now," Mississippi Twilight: *Caroline arrives at the gym to see them prepping for the Roaring Twenties dance, not for the '70s dance.*
2. "Dying to Be Born," Civil Twilight: *Elena and Damon find Jeremy at the batting cages.*
3. "Redemption," The Strange Familiar: *Caroline and Tyler meet up in the woods . . . then head down to the cellar.*

4. "Never Let Me Go," Florence + The Machine: *Elena and Damon make out. Like crazy.*

5. "When the Light Dies Out," Christel Alsos: *In the car, Rose explains to Jeremy why she's a Delena shipper.*

3.20 "Do Not Go Gentle"

1. "We Are the Tide," Blind Pilot: *Elena and Caroline decorate the gym for the dance.*

2. "That Man," Caro Emerald: *At the dance, Caroline talks to Matt and then Tyler; Elena and Stefan arrive.*

3. "You Do Something to Me," Sinéad O'Connor: *Elena and Stefan slow-dance.*

4. "The Man I Love," Helen Forrest: *Klaus cuts in on Caroline and Tyler's dance.*

5. "Be Still," The Fray: *Alaric says goodbye to Jeremy, then comes outside the crypt to see the whole group gathered.*

6. "Medicine," Daughter: *Jamie takes Bonnie home; at the Grill, Matt and Jer drink to Alaric.*

3.21 "Before Sunset"

1. "Reno," The Gods of Macho: *As he slowly burns, Alaric drags Caroline across the school parking lot.*

2. "Start to Run," Middle Class Rut: *Klaus attacks the Gilbert house with makeshift weapons.*

3. "Light," Analogue Revolution: *On the porch, Elena talks to the Salvatore brothers about making a choice.*

4. "Act on Impulse," We Were Promised Jetpacks: *Stefan and Damon drive Klaus's desiccated body to the Atlantic.*

5. "Ache," James Carrington: *Alone painting Alaric's old room, Elena passes out.*

3.22 "The Departed"

1. "So What," Pink: *Elena's clock-radio alarm goes off — in 2009.*

2. "Wasted," Low vs Diamond: *Bonnie, Matt, and Elena walk outside school.*

3. "Airplane," Shadow Rewind: *Alaric approaches Jeremy at the Grill.*

4. "Sick Muse," Metric: *At the bonfire, Elena calls home for a ride.*

5. "Dauðalogn," Sigur Rós: *The final sequence of the episode is set to this haunting soundtrack, from the underwater scenes to Alaric's ghost visiting Jeremy.*

Epic Storytelling

An Interview with Joshua Butler

Joshua Butler has been with *The Vampire Diaries* from the very beginning. He edited the pilot, "The Night of the Comet," "You're Undead to Me," "The Turning Point," "Miss Mystic Falls," "Founder's Day," and "Klaus," and was in the director's chair for "A Few Good Men," "Daddy Issues," "Klaus," "The Hybrid," "Homecoming," and "Do Not Go Gentle." Outside of Mystic Falls, Joshua has worked on other TV series such as *Kings*, *Warehouse 13*, *The Secret Circle*, *Ringer*, *Friday Night Lights*, and Kevin Williamson's new series *The Following*.

How did you get into television editing and directing? Were you specifically interested in genre work?

For college, I did the Production Program at the University of Southern California School of Cinema-Television, which focuses on directing but rightly insists that each student learn as much about every aspect of production as possible. While I was there, I trained on what was then a revolutionary new editing system called Avid. After I graduated — as I was promoting the student film I wrote and directed — my day job became Avid editing, and I was being hired by post-production facilities simply because I knew how to work the machine. Ultimately, I fell into an opportunity to edit a pilot for the

USA Network called *Good vs. Evil* and that led to me directing some episodes on the series. Because my break was on a science-fiction/fantasy show, I became known as a "genre" director and ended up doing a lot of fun series and movies-of-the-week for USA and their sister network, the SyFy Channel. Luckily I am a huge fan of genre film and television, so directing vampires, werewolves, witches, doppelgängers, mutants, aliens, etc. came quite naturally to me. As I always joke, someday I'll get to make a show or a movie where the cast consists of regular human beings just talking to each other, but in the meantime I'm having fun with fangs and stakes and guns.

How would you describe *The Vampire Diaries*' style?

Kevin Williamson, Julie Plec, and Marcos Siega had a very clear idea of what they wanted when they made the *TVD* pilot. Kevin and Julie were all about "epic" storytelling, and Marcos chose an appropriate shooting style — high-contrast lighting and the use of long lenses — to deliver the "epic," creating beautiful cinematic frames that allowed viewers to feel intimately connected with the characters and connect to the nuances of their emotions. In the editing room, we made sure that we "opened up" scenes, allowing for looks, gestures, "moments" that suggested the deep yearnings underneath the surface of Kevin and Julie's wonderful dialogue. We also found that by letting these unspoken moments breathe, we had the opportunity to interweave songs into the episodes that could elevate and comment on the subtext. I think there are two moments in the pilot that define what *TVD* does so well musically: Placebo's cover of "Running Up That Hill" pulsing as Stefan seeks out Katherine's photo, and The Fray's "Never Say Never" making our hearts jump when Elena lets Stefan inside her house for the first time.

You've been with the show from the beginning; would you say it has evolved stylistically since the pilot?

It's been a fascinating journey for me, from editing the pilot to directing my sixth episode, "Do Not Go Gentle." There's a wonderful moment in that show, written by Michael Narducci, where Stefan comes to Elena's door to pick her up for the Decade Dance.

It's a deliberate callback to the pilot, where Elena and Stefan are once again experiencing the wonderful awkwardness of falling in love. While I was directing this scene, I realized that after three years we were still remaining faithful to what Kevin, Julie, and Marcos established in the pilot — lingering looks, extreme closeups, "epic" silences that speak volumes. There is a continuity that has been maintained throughout the 66 episodes, and that comes down to Kevin and Julie being so passionate about retaining the show's stylistic elegance on set while continuing to elevate every emotional beat in the editing room.

At what point do you, as director, get involved in an episode? Could you provide a sense of the timing from when you'd first get your hands on a script to the episode airing?

As a director, I start prepping seven weekdays before the first day of shooting. Then there are, on average, eight days of filming. Since we get weekends off, the prepping and shooting process for each episode is about three weeks in total. Then there is about a month of editing, visual effects, sound design, scoring, mixing, coloring, etc. before an episode is finished and ready to air. Sometimes when there are "accelerated" airdates — usually for the episodes that air right before the holiday hiatus — the post-production time gets shortened to two weeks, but for the most part, it's a seven- to eight-week process from script to screen.

What's the biggest challenge of directing an episode of *TVD*?

Because the show exists mostly in closeups of these beautiful actors' faces, every flicker of emotion, every beat, every shade of their performances will be felt that much more strongly. The challenge as a *TVD* director is to make sure all the subtlety that Kevin and Julie value so highly gets captured on film. Luckily the casting on this series is impeccable, and everyone is ready and willing to give everything they have as performers and as human beings. I don't know any other show on television that plumbs the depths of an actor's soul the way *TVD* does.

Do you have a preference for studio or location filming?

Pascal Verschooris, our genius producer in Atlanta, has over the seasons secured five soundstages that contain a stunning number of sets. From the entirety of Elena's house and the Lockwood mansion and the Mystic Grill to an actual photorealistic section of forest that I used while directing "Do Not Go Gentle," studio filming on *TVD* is an absolute pleasure. [Director of photography] Dave Perkal and his team light the sets

beautifully, and the cast and crew are much happier when they're not shooting in the cold or rain or both.

Understandably, the actors, showrunners, and writers get a fair amount of attention from the fans. Is there an unsung hero on the TVD crew, someone integral to the making of show that we just don't know about?

There are so many heroes on the *TVD* crew I don't even know where to start. If I had to pick one person to single out who really is an "unsung" hero, I'd have to choose Lisina Stoneburner. She is *TVD*'s acting coach and has been since the very beginning. Not only does Lisina work with the cast and guest stars at all hours of the day and night, she makes herself available to all the directors on set. Lisina's an invaluable resource and a joy to be around.

What other shows do you watch or admire? Are there other filmmakers or TV directors that inspire you or your work on TVD?

I do love genre television and have great admiration for all the filmmakers who work in this very specific medium. The network shows I currently watch and admire (other than *TVD*) include *Once Upon a Time, Grimm, Supernatural, Nikita, Person of Interest,* and *Pretty Little Liars*.

There's a little bit of everything in an episode of *TVD* — "The Hybrid" is a great example of that. Horror, drama, comedy, romance. How do you establish that tone?

I think "The Hybrid" is a great example of how *TVD* gets away with what, on paper, shouldn't work. It doesn't seem logical that a show can go from horror to drama to comedy to romance and back again, sometimes from scene to scene. But it *does* work, and that's because the performances and the stories are always grounded in real human emotion and universally shared experience. No one is ever winking at the audience. Every actor embraces the supernatural and genre elements and treats them simply as what their characters happen to be going through in their lives. So as a director, the key is to find the humanity in each moment of fantasy and never let anything in the story become exaggerated or artificial.

Tell me about developing the "hybrid zombie mountain man" look — it was pretty gruesome! How much of the special effects work is done on the day versus in post-production?

The "hybrid zombie mountain man" look was mostly done practically with make-up designed by Essie Cha and her team. There were a few digital touch-ups, as there always are, and the computer always has to help with pulsing veins and transitions from one look to another. But for the most part, the wonderful gruesomeness was achieved on set.

Let's talk Klaus. You directed some key Klaus episodes. Is it difficult to maintain a character who is loved by fans but still a viable threat, without him losing his bite (so to speak)?

I am so lucky when it comes to Klaus. I was the first director to introduce his character on the series, and then I was able to be there on set for many of his life-changing moments: his crushing failure to produce hybrids, the realization that Stefan is his only true friend, his epic confrontation with a father who gave him a thousand years of shame and guilt, his explosion of rage at a mother who tried to destroy the "abomination" she created. I love Klaus. And I agree that it should be difficult to keep Klaus both lovable and threatening, but when you have Joseph Morgan playing the role . . . well, it's not difficult at all. Joseph nails it on every level. He gives Klaus humanity, sensitivity, vulnerability, charm . . . while still scaring the hell out of you.

Tons of extras and My Morning Jacket performing in "Homecoming." The 1920s Decade Dance in "Do Not Go Gentle." How do you manage such complex episodes?

On the back of the second-season DVD set, there's a quote: "Every episode is a big episode." That couldn't be more true. It feels like every single episode could be — on any other series — a finale. But that's the brilliance of what Kevin and Julie do. They shoot for the stars every week and in the process have raised the bar on "event television." Any director who works on *TVD* must be prepared to execute a truly epic storyline with often logistically difficult shooting circumstances. But the good news is that the assistant directors — Michael Allowitz and Rudy Persico — are the best of the best at coordinating complicated schedules and hundreds of extras and visiting rock bands, etc. Michael and Rudy are fearless, and that inspires the directors to be fearless as well.

Alaric's death was a hugely emotional moment for the audience. What was it like filming "Do Not Go Gentle"?

I was an emotional wreck — in a good way — while filming "Do Not Go Gentle." Michael Narducci, who wrote the episode, was with me on set and I was hugely grateful for his calming presence. Because I've been with the series so long, almost every scene in that episode had huge emotional resonance for me. I still tear up just thinking about Alaric telling Elena and Jeremy that taking care of them was the closest he ever came to the life he always wanted.

How much do you have the audience in mind as you're directing?

The good news is that I *am* the audience for *TVD!* When I direct, it's like being an audience member who has this incredible opportunity to interact with my favorite series.

So many commercial breaks — a helpful structuring device or the bane of your existence?

Kevin and Julie embraced the commercial breaks from the very beginning, and have subsequently challenged everyone who works on the show — writers, directors, actors, editors, etc. — to find ways to make every single break into a there's-no-way-I'm-going-to-change-this-channel moment.

TVD is known for its cliffhangers; has there been any one moment that shocked you the most?

I know this is probably everyone's #1 answer, but Katherine chopping off John's fingers at the end of season 1 is in my opinion one of the most shocking moments in TV history.

Which episode that you edited is your favorite? That you directed? What's your favorite episode that you didn't work on?

I love all the episodes I've worked on, but I have an extra special place in my heart for "Klaus" — which I both directed and edited. Kevin and Julie's incredible script, the opportunity to direct those luscious flashbacks, working so closely with Nina Dobrev and Daniel Gillies on their characters' truly special relationship, introducing the extraordinary Joseph Morgan to the *TVD* world . . . all of it added up to a truly awesome experience. As for my favorite episode that I didn't work on, I'd have to say "The Reckoning." Brilliantly directed by John Behring, brilliantly written by Michael Narducci, brilliantly shot by Dave Perkal, brilliantly edited by Lance Anderson, brilliantly acted and produced and scored and sound-designed . . . I could go on. Key word is "brilliant." That episode floored me.

Will we see your name in the credits of TVD season 4 or on other upcoming projects?

I will be back as a director on season 4 of *TVD*, and I'll also be directing *Nikita* and Kevin Williamson's new FOX show *The Following*. Plus I'm writing and directing a horror film that I'm really excited about.

Thank you, Joshua! You can find Joshua Butler on Twitter at @TheJoshuaButler.

𝓜𝓸𝓾𝓽𝓱 𝓝𝓸𝓲𝓼𝓮𝓼

An Interview with Price Peterson

Price Peterson writes for TV.com, and that's where you'll find his incredibly popular photo recaps of *The Vampire Diaries*. The mix of LOLcat format, insightful commentary, and fall-off-your-chair hilarity in Price's recaps make him a must-read.

First things first: is "Price Peterson" your real name?
Yeah, I know it sounds like I'm a character on *Dynasty* or whatever, but that's because alliteration is classy! If it makes you more comfortable (or if you work at Starbucks), you can just write "Bryce." That might as well be my name considering how often I respond to it without correcting people.

"TV.com writer, specialty: photo recaps" is a pretty specific job. How did you end up with that gig?
Being bad at writing. I am legit terrible at (a) forming critical opinions and (b) expressing them coherently. What a chore. My main problem is I like 90% of everything I watch and being forced to explain why I like (or don't like) something is a bummer. I prefer to focus on things I like and it's easier to just SHOW people why. "Look at this picture, I loved this part." Also it just makes me laugh to take a serious moment and paint it in the dumbest possible terms. That's

why all the characters in my recaps have serious expressions on their faces but seem to be speaking in some kind of slangy, LOLcat pidgin-speak. That just makes me laugh.

How do you choose which shows to recap?

It has to be something I would've watched for fun on my own, and it has to be something that's semi-serious. I don't like making fun of comedy, that just seems lame to me, but *The Vampire Diaries* is just serious enough that it's fun to tease. You won't see me commenting too much on Damon's one-liners, for example, because those were already funny as-is.

What are your three favorite things about *The Vampire Diaries*?

Its ambitious storytelling. The deep talent of its cast and guest stars. But #1 would be the fandom. That sounds like pandering but it's fact. It takes a pretty special group of people to not only embrace a geek property so passionately but also allow some dunce like me to have fun with it too.

I know it takes a heck of a long time to put together a photo recap that manages to be both hilarious and insightful. What is your process?

First I watch the show while capturing footage to my laptop. I don't take notes or live-tweet or anything because I just want to enjoy the episode and let my mind play around in that world for an hour. It's a fun world to play around in! Then I'll go re-watch the footage and grab freeze frames of important moments and conversations. Sometimes I'll have ideas for jokes already, but usually not. I'll end up with something like 300 images. Then I'll try and whittle them down to less than 100, at which point I'll color-correct, resize, and crop them all. Then I'll go through and write captions on all of them. Then I'll realize the sun is coming up and I'll start panicking that I'm already behind schedule.

After exporting and uploading all of the images, I'll start writing the recap, which often involves just filling in the story between each image. If I'm lucky, I'll get done by lunch time, at which point I'm too excited to see everyone's feedback to actually go to bed. All told it takes about 14 hours to do, but a lot of that is because of the sleep deprivation. My brain really stops working around 4 a.m. and it all turns into a slow-motion blur after that. The cool thing is, because almost all of my recaps were written in a delirium, I have no recollection of having written 98% of them. Sometimes I'll re-read something and be totally baffled about  what exactly I was thinking at the time. I'm still not sure I understand all the Snickers jokes except that I was probably really hungry that night.

The people who make the shows you recap have been enthusiastic and attentive to your recapping — particularly *The Secret Circle* (R.I.P.), but also the *TVD* cast and crew. Does that shape the way you write your posts?

Receiving that kind of acknowledgment was not something I expected to have happen. The feeling is kind of hard to describe: what is both wonderful and uncomfortable at the same time? If I'm being honest, I think it has affected the tone of my recaps, yes. Don't get me wrong, I'm still being 100% honest in what I write, it's more a matter of, in the whole spectrum of my personal opinions about something, I've made an effort to focus more on the positives. Not just with regard to *TVD* or *The Secret Circle*, but across all the TV coverage I do. It is legitimately my job to have opinions about things, but just from a mental health standpoint, I don't want to spend a lot of my waking hours bumming people out. It makes me sad to read negative reviews of the things I *like*, so I can't even imagine what it would feel like to read negative reviews of things I've WORKED on. That being said, knowing that certain crewmembers might read my recap and be happy about the work they've done is a nice thought, but I would never write something untrue just for their benefit. I have a bigger obligation to the viewers and commenters who aren't involved in the shows. They're the ones I'm writing for; they're the ones I want to invite over for a pizza party in the big virtual living room that is TV.com.

There are a lot of recurring gags in your *TVD* recaps — most famously "Is it Friday yet?" Do you have a favorite? Or a least favorite you wish you could kill but your pesky readers love so much?

One person's recurring gag is another person's lazy writing. Thinking of fresh new jokes at dawn is hard to do! So while I'm not positive that "Is it Friday yet?" or "mouth noises" are even funny anymore, it's gratifying when people remember jokes and quote them back to me. It feels good to think I've written anything memorable.

Comments! You get hundreds and hundreds on your posts. Do you have a favorite reader-reaction moment or story?

In a general sense, just getting to know the regular commenters has been a blast. Some really distinctive personalities are in the mix now and that makes me so happy. They're really funny and more importantly they have better comprehension of the *TVD* world than I do. I am constantly overlooking details or forgetting backstory, so I love how informative the commenters can be. I think my season 3 finale recap has something like 1,600+ comments, which is certainly a record for TV.com but it's also a big point of pride for me. I don't know, I realize that's bragging, but it's mostly a testament to how watercooler-worthy *TVD* is. People just want to talk about it!

Name your Season 3 favorites and why!

Character Caroline. At this point it kind of seems like I shouldn't have to explain this?

Character sub-category: Original Klaus. Because Joseph Morgan. My heart will hurt if he's not back for season 4.

"Mouth noises" moment Damon and Elena at the motel. I loved that it was this huge, epic moment and there was a vending machine in the background. This show in a nutshell.

Death scene Elena's watery demise was hypnotically beautiful.
Episode "Our Town" was equal measures poetic and horrifying.
Episode to recap Probably "The Hybrid," what with all the Tennessee werewolf stuff and Tyler coming out to his mom and Alaric's indie rock haircut. Just good TV all around.

For the heroine of the show, Elena Gilbert garners rather a wide range of audience response. What are your thoughts on the character and her undead future?

Elena has always been a frustrating character, but it's not necessarily to the show's detriment. As an audience surrogate, she has had to essentially be the straight-man to all the wild shenanigans going on around her, and that's a tough job. The problem is that too often things revolve around her when they shouldn't, or she'll behave like a tragic martyr when she should really just go home and take a nap. It'll be pretty interesting to see what Vampire Elena will be like. It's a change that will significantly alter the tone of the show, but it will hopefully also reboot things enough that the show can avoid repeating itself too much. There was only so much you can do with Human Elena, and this opens up a whole new world of foolishness on her part. Plus I'm dying to see what will happen between Elena and Katherine. Personally, I'm hoping for a bizarro element where either Elena or Katherine strikes up a romance with two human brothers.

Is there a character you think should've stuck around longer in Mystic Falls? Anyone gone too soon?

Lexi and Anna were two great characters killed off too quickly during season 1's more trigger-happy days. I'm glad they both got to return in season 3. I don't know. Pearl? Sean Faris's towel? If I'm being honest, I don't mind the deaths that much. The high death toll keeps things interesting, and now that ghosts are an integral part of the story it seems like there's always a chance we'll get to see familiar faces again. Except for Aunt Jenna getting banished to the Other Side permanently. Didn't that seem slightly vindictive on the writers' part? You're telling us she was at peace after having been brutally murdered twice in one night?

Back in 2009, when the series debuted, it was marketed as primarily a story about a love triangle and to a large extent that view persists — both within a portion of the fandom and with people who have never seen the show (the "Twilight for TV" impression). What are your thoughts on the way *The Vampire Diaries* is marketed versus the content of the show itself?

Well, personally I couldn't be more bored with the love triangle. I just think, narratively, that love triangles are not interesting. In real life, it is VERY easy to just say, "I want this one and not that one. Everybody else just move on." You know? Love triangles just seem so contrived to me. But, yeah, that puts me in the 1% of the human population. So The CW is probably correct in playing up the love triangle. That's a pretty solid point of entry for most people, but once they tune in I think it doesn't take long for people to notice how much better *every other element of the show is* besides the love triangle. So, come for the three-way, stay for the afterparty.

Three seasons into the show, there are unanswered questions galore from the major to the minor. What is the most pressing of the lingering questions for you?

Did slavery even *happen* in Mystic Falls? I'm not trying to be controversial, I'm simply baffled as to how something so overwhelmingly important to that town (and the Bennetts in particular) could be straight-up ignored like that. It's pretty troubling and maybe the #1 most legitimate criticism against this show.

Let's talk ultimate *TVD* endgame. The year is 2015. It's the series finale. Where would you like to see things end up?

Holy jeez. I mean, I'm not sure anyone wants to see a bunch of immortal vampires in sleek eveningwear sipping champagne and exchanging quips. Like *Gossip Vampire Girl* or something. I'd personally grow pretty bored of that. Here's what I'd love to see: Bonnie's last dying act can be a spell that turns every last one of the gang back into normal human beings. In the last scene, they'd all re-enroll at Mystic Falls High and actually attend class. You know, regular teens just starting over and doing it right this time.

If you had a guest role on an episode of *The Vampire Diaries*, who would you like to play?

I'd just want to be a random citizen of Mystic Falls just hanging out in the background of any scene going, "Um, what? Hold up."

You've started recapping *Teen Wolf*. Should those of us TVDers not yet watching the series tune in? What else do you get up to at TV.com that we should know about?

Yes, I love *Teen Wolf*. And just FYI, *Teen Wolf* seems to love *The Vampire Diaries* just as much as we do. There are a lot of similarities — BOTH of Tyler's parents also play parents on *Teen Wolf*. But the biggest *TVD* influence on *Teen Wolf* is just how go-for-broke crazy *Teen Wolf*'s storytelling has become. If all shows could learn a lesson from *The Vampire Diaries*, I hope it's that one.

Other than that, I like to photorecap cheesy TV movies under the banner of "We'll Watch It For You." I'm hoping to do more of those this year. (I cannot believe my job sometimes.)

Any other series/books/movies you'd recommend?

I love *Girls* and *Homeland* and *Childrens Hospital* and anything by Tim and Eric. As for books, I'm still learning how to read. [I answered these questions and write all my recaps via dictation software.]

When you are not tirelessly working at being the funniest person on the internet, what do you, Price Peterson, like to do?

I like to eat candy and sleep, mostly. Someday I hope to learn how to write gooder.

Thank you kindly! You can find an archive of all of Price Peterson's photo recaps at tv.com/news/the-tv-com-photo-recap-treasury-26826/ and he tweets at @PricePeterson.

Director's Take

An Interview with J. Miller Tobin

Director J. Miller Tobin has been at the helm in Mystic Falls for seven episodes: season 1's "The Turning Point" and "Isobel"; season 2's "The Return," "Katerina," and "The Last Day"; and season 3's "Ordinary People" and "The Murder of One."

How did you get into directing for television, and specifically for _The Vampire Diaries_?

Well, that's sort of two stories. Initially, I was an assistant director for many years in New York and started working with Tom Fontana, who's the executive producer and writer/creator of _Homicide: Life on the Street_ and _Oz_. I did a couple of pilots for him and then I AD'd _Oz_ for four seasons. I started directing on season 3; I did one show in season 3, two shows in season 4, and he brought me back to do one show in season 5. So that's sort of where I got started, where I bumped up from assistant directing to directing. I got signed by an agent, and ultimately ended up moving to L.A. and started working pretty much right out of the gate after I moved to Los Angeles. That was 10 years ago now, so I've been working full-time as a director for almost 10 years.

Episodic television directors are all freelance, so we jump from show to show every year. And as I say the good news is every year's different and the bad news is every year's different. You never quite know what your season's going to bring. I'd been working for The CW a fair bit at that point, doing *Gossip Girl* and *Supernatural* and a bunch of their other shows, so when *Vampire Diaries* popped up, Warner Brothers recommended me to Marcos Siega, who was the producer/director on the job, and he hired me to do show 9 of the first season. That was "The Turning Point," that was the first episode I did for them, and subsequently they hired me to do a second one that season in the spring ["Isobel"].

And at that point, conversation started about my coming in as producer/director for the second season, which I did for half of the second season. I ended up leaving the show, but I still direct the show on a regular basis. I did two last year, and I think I'm going to do one or two next year.

From a viewer's perspective, the shows you work on seem very different — like *Gossip Girl* versus *The Vampire Diaries*. How do you adapt from one series to the next?

When I start a new show, especially one I haven't done before, I just sit down and watch as many episodes as I can stand and read all the scripts. I definitely get caught up on story, especially the shows leading up to what I'm trying to shoot. So I'll watch previous shows, I'll watch cuts of recent shows, I'll read all the scripts, so I know where I am in the arc of the season in terms of telling that particular piece of the story. It's about completely immersing yourself in the show: in the culture of the show, who the characters are, what their backstory is, what their history is, watching how the show is shot from previous episodes. Meeting the crew, talking to the crew, trying to figure out what the look of the show is. Every show's got its own thing going; it's got its own look or its own style. Some are more forgiving than others, some have very specific styles — "We shoot the show hand-held," or "We shoot the show long-lens," "We shoot the show this way or that way." Most shows are not that specific, but more often there will be a "visual style" for the show, and I adopt that.

Vampire Diaries is a long-lens show; it's a gothic, horror show, so there are camera moves and lots of long flowing camera angles and long lenses. It's part of why it looks so cinematic and beautiful.

You've directed some key *Vampire Diaries* flashback episodes: "Katerina" and "Ordinary People." "Katerina" gave us a wealth of backstory on Katherine, while "Ordinary People" was the episode fans were waiting for in this "Season of the Originals." What's it like working on these episodes?

The challenge on those is always creating the world of the flashbacks. One of the most challenging was probably the Originals in what we were calling "Viking times"; you know it was 1000 or 1200 AD when they were in the New World living in the village. That's a tremendous amount of art direction, production design, construction, costumes, accents — how do they speak, how do they hold themselves, how do they move? There's a lot of time and energy that goes into creating that world and making it plausible and real and believable for that time period.

And then you have to figure out the story that's being told in present day, which always references that. So you're talking about the transitions in and out of the flashbacks and what those connective tissues are, and what those pieces are that take you. In the case of Claire Holt as she narrates the story of her family, how do you go from her to the scene that she's describing? How do you transition? Most of that is on the page, in the script, but it's my job to figure out how to tell those pieces of the story visually. Some of it's scripted, some of it's not — you're just creating transitions in camera, but that's the fun part. That's what we get to do, we get to make all that up and figure it out.

Though "Ordinary People" was not the audience's introduction to Rebekah, it was a big episode for Claire Holt. What are your thoughts on her work?

Claire's fantastic. I had actually met her on *Pretty Little Liars*, so I knew her going into *Vampire*. She's an enormously talented actor — a very bright, very smart, very talented woman — and it's always just a pleasure to work with people like that. And she works really hard. She's got an incredibly strong sense of work ethic, which is fantastic, because again, especially in the Viking episode, she had a tremendous amount of work to do both in present day and flashback and she just was absolutely terrific. She came to work every day

J. Miller Tobin on set with the two sides of Nina Dobrev
(photos courtesy J. Miller Tobin)

gung-ho and willing, anxious to be there and happy to be there. And that makes a huge difference when you have that much work to do. Claire's kind of amazing in that she brings such charisma to the part, and I just have a tremendous amount of respect for her.

When we did the "Katerina" episode, Nina came in and she had to play both parts twice for almost 10 pages over the course of two days. The way we broke it down, the way we decided to do it, is she played Elena for all of those 10 pages of scenes on one day and then she played Katherine on the second day. And she had a very specific idea; she had done a lot of thinking and homework. She came in very prepared and very ready to go, and that just makes my life easy when you're working with talented, invested actors like that, like Claire and Nina.

The Vampire Diaries can be rather a violent show; is there a limit to what you can show or guidelines from the powers-that-be? The tearing of Damon's wrists in "The Murder of One" comes to mind as a particularly gruesome moment . . .

It was! It's interesting; my premise is you probably shoot more than they're going to want to see. You find that line, and you push it right to the edge. You always try to find how much they're actually going to let you put on air.

In that case, we shot it a couple of different ways, and I tried to protect them so that if it was too much, they could cut it out. Ultimately they left it in, and it worked. What we try to do is make it a fleeting thing — we panned up and then we panned off. We cut to the hand, you see the violence of what's happening to his arm and then we pan off it, so you get a little whisper of what's going on. That's actually, I think, ultimately more effective than really seeing something closeup and graphic and intense. You really want to feel what the character is feeling as much as anything else. There's a tremendous amount of blood on *Vampire Diaries* — we go through it by the bucket — but a lot of [the violence] is implied, a lot of it is about what's happening to the people.

It's not a slasher show; it's not about the violence, it's about the violence that's happening to our beloved characters and how they respond to that. To me, that's always the premise: how do we make this horrific for the audience on behalf of these characters? So in Damon's case, you want to feel the excruciating pain that he's going through. So it's just as important to see what's happening on his face as it is to see what's happening on his body. That being said, we shot it as graphically and bloodily as we possibly could.

Tell me a little bit about visual effects and stunts: would you rather be creating those scenes during filming or in post-production?

We do as much as we possibly can practically. Visual effects have become the norm in a lot of shows; the more you do practically, the more you do on set, the more it lends to the credibility and the reality of the scene. The blood looks better, the blood always looks real. I'm a big proponent of doing as much practically as possible, and then fixing whatever you can't do on the day later — and they can certainly do a lot, a tremendous amount. But again, try to get it on set, try to make it work the first time out, try to make it work for the director, try to make it work for the camera. I think there's a visceral quality to the stuff that you do practically that translates through the screen; its part of that visual storytelling and I think the audience responds better to it. The actors react more instinctively, more naturally, when it's actually happening to them on the day as opposed to "Imagine that you're covered in blood."

Is there a particular effect or stunt that stands out for you from one of your episodes?

Flipping the car in "The Turning Point" was a big one, and then the aftermath — of Nina hanging upside down, the guy that she hits who gets up and sort of breaks himself back into shape, and looks like a spider. I was just so happy with the way that turned out. It was so violent and so upsetting, and you were so scared for Elena and then this guy gets up and he's silhouetted and terrifying and he starts walking towards her. I just think that turned out really, really well.

We do a lot of fight sequences on the show; I've done a couple of Damon-Stefan fights. In "The Murder of One," we did the killing of the vampires with the sort of "plague"; we did the killing of the Original in the stairwell in the alley. You know, every episode of *The Vampire Diaries* has *some* of that. You end up doing a couple of sequences. I didn't do the underwater stuff at the end of the season ["The Departed"], but it was clearly a huge amount of work. A very risky and interesting way to go out on the end of the season. That's what the writers are great at; they come up with stuff, and you do as much of it as you possibly can. Sometimes it's too big and you have to pare it back, but everybody on the show works very hard to make it happen. That's the fun part to figure all that stuff out.

Like the fun of killing Originals in the town square . . .

That Covington town square plays for Mystic Falls; that corner building plays for the exterior of the Grill, and that stairwell's practical. That's all practical street. The people on the show have nicknamed it "Stab Alley" because so many people have been killed down there. It's a great location, it really shoots well, it really feels creepy. And to be down in that hole, you can really take advantage of the stairs.

In this particular case, they really wanted it to feel kind of operatic and grand when Finn gets killed — him lying back on the stairs and Sage comes down to him and being forced back when he bursts into flames. It was intentionally designed to be somewhat grand and a little bit operatic. That's not necessarily the norm for the show, but they felt like with that death, you could take advantage of that and play it a little bit more dramatic than you might otherwise.

Product placement seems to be here to stay, particularly for series on The CW. Do you have any thoughts on incorporating those moments? Does everyone groan on set, or just get on with it?

It's become so much the norm on pretty much every show. It doesn't happen in every episode, but on every show you end up doing the stuff. On *Gossip Girl*, it's cell phones; on *Vampire Diaries*, it was Ford and I don't remember what else they placed, but Ford was a big one.

Cars are a little bit trickier because you have to integrate that into a scene. Whenever you see someone pushing a button and saying something to the car and the car answering back, you know it's product placement. Sometimes it's very simple: Caroline drives a Ford Fiesta and she gets in and you sort of find a nice way to feature the Ford logo. That's easy. When she has to use the in-sync system and touch the buttons and say "give me directions to . . ." or "call" or "play this song," then it becomes less about storytelling and more about product placement. But it's a benefit to the show: the studio gets money and the show gets money, and it helps pay for all of those big stunts and effects and things that we get to do. And it really does help to defray the costs in a beneficial way for the show.

I think everybody sort of bites their tongue and puts up with it. No director wants to be shooting a commercial inside of an episode and no actor wants to be doing a commercial inside of an episode. That being said, it's become the norm; there's a lot of benefit to the show, and I think everybody decides it's worth the extra effort to get the financial benefit and have the capacity to do these other things.

In season 2, you not only directed three episodes but produced. Describe what that role was like.

Basically the producer/director — especially when the writers and post-production are all in Los Angeles — is the creative liaison between the writers and the editors in Los Angeles and then the production team on the ground in Atlanta. So there's a lot of back and forth. The way I approached the show was to prep. You hire the best directors you can find, you get them in — some of them know the show, some of them don't. You make sure that they are familiar with the show, that they know the mythology, that they understand who the characters are and how the show is shot and all of that. You give them whatever tools you can in terms of equipment or art direction or logistical support. You try to help them find the best locations. You oversee casting and location scouting and all that. And then you let them go and shoot their show.

You do spend a certain amount of time on set just making sure things are running smoothly. You spend a lot of time dealing with the actors and dealing with their personal and professional concerns — it could be the script or the story or their call time — they don't want to come in that early or they don't want to stay that late. There's a lot of problem solving; there's a lot of management in the job dealing with the cast and the crew and dealing with things that aren't going well. Obviously, your job is to make things go well, so very often the problems end up in your lap and you're expected to negotiate or deal with things.

My biggest complaint about doing the job was that I wasn't directing as much as I wanted to. I directed two episodes out of the first half of the season ["The Return" and "Katerina"], two out of 13 as opposed to when I'm working full-time as a director, I would have probably directed six episodes [on various series] over the course of that six months. I really missed directing. As opposed to directing, I was being a manager and I really found that a difficult transition. One of the reasons I decided to leave the job was I directed episode 9, "Katerina," and I realized this was the fun part, the part that I really enjoy doing. So I decided to segue out of the job, and luckily Julie and Kevin decided to keep me on as a director, so I came back and directed shortly after that at the end of that season ["The Last Day"]. And I did two episodes of season 3, and I think I'm back next year.

How would you say the series has evolved since season 1?

Well, it's very much less about the teen drama of our characters; they've all grown up a tremendous amount. Obviously, the first two seasons were very much hinged in and around high school. And I guess ostensibly they're all still in high school, but we don't really shoot at the school very much anymore. Once they really started introducing the idea of the Originals, there became a greater mythology to the show. The original mythology between Elena and Katherine and who the doppelgänger was and why she was important and what all that meant, and we started to develop that, and then the revelation of the Originals — Daniel Gillies and Claire and Joseph — when you start meeting all those people, that became the overriding sort of battle on the show.

In the third season, it became less about the love triangle, and it became much more about the global sort of mythological elements of why Elena was so important and what it meant to the Originals. And that's when you started getting much more of the bigger-episode flashbacks. The first few were all about the brothers and their creation as vampires, who they were, where they came from. Once all of that was established, I think the writers felt the need to open up the show into a bigger, global perspective.

I think that's a natural progression on most shows. *Supernatural* went through that. They evolved from two guys on the road, sort of bounty hunters, to the battle with angels and demons. For shows like this, you have to keep upping the ante and growing the world and raising the stakes in terms of their battles and their fights. They tend to start fairly local as they did with *Vampire Diaries*, in terms of boys showing up at the high school — who these guys are, what they mean, are they dangerous or are they safe, who's in love with who and what's going on and how unpredictable are they? And then it starts to spread out and you introduce new people from outside the world. That, and everybody ends up with some sort of supernatural powers, so you need to introduce extra people. Poor Matt is the only one who doesn't have any power at this point.

Do you have a particular favorite of the episodes you directed?

I was really happy with the "Katerina" episode; I was really happy with "The Turning Point" — though it feels like that was a really long time ago now. And I was very happy with the Viking vampire episode; again, I thought Claire did such a tremendous job with that. Each episode has a lot going for it; you invest yourself pretty deep, so it's a little hard to pick one over the other. You put a lot of energy into making the best show you possibly can.

What about an episode that you didn't work on? Any standouts?

The well episode ["Plan B"] was a really interesting episode. John Behring did a really good job with that. John's episode, the finale of this season was a really great episode; really huge in terms of the mythology of the show and in terms of the production, obviously with the fate of Elena being held in the balance. There are wonderful shows in every season; the premieres and the finales tend to be big shows and they're always fun ones to watch. There's always big splashy stuff inevitably in the beginning and the end of the season.

Besides *TVD*, what's coming up for you in the 2012–2013 TV season?

Actually, I have a pretty interesting season: I'm doing *Alphas* right now, I just finished *Covert Affairs*, I'm going to do a couple of *Revenge*s this year, which I like; I did one last year. I'm doing two new shows that I'm excited about: the first one is *666 Park Avenue*, which is a new ABC show. The devil has a building in Manhattan; it's sort of *Rosemary's Baby* with Terry O'Quinn and Vanessa Williams and Rachael Taylor. I think it's going to be really fun. It's another sort of supernatural show, which is my favorite genre. And then I'm doing another new ABC show called *Red Widow* with Radha Mitchell and Lee Tergesen, which I'm excited to work on as well. It's going to be an interesting season; I'm breaking away slightly from The CW world, but I'm still trying to keep my foot squarely in the supernatural camp. It's the stuff I watch, and the stuff I enjoy shooting the most. I'm happy to do those shows.

Thank you, Miller!

Ms. Mystic Falls

An Interview with Julie Plec

Julie Plec is executive producer, writer, and co-creator of *The Vampire Diaries*. (When you feel *all the feelings* while watching *TVD*, you have Julie to thank.)

"Showrunner" wasn't a career choice people could aspire to until very recently. What did you set out to be when you were starting your career, and how did you get to where you are now?

I moved to L.A. without a clue of what exactly it was I wanted to do, just knowing that I wanted to be a part of the entertainment business. After playing a lot of different roles in the film/TV world (assistant, development executive, producer, etc.), I got an opportunity to write a script on a television show I was producing called *Kyle XY*. People liked it, asked me to write another one, and then another. Because I was already a producer, the leap to showrunner wasn't too big to take. Showrunning lets me combine all the skillsets I've built over 18 years working in Hollywood into one crazy/difficult/harrowing and yet completely exciting job.

The thing that fascinates me most about writing for television is its collaborative nature. Could you describe the process and give us a peek inside the writers room?

The most fun you'll ever have (or maybe I should say the least stress) as a writer on a TV show is that glorious time "in the room" before any scripts are due, before anything is filming. That's when a group of creative people sit around a table and just, basically, shoot the shit. We talk character, mythology, story. We pitch bad town events and "season 10" episodes (code for: this is a really bad idea, but . . .).

The basic process for each episode is we start with a blank whiteboard (very daunting). We say, "Where did we leave off with all our characters? Where do we want them to go by the end of the episode? What's the big, emotional WOW?" Then we start talking mythology, plot, moments, etc. Slowly but surely, we are able to take our broad-stroke ideas and turn them into "beats on the board," and then ultimately a story structure that's written up on the board — six acts plus a teaser. Inevitably, our first run at the script is a total disaster. Sometimes we can't see the problems until we've written a draft of the script and we have to do what's called a "re-break" of the story (erase the board and start over) and then a rewrite of the script. We sweat, suffer, hate ourselves, pray for a breakthrough, think outside the box, rein ourselves back in, dig back into character, remind ourselves why we're telling this story and what its emotional worth is, and somewhere at the end of that pretty freakin' painful process is a shooting script. Then we dust ourselves off and start it all over again for the next episode.

Are there particular *TVD* writers with an aptitude for writing a specific character or type of scene?

Caroline Dries has the voice of the show better than anyone I've seen — sometimes better than Kev and me. Mike Narducci is the king of the epic Originals moments. If Klaus is being Shakespearean and epic, odds are good Nardooch wrote it. No one has ever been able to top Kevin for Damon one-liners, but Elisabeth Finch, who is new to the team, has dropped in a few stealth bombs that have been wickedly funny. Rebecca Sonnenshine is responsible for the "give birth to a ship in two minutes flat" monologue Klaus tells Caroline before he heals her from the werewolf bite.

The pace of production on the series is unbelievably quick, and yet you guys pull off incredible flashback sequences. Could you describe how those episodes come together?

We consider the flashback episodes to be our production triumphs. We usually give the department heads an advance warning, so they can start checking rental houses, building costumes, designing sets, etc. Jennifer Bryan in season 1 had enough of a heads-up for "Lost Girls" that she was able to design and build Katherine's "travel gown," for our first look at Katherine when she gets out of the carriage. Leigh Leverett in season 3 almost lost her mind trying to dress everyone for "The End of the Affair" because between *Boardwalk Empire* and another '20s-themed movie shooting at that time, all the rental houses were slim-pickin's. Garreth Stover, our production designer, designed and built the entire Viking village in "Ordinary People" in the backyard woods of our production office (where he has also built the old cemetery, the church ruins, the Lockwood cellar, etc.). Even though it's exhausting and stressful for our production team, they all can take away an enormous amount of pride from their work on these episodes. Our producer Pascal Verschooris is the hero and the champion of all of it.

With three seasons under your belt, is it challenging to maintain the balance between evolving the series and keeping true to its origins?

The challenge always has been and always will be tone. How to keep it honest, grounded, and real in the midst of some pretty extraordinary circumstances. Sometimes it gets away from us, especially with the magic stuff. But when we find ourselves getting out of control, we try to bring it back to the most human, relatable moment we can think of. So even in an episode like "Do Not Go Gentle" where the layers of witch science and mythology almost collapsed on top of us, we were able to say goodbye to one of our favorite characters, Alaric, in a simple, beautiful, and poetic moment.

You are wonderfully involved in the fandom, watching fan videos, tweeting, and reading reaction posts. I imagine it's difficult not to

anticipate fan reaction while writing. How much is the audience in your head?

The audience is always in our minds and as a result we often have to be careful of letting the "loudest" voices drive our choices. The kind of effusive praise and, equally, harsh criticism we get from some of those voices can embed itself deeply in our minds and can impact the way we look at certain relationships, characters, etc. So our job is to hear it and then fight against it — try to clear our minds of it so we can make the right creative choices for the story we're telling and for the characters that we control. No one likes to work in a bubble, but sometimes you have to shut everything else out so you can look back inside yourself and say, "What do I think is the right way to go here?"

Season 3 was hailed as the season of the Original family. Tell me about putting that group of actors together, and building their story from what was established in season 2.

Ahhh, the Originals. So much kismet, serendipity, and blind luck. First of all, the idea of the Original family didn't even exist until Daniel Gillies was so magnificent in his portrayal of Elijah that we decided we needed to find a way to keep him around. For Klaus, we auditioned locally and internationally, and Joseph Morgan was the obvious choice. No one else even came close. Funnily enough, Paul Wesley had pitched me Joseph months before and I had completely forgotten.

Claire was a gift from *Secret Circle* heaven. She had auditioned for the role of Diana, and Kevin had fallen in love with her as an actress. So when it came time to cast Rebekah, her audition flew to the top of the pile, because everyone was already such big fans.

Nathaniel tested for the role of Stefan when we did the pilot. Tony Birkley, the casting director at WBTV, called me when we were looking to flesh out the Original family and said, "Remember Nathaniel? Take another look at him. His facial structure is uncannily similar to Daniel Gillies'."

Let's talk season 3 highlights. What was your favorite moment for each of the characters?

Damon Giving Elena her necklace back for her birthday. Watching

Elena fall asleep while he lies in her bed. Playing moderation coun-
selor to Stefan, telling him, "I want to help you." Sitting (shirtless!)
by the window in the motel room, completely still and unaware that
Elena is watching him. Cradling Alaric in his arms when he dies.

Caroline "Daddy, please stop hurting me." Cheerleader versus
cheerleader on the football field with Rebekah. The entirety of episode 3.13 when her dad dies. And, of course, the "Happy Birthday,
Caroline" scene with Klaus.

Bonnie "Ghost World," "Ghost World," "Ghost World." Watching
her realize her boyfriend is "cheating" on her, save the town from
tomb vampires with a little ghostly help from her Grams, and telling
Jeremy she deserves better than him.

Jeremy Saying goodbye to Anna. Chopping off the hybrid's head.
Realizing if Alaric is a ghost then that means his sister is dead.

Tyler Season premiere hot sex with Caroline. "Coming out" to his
mom. Telling Klaus, "I'm not your little bitch anymore."

Klaus The entirety of "The Reckoning." His smirks and arrogance
at the dinner party with Stefan and Damon and Elijah; "You've
missed so much." Healing Caroline. Telling his mom, "You will
never destroy me."

Stefan The phone call to Elena. Trying to fight Klaus's compulsion
so he wouldn't hurt Elena. Stefan the asshole on the track field. The
look in his eyes when Elena says, "I kissed Damon." The closet face-
to-face in Chicago with Elena.

Alaric "You're not a lost cause, Ric. You're just . . . lost." "You're
going to recycle the same crap-ass apology you gave Mason
Lockwood?" The shift from Alaric to Alaric-Hyde when Meredith
is in the kitchen making a sandwich. The final Damon-Alaric-
Bourbon ship moment in the crypt before he dies. Him dragging
Caroline through the sunny parking lot.

Elena Seeing Stefan for the first time in the closet in Chicago.
"Training" with Alaric in the woods as she puts on her wolverine
spike-glove. "Training" with Damon as he teaches her how to find
a vampire's heart. Telling Stefan, "I won't be in love with a ghost for
the rest of my life." Telling Stefan how devastated she is that he tried
to drive her off Wickery Bridge. Her underwater death scene.

Is there a particular episode of *TVD* that you're most proud of?
Season 1 — "Lost Girls" and "Founder's Day."
Season 2 — "Plan B" and "Masquerade."
Season 3 — "The End of the Affair" and "The Reckoning."

Lightning round questions about what the future of the series may hold! Answers will be considered as "not for always but for right now." Will we ever . . .

- **meet Bonnie's dad?** Yes.
- **see Elijah's vamp face?** Maybe.
- **meet Tatia?** Doubtful.
- **learn about the Salvatores' mother?** Yes, probably.
- **have a mayoral election in Mystic Falls?** This season! (Maybe.)
- **see Kelly Donovan again?** I hope so.
- **see Mikael again?** I hope so, in flashback.
- **meet the Mystic Falls High principal?** Hmmm, good question.
- **see Elena take romantic interest in a non-Salvatore?** Doubtful any time soon.
- **find out what happened to Jeremy's Denver dog?** Adopted, living with a nice family in Colorado Springs.
- **learn the name of Elena's teddybear?** Maybe we should take requests via Twitter.
- **find out which "one Miley song" Stefan likes?** Hah! It's "The Climb."

If Mystic Falls High School presented a musical, what would it be?
Les Misérables.

Taking the whole Klaus-Tyler possession thing a little further: let's say a wacky possession spell takes hold in Mystic Falls; it's Freaky Friday with body swapping galore. Which cast members would you like to see possessed by a different character?
Don't laugh, I wrote a *Buffy* body-swapping episode as a writing sample years ago (Spike with Xander, Dawn with Anya, Buffy with Willow). I love stuff like that. The only one I can think of off the top of my head would be Matt Donovan with anyone supernatural.

What was the last great book you read?

The Leftovers by Tom Perrotta. Great book about loss, grief, and spirituality — yet somehow funny.

What other shows do you watch or admire? Are there other screenwriters or TV writers that inspire you, or your work on *TVD*?

I love *Homeland, Scandal, Game of Thrones*. I'm a huge fan of Shonda Rhimes, Joss Whedon, Aaron Sorkin, not to mention the brilliant Kevin, and friends from my past who have done so well for themselves — including Greg Berlanti, Damon Lindelof, and Ryan Murphy.

Thank you, Julie! You can find Julie Plec on Twitter at @JuliePlec.

The Vampire Diaries Timeline

Despite the fact that *The Vampire Diaries* makes no pretense of establishing a timeline, here is an attempt to organize the information provided in the first three seasons into a history of the last thousand years in the *TVD* universe. A question mark indicates that a date is only an estimate; a ● marks a full moon.

In the beginning . . .

c. 975?–1000 — Esther and Mikael lose their first child to a plague, travel to the New World, and live in peace as they raise their six children ("Ordinary People").

c. 1000 ● — Henrik is killed by a werewolf ("Ordinary People").

c. 1000 — Esther turns her remaining children and Mikael into vampires and places the hybrid-binding curse on Klaus ("Klaus," "Ordinary People"). The white oak tree is burned. Klaus kills Esther; Ayana preserves Esther's body with magic. Klaus and Elijah begin faking documents about the curse of the Sun and Moon ("Klaus"). At some point in this era, the "witches," perhaps Ayana, forge the daggers that can put an Original into a death-like state when coated in the oak's ash ("Klaus").

c. 1100 — Still in what would become Mystic Falls, Finn and Sage fall in love; he turns her ("The Murder of One"). Klaus daggers Finn ("Bringing Out the Dead"). At some point, the remaining children return to the Old World ("Ordinary People," "All My Children").

Dark Ages — Vampires punished those who threatened to expose their kind with 50 years in solitary confinement, according to Stefan ("You're Undead to Me").

The 1400s–1700s

c. 1400 — The calendar markings on the cave wall indicate a white oak tree grew in Mystic Falls and was a spot for worship for the native people ("All My Children").

1400s — According to Vanessa, the Sun and Moon Curse dates back 600 years to when the Aztecs were being plagued by vampires and werewolves ("Bad Moon Rising"); later Elijah reveals to Elena that the historical documents were fakes ("Klaus").

1450 — Rose is born ("The Descent").

1464? — Pearl becomes a vampire; she has "400 years on" Damon who is turned in 1864 ("There Goes the Neighborhood"). Presumably, Anna also became a vampire around this time.

1490 — Katerina Petrova gives birth to a baby girl who is taken from her ("Katerina").

1492 — Katerina meets Klaus at his birthday celebration; she and Elijah spend time together ("Klaus").

Night before the sacrifice, 1492 — Katerina escapes and becomes a vampire; Trevor and Rose begin running from Originals ("Katerina," "Rose").

Shortly thereafter, 1492 — Katerina discovers that her entire family has been killed by Klaus.

1659? — Lexi is born; she lives to be 350 years old ("162 Candles").

1692 — The Bennett family moves from Salem to Mystic Falls ("Haunted"). They are among a larger group of settlers who moved to the area to flee persecution ("The Dinner Party").

1755 — The Saltzman family comes to America from Germany ("History Repeating").

1790? — A hundred witches are rounded up and burned at the stake in Mystic Falls ("The Dinner Party").

1792 — Mystic Falls cemetery is established ("Pilot").

The Rise of the Salvatores: The 1800s

October 9, 1810 — Giuseppe Salvatore is born ("Children of the Damned").

Early November 1847 — Stefan Salvatore is born ("Lost Girls," "162 Candles").

1860 — The town of Mystic Falls is founded ("Under Control"); the town jail is built, with a special cell for vampires ("Disturbing Behavior").

1861–1865 — The American Civil War. At some point in this era, Giuseppe Salvatore impregnates a maid, who bears him a child; the child carries on the Salvatore name after Stefan and Damon's deaths, despite being illegitimate ("1912").

January 23, 1864 — According to his tombstone, Giuseppe Salvatore dies ("Children of the Damned"). This date conflicts with many other details in the timeline and is likely a production error.

April 1864 — According to Vanessa (and to Isobel's research), Katherine arrives in Mystic Falls ("Bad Moon Rising").

June 1864 — Johnathan Gilbert begins writing the journal that Jeremy finds ("History Repeating").

September 1, 1864 — The beginning of the Atlanta Campaign fires, which Katherine uses as a cover story ("Children of the Damned"). Presumably, Katherine arrives at the Salvatore estate shortly thereafter. This date conflicts with Isobel's research ("Bad Moon Rising").

September 24, 1864 — The first Founder's Ball is held ("Family Ties"). Katherine confronts George Lockwood at the ball ("Memory Lane"). Damon is rebuffed when he visits Katherine in her bedroom after the ball; Stefan has just professed his love for Katherine ("Memory Lane"). Some time soon after the ball, Katherine reveals to Stefan that she is a vampire ("Lost Girls").

1864 — A comet passes over Mystic Falls ("The Night of the Comet").

The Battle of Willow Creek / The Vampire Purge — Mr. Tanner says that the Battle of Willow Creek took place in 1865 ("Pilot"), but the flashbacks suggest it was actually in late 1864. On the day of the battle, Katherine meets with George Lockwood to go over their plan to fake her death ("Memory Lane"). Damon is also with Katherine at some point on that day and sees her in possession of Emily's crystal ("History Repeating"). Stefan speaks to his father about the vampire situation and unwittingly drinks vervain, which leads to Katherine's capture ("Children of the Damned"). Damon makes a bargain with Emily for Katherine's safety ("History Repeating"). Stefan and Damon are shot trying to rescue Katherine ("Family Ties," "Blood Brothers"). Either one or both of the brothers watch the church burn ("History Repeating" conflicts with "Blood Brothers" on this detail). Before Katherine leaves Mystic Falls, having been released from the church before it was set afire, she gives George Lockwood the moonstone and she sweetly promises (the then-dead) Stefan that they'll be together again ("Memory Lane").

The day after the Battle of Willow Creek — Emily gives the Salvatore brothers their rings; Stefan confronts his father and inadvertently kills him; Damon promises Stefan an eternity of misery ("Blood Brothers").

Shortly thereafter, 1864 — Stefan kills Thomas and Honoria Fell and Johnathan Gilbert (temporarily); Stefan meets Alexia Branson; Damon leaves Stefan in Lexi's care ("The Dinner Party").

1865 — Damon "made sure" vervain won't grow in Mystic Falls ("Family Ties").

? — Katherine surreptitiously lets the founders know that Emily Bennett is a witch, and she is killed ("The House Guest"). Somehow, Emily's grimoire ends up buried with Giuseppe Salvatore despite the timeline problem . . . ("Children of the Damned").

? — The Salvatore crypt is built sometime after Giuseppe's burial, but before Zachariah Salvatore's murder ("Children of the Damned," "1912").

The 1900s

1900? — The Salvatore boarding house is built ("Lost Girls").

July 2, 1910 — Construction begins on Wickery Bridge ("Break on Through").

c. 1910 — Klaus daggers Kol ("Bringing Out the Dead").

1911? — Lexi tries to set up Rose on a date with Stefan ("Rose").

February 11, 1912 — Construction of Wickery Bridge is completed ("Break on Through").

1912 — The brothers see each other for the first time since the events of "The Dinner Party" for their nephew Zachariah Salvatore's funeral. Samantha Gilbert murdered him as well as another councilman. Sage teaches Damon to seek pleasure in killing. Stefan lets the Ripper out ("1912"). The white oak tree is used to build the Wickery Bridge ("Break on Through").

1917 — Stefan slaughters a migrant village in Monterey ("As I Lay Dying").

1922 — Samantha Gilbert confesses to the murders and is put in an asylum, where she kills a nurse, a guard, and eventually herself ("1912," "Break on Through").

March 12, 1922 — Stefan is in Chicago and writes in his diary about meeting a woman, presumably Rebekah ("The End of the Affair").

April 1922 — Stefan records in his diary that Lexi found him and is trying to help him again ("The End of the Affair").

June 1924 — According to his diary, Stefan is back feeding on animal blood after his ripper stint ("The End of the Affair").

1935 — Stefan is managing his cravings, and Lexi's project is to get him to laugh ("The End of the Affair").

1942 — The start date for Anna's research into vampire attacks in the Mystic Falls area ("Bloodlines").

1952 — After 30 years of Lexi's help, Stefan finally begins to feel like himself ("The End of the Affair").

June 12, 1953 — "Uncle" Joseph Salvatore is killed at the Salvatore boarding house, presumably by Damon ("Family Ties," "You're Undead to Me").

1953 — Four people are killed by "animal attacks" in Mystic Falls ("Bloodlines"); that number likely includes Joseph Salvatore.

April 2, 1954 — The first restoration of Wickery Bridge begins, according to the preservation society's sign ("Break on Through").

1962 — Five people are killed by "animal attacks" in Mystic Falls ("Bloodlines").

October 1969 — Stefan meets Sheila at an antiwar demonstration ("Bloodlines").

August 16, 1972 — Abby Bennett is born, according to the document from the DMV ("The Ties That Bind").

1974 — Three people are killed by "animal attacks" in Mystic Falls ("Bloodlines"). Slater is made a vampire and begins accumulating college degrees ("Katerina").

October 17, 1975 / January 18, 1978 — Isobel Flemming is born: the earlier date is on her driver's license ("A Few Good Men"), the later one on her tombstone ("Know Thy Enemy").

February 4, 1976 — Alaric Saltzman is born ("Break on Through").

1980s — Elizabeth Forbes and Kelly Donovan go to high school together ("Lost Girls"); Kelly Donovan and Miranda Sommers are best friends

("There Goes the Neighborhood"). Miranda is also best friends with Abby Bennett ("The Ties that Bind").

1983 — Anna sees Katherine in Chicago ("Fool Me Once").

Late 1980s? — Elizabeth Forbes and Logan Fell have known each other since he was six ("The Turning Point"). Kelly Donovan babysits Jenna Sommers ("There Goes the Neighborhood").

Spring 1987 — Lexi and Stefan attend a Bon Jovi concert; Katherine stalks Stefan ("Masquerade").

1989? — Damon meets Bree and asks for her help getting into the tomb ("Bloodlines").

August 20, 1991? — Vicki Donovan is born ("Lost Girls").

Early to mid 1990s — Jenna Sommers and Mason Lockwood attend high school together, along with Logan Fell ("Memory Lane").

1993? — Isobel leaves her hometown of Grove Hill; Elena is born in late August/early September ("A Few Good Men").

1994 — Jeremy Gilbert is born ("The Night of the Comet"). Stefan and Damon see each other for the last time before fall 2009 ("Pilot").

March 14, 1994 — Aimee Bradley is born ("Rose").

1996 — Abby lures Mikael away from Mystic Falls, entombs him in Charlotte cemetery, and stays in North Carolina ("The Reckoning," "The Ties That Bind").

Late 1990s — Logan babysits Caroline ("The Turning Point").

The 2000s

2001/2? — Ten-year-old Tyler sees his uncle Mason; he doesn't see him again until after Mayor Lockwood's death ("The Return"); Caroline's parents split up ("Bringing Out the Dead").

May 4, 2007 — The date of "death" on Isobel's tombstone ("Know Thy Enemy"); presumably her parents chose the date she disappeared, which conflicts with the timeline established in "Blood Brothers" that suggested Damon turned Isobel in 2008.

May 23, 2009 — Elena meets Damon, but he compels her to forget their encounter ("The Departed"). Grayson and Miranda Gilbert die in a car accident ("Pilot"); Stefan rescues Elena ("Bloodlines").

May–September 2009 — Stefan observes Elena and investigates her family history ("Bloodlines").

Summer 2009 — Matt and Bonnie work as lifeguards together ("The Reckoning").

August 2009 — Katherine compels Jimmy to attack Mason; Mason kills him, which triggers his curse ("Kill or Be Killed").

August 31, 2009 — Mason writes in his journal about how different he's felt since killing Jimmy ("The Sacrifice").

Season 1 Begins

September 6, 2009 — Damon kills a couple who is driving home from a concert ("Pilot").

September 7, 2009 — First day back to Mystic Falls High ("Pilot").

September 8, 2009 — Damon attacks Vicki during the party by the falls ("Pilot").

September 9, 2009 — The comet passes over Mystic Falls ("The Night of the Comet").

September 10, 2009 — Caroline wakes up with Damon; Stefan tries out for the school football team; Caroline and Damon crash Elena's dinner party with Bonnie and Stefan ("Friday Night Bites").

September 11, 2009 — Stefan gives Elena the vervain-filled necklace; Damon kills Coach Tanner ("Friday Night Bites"). (This date actually was a Friday.)

September 15, 2009 ● — Mason turns into a wolf for the first time ("The Sacrifice").

September 24?, 2009 — The Founder's Ball is held; the date here is based on the original Founder's Ball, which was held on the 24th. Stefan captures Damon and locks him in the cellar ("Family Ties").

September 27?, 2009 — Three days after leaving Elena a cryptic voice-mail message, Stefan tries to fix his relationship with her by making dinner for her ("You're Undead to Me").

September 28?, 2009 — The Sexy Suds Car Wash is held at the high school; Damon attacks Vicki and kills her friends; Elena figures out that Stefan is a vampire; Stefan asks her to keep his secret ("You're Undead to Me," "Lost Girls").

September 29?, 2009 — Damon turns Vicki into a vampire; Logan is killed ("Lost Girls").

There's a jump in the timeline here. Between "Lost Girls" and "Haunted" only a few days pass, but "Haunted" takes place at the end of October.

October 31, 2009 — Vicki is staked by Stefan ("Haunted").

Early November 2009 — Bonnie reveals her powers to Elena; Stefan turns 162; Damon kills Lexi ("162 Candles").

Mid-November? 2009 — Emily possesses Bonnie and destroys the crystal; Logan returns, now a vampire. Stefan has been asking Damon for "months" why he returned to Mystic Falls; Alaric mentions to Jeremy that they are halfway through the school semester ("History Repeating").

The following day ● — With a full moon overhead, it's Career Night at Mystic Falls High School; Elena and Stefan have sex for the first time; she discovers the portrait of Katherine; Noah causes her to crash her car ("The Turning Point"). Damon rescues Elena from the car wreck ("Bloodlines").

The following day — Damon takes Elena to Atlanta to visit Bree; Bonnie falls into the tomb and Stefan rescues her ("Bloodlines").

The following day — Elena arrives back in Mystic Falls, and Stefan reveals that he rescued her from the car crash that killed her parents in May and that she is adopted ("Bloodlines").

December? 2009 — The 1950s Decade Dance is held at the high school; Caroline passes a Christmas display in a store window ("Unpleasantville").

Shortly thereafter — Stefan unearths the grimoire that was buried with his father; both Elena and Bonnie are kidnapped ("Children of the Damned").

The following day — The tomb opens; Duke has a party at the old cemetery where people are wearing winter coats and hats; Sheila Bennett dies ("Fool Me Once").

Winter 2010 — An ill-fated hiker tells Harper the year; the Bachelor Auction is held at the Grill ("A Few Good Men").

No indication of time of year for "There Goes the Neighborhood" or "Let the Right One In."

One month before Founder's Day ● — Johnathan Gilbert returns to Mystic Falls; the kickoff to Founder's Day party is held on the night of a full moon; Stefan gives in and drinks human blood ("Under Control").

Three weeks? before Founder's Day — Bonnie returns to Mystic Falls; the Miss Mystic Falls competition is held; Elena and Damon lock up a blood-drunk Stefan ("Miss Mystic Falls").

A few days later — Stefan refuses to eat; Elena convinces him not to commit suicide; Isobel shows up at the Grill ("Blood Brothers").

The following day — The Mystic Falls High students prepare floats for Founder's Day; Elena meets her birth mother, Isobel ("Isobel").

The following day — Isobel gets the Gilbert invention from Elena and gives it to Uncle John ("Isobel").

Founder's Day — The tomb vampires, Anna, and Mayor Lockwood are killed; Tyler, Matt, and Caroline are in a car accident; Katherine impersonates Elena, kisses Damon, and attacks Uncle John ("Founder's Day").

Season 2 Events

The following day — Mason returns to Mystic Falls for his brother's wake; that night, Damon "kills" Jeremy and Katherine "kills" Caroline ("The Return").

The following day — Caroline completes her transition to a vampire; the school hosts a carnival ("Brave New World").

Full Moon ● — Alaric, Damon, and Elena go to Duke University. Caroline gets a daylight ring from Bonnie. Mason turns into a werewolf. Tyler discovers the Lockwood secret. ("Bad Moon Rising")

The following day — Caroline wakes up to find Katherine in her bedroom ("Bad Moon Rising").

The following day — (Assuming this is not the same day that Katherine wakes up Caroline because Katherine's wearing a different outfit when she shows up at the Salvatore boarding house.) Jenna hosts a barbecue; Katherine reveals to Stefan the real story behind the Vampire Purge of 1864 ("Memory Lane").

August 2010 / the following day — The day of the Historical Society Volunteer Picnic; that night, Sheriff Forbes is put in the Salvatore holding cell until the vervain is out of her system ("Kill or Be Killed"). The flashback to "one year ago" in "Kill or Be Killed" is later revealed to have taken place in August 2009 ("The Sacrifice"), meaning the present-day events take place in August 2010. (The timeline is later muddled, because

"The Birthday" also takes place in August or early September 2010 [being a year after the events of the pilot episode].)

Three days later — It takes three days for the vervain to leave Liz's system ("Kill or Be Killed"). The gang sets up for the Masquerade Ball. Mason is tortured and killed by Damon. ("Plan B")

Masquerade Ball — Katherine kills Aimee; Tyler triggers the curse by accidentally killing Sarah; Katherine is captured and put in the tomb; Elena is kidnapped ("Masquerade").

The following day — Elijah kills Trevor; Damon and Stefan rescue Elena ("Rose").

The following day — The Martins arrive in Mystic Falls; Elena visits Katherine at the tomb; Rose and Damon visit Slater; Elijah compels Slater to kill himself ("Katerina").

It's not clear how many days, if any, pass between "Katerina" and "The Sacrifice," but since Slater's body is still undiscovered in "The Sacrifice" it's safe to assume the timeline is continuous.

That night — Late at night, Jonas steals various artifacts from Elena's room ("The Sacrifice").

The following day — Jeremy manages to get the moonstone out of the tomb; Stefan is stuck in the tomb with Katherine; Elijah kills three vampires ("The Sacrifice").

The following day — Tyler calls Mason as he gets ready for the full moon ("By the Light of the Moon"). (Assuming this is a separate day since he's wearing a different shirt than in "The Sacrifice.")

Full Moon ● — Tyler makes his first transformation. Rose is bitten by Jules. ("By the Light of the Moon")

The following day — Jules wakes up in bloodbath campground; Rose dies ("The Descent").

The following day — The werewolves kidnap and torture Caroline ("Daddy Issues").

The following day — Stefan and Elena go to the lakehouse. Tyler leaves town with Jules ("Crying Wolf")

The following day — (Assuming it's the next day, since news of Tyler's departure is just spreading.) Elijah is killed (twice). Katherine is freed from the tomb. ("The Dinner Party")

The following day — The Grill burns down; Luka and Jonas Martin are killed ("The House Guest"). Jenna meets Isobel ("Know Thy Enemy").

The following day — Isobel kills herself; Katherine is kidnapped; Alaric is possessed by Klaus ("Know Thy Enemy").

The Decade Dance — Bonnie fakes her death to fool Klaus; later that night, Elena takes the dagger out of Elijah ("The Last Dance").

The following day — Elena spends the day with the newly resurrected Elijah, learning the true curse ("Klaus").

The Sacrifice ● — Damon force-feeds Elena his blood; Stefan and Elena go for a climb by the falls. Damon gets bitten by Tyler ("The Last Day"). Klaus breaks the curse, killing Jenna, Jules, and Elena, and transforming into a true werewolf-vampire hybrid ("The Sun Also Rises").

Next morning — Elena and Jeremy bury Jenna and John ("The Sun Also Rises").

The following day — Klaus "kills" Elijah. Jeremy dies but Bonnie resurrects him. Stefan and Klaus make a bargain. ("As I Lay Dying")

By moon cycles, it is two months from Founder's Day to the events of the finale. By time markers within episodes, it is only 26 days.

Season 3 Events

Summer — Klaus and Stefan chase werewolves (and kill tons of people), while Elena and Damon track them ("The Birthday").

Day 1 of season 3 timeline (late August/early September 2010) — Two months after the events of "As I Lay Dying," Elena turns 18; Stefan kills Andie Star ("The Birthday").

Day 2 ● — Elena, Alaric, and Damon track down Stefan in the Smoky Mountains; Klaus's hybrid experiment fails ("The Hybrid").

Day 3 — Caroline is tortured by her father; Elena and Damon go to Chicago; Rebekah is awakened ("The End of the Affair").

Day 4 — In Chicago, Katherine kills Gloria to save Stefan; Damon attacks both Alaric and Bill Forbes at the barbecue at the Lockwoods' ("Disturbing Behavior").

Day 5 — Bill Forbes leaves town; Damon and Katherine go on a road trip; Klaus drags Stefan back to Mystic Falls ("Disturbing Behavior"). That night, Tyler is turned into a hybrid, Stefan is forced to flip the switch, and Katherine and Jeremy locate Mikael ("The Reckoning").

Day 6 and 7 — Katherine tries to revive Mikael but he is unresponsive ("Smells Like Teen Spirit").

Day 8 — The first day of school, established as one year after the events of the pilot. Vicki tries to kill Elena at the Spirit Squad bonfire; Bonnie's magic is used to open the door to this side for the ghosts ("Smells Like Teen Spirit").

Day 9 — The Night of Illumination ("Ghost World").

Day 10 — Elena learns the Original family history from Rebekah; Mikael confronts Stefan and Damon ("Ordinary People").

Day 11 — As part of their plot to fool Klaus, Elena stakes Mikael; Klaus leaves Portland to return to Mystic Falls ("Homecoming").

Day 12 — Homecoming. Rebekah is daggered; Mikael is killed ("Homecoming").

Day 13 — Klaus discovers that his coffins are missing ("Homecoming").

Day 16? — Sunday, likely the one directly following Homecoming Friday. Alaric is run over saving Jeremy; Stefan enlists Bonnie to help him hide the coffins ("The New Deal").

Day 17 — Caroline turns 18; a fundraiser for the Wickery Bridge revitalization is held at the Lockwoods ("Our Town").

Day 18 — Jeremy leaves Mystic Falls for Denver; Brian Walters is found dead ("Our Town").

Day 19 — Bonnie tracks down her mother; Damon undaggers Elijah ("The Ties That Bind").

Day 20 — Bill Forbes dies; Kol, Finn, Rebekah, and Esther are resurrected ("Bringing Out the Dead").

Day 21 — The Mikaelson family holds a ball ("Dangerous Liaisons").

Day 22 — Esther tries to kill her family; Abby is turned into a vampire ("All My Children").

Day 23 — Alaric spends the day in jail; they realize he is the Mystic Falls Murderer ("1912").

Few days later — Damon, Sage, and Rebekah manipulate each other; Alaric attacks Meredith ("Break on Through").

Next day — Abby leaves Jamie and Bonnie ("Break on Through").

Next day — Bonnie breaks the "united as one" spell; Matt kills Finn;

Rebekah tortures Damon ("The Murder of One"). Damon and Elena leave for Denver ("Heart of Darkness").

Next day — Tyler returns; Esther possesses Rebekah ("Heart of Darkness").

Next day — The 1920s Decade Dance ("Do Not Go Gentle").

Next day — Alaric terrorizes the gang; Klaus is desiccated ("Before Sunset"). Late that same night, Elena dies ("The Departed").

By time markers within episodes, it is approximately 31 days between "The Birthday" and "The Departed."

Seasons 1 and 2 Refresher

1.01 "Pilot" Stefan and Elena meet on the first day back to school at Mystic Falls High. Vicki Donovan is attacked by Damon in the woods.

1.02 "The Night of the Comet" Damon antagonizes his brother, dangling Vicki off a roof over the town square, as a comet passes over town. Stefan and Elena kiss.

1.03 "Friday Night Bites" Stefan joins the football team, but then Damon kills Coach Tanner, ending the football season prematurely. Caroline debuts her new boyfriend (and penchant for neck scarves): Damon.

1.04 "Family Ties" At the Founder's party, Stefan manages to capture Damon by spiking Caroline's drink with vervain. Vicki leaves Tyler behind for Jeremy Gilbert.

1.05 "You're Undead to Me" It's the Sexy Suds Car Wash! Bonnie sets water on fire. Elena figures out Stefan's a vampire. Damon escapes from the Salvatore Holding Cell and attacks Vicki as she parties in the graveyard.

1.06 "Lost Girls" The first flashback episode brings us our first glimpse of Katherine and a heck of a lot of backstory on how Stefan and Damon became vampires. Bored, Damon turns Vicki — but not before their classic dance party moment.

1.07 "Haunted" Halloween in Mystic Falls marks the first death of a major character, as Stefan stakes Vicki, on the loose and hungry for Gilbert blood.

1.08 "162 Candles" Stefan's BFF Lexi comes to town on his birthday, the one day he isn't allowed to brood, and Damon kills her to cover up his own bloody tracks. Bonnie reveals to Elena that she's a witch in one of the series' most magical moments of magic.

1.09 "History Repeating" The girls hold a séance and Bonnie is possessed by her ancestor Emily Bennett, who destroys the tomb-opening crystal. Alaric Saltzman makes his debut.

1.10 "The Turning Point" Damon deals with Logan Fell, now a vampire, while Tyler and Jeremy come to blows at the school's Career Fair. Stefan and Elena sleep together for the first time. She discovers Katherine's portrait, takes off, and ends up in an accident, after a vampire in the road causes her to crash her car.

1.11 "Bloodlines" Damon takes Elena on a road trip to Georgia where she gets nice and drunk and saves his life from Lexi's angry ex. Stefan helps Bonnie get her powers back. Elena finds out she's adopted.

1.12 "Unpleasantville" It's the 1950s Decade Dance at MFHS. Uninvited vampires crash the party, but the Salvatore brothers kill Noah. Matt and Caroline kiss.

1.13 "Children of the Damned" Pretending to work with Damon, Elena and Stefan race to find the location of Emily Bennett's grimoire before he can. In flashback we see the events leading up to Katherine's capture. Bonnie and Elena are kidnapped by Ben and Anna.

1.14 "Fool Me Once" The tomb opens — and Katherine isn't in it.

1.15 "A Few Good Men" Damon goes on a bender. A bachelor auction is held at the Grill. Elena finds out that her birth mother is Isobel, Alaric's not-so-dead wife.

1.16 "There Goes the Neighborhood" Caroline and Matt and Elena and Stefan go on a double date. Damon makes out with Matt's mom. Two tomb vampires attack the Salvatores.

1.17 "Let the Right One In" A storm moves into Mystic Falls. Stefan is kidnapped and tortured. Damon, Alaric, and Elena rescue him. Caroline discovers Vicki Donovan's body.

1.18 "Under Control" At the kickoff to Founder's Day party, Stefan tries to manage his thirst for human blood and fails. Tyler makes out with Matt's mom. Uncle John Gilbert arrives with a magic ring.

1.19 "Miss Mystic Falls" Caroline wins Miss Mystic Falls. Stefan attacks Amber Bradley.

1.20 "Blood Brothers" Starving himself in the Salvatore holding cell, Stefan flashes-back to the night he and Damon became vampires.

1.21 "Isobel" Elena meets her birth mother, Isobel, who demands the Gilbert device from her. Bonnie pretends to deactivate it.

1.22 "Founder's Day" As the town celebrates its sesquicentennial, the tomb vampires face off with the vampire-hating members of the founding families. Damon kisses Katherine, thinking she's Elena, and Katherine chops off Uncle John's fingers.

2.01 "The Return" The Lockwoods, including Uncle Mason, mourn the mayor. Katherine makes her presence known. Damon snaps Jeremy's neck.

2.02 "Brave New World" Caroline becomes a vampire and kills Carter at the school's carnival.

2.03 "Bad Moon Rising" Alaric, Damon, and Elena go to Duke to investigate werewolves; Tyler learns that Mason is one.

2.04 "Memory Lane" Katherine and Stefan relive some 1864 memories. After Jenna's friendly barbecue, Damon makes an enemy of Mason Lockwood.

2.05 "Kill or Be Killed" At the historical society picnic, Mason and the Salvatore brothers face off; Liz Forbes finds out that Caroline, Damon, and Stefan are vampires.

2.06 "Plan B" The gang finds the moonstone in the bottom of a vervain-filled well. Damon kills Mason. Caroline compels her mother.

2.07 "Masquerade" At the masked ball, Katherine kills Aimee Bradley and orchestrates Sarah's death so Tyler triggers his werewolf curse. She is captured and entombed.

2.08 "Rose" Elena learns about the Originals from her vampire captors Rose and Trevor. Elijah makes an impressive debut.

2.09 "Katerina" Elena turns to the entombed Katherine for answers about being the doppelgänger.

2.10 "The Sacrifice" After Jeremy's botched attempt to get the moonstone from the tomb, Stefan ends up in there with Katherine. Elena tries to turn herself over to Klaus.

2.11 "By the Light of the Moon" Tyler turns into a werewolf. Elijah and Elena make a deal. Jules, in wolf form, bites Rose.

2.12 "The Descent" Rose dies from her werewolf bite.

2.13 "Daddy Issues" The werewolves and vampires face off, with Caroline getting the brunt of the attack. John Gilbert returns to town.

2.14 "Crying Wolf" Stefan and Elena go to the lakehouse; Stefan kills Brady. Bonnie pries information about the sacrifice from Luka.

2.15 "The Dinner Party" While Stefan and Elena talk about his ripper days and the first time he met Lexi, Damon and Andie host a dinner party. Elijah is daggered twice.

2.16 "The House Guest" The unwelcome house guest Katherine proves to be helpful in taking out Jonas. Caroline sings "Eternal Flame," the Mystic Grill burns, and Matt finds out his girlfriend is a vampire.

2.17 "Know Thy Enemy" Katherine double-crosses the Salvatore brothers but is crossed herself by Isobel who is compelled by Klaus who arrives in Mystic Falls . . . in Alaric's body.

2.18 "The Last Dance" At the 1960s Decade Dance, AlariKlaus terrorizes the gang, and Bonnie, using the power of 100 dead witches, fakes her own death.

2.19 "Klaus" Jenna learns about vampires, Elena learns about the Originals and the real curse from Elijah, and Klaus returns to his own body.

2.20 "The Last Day" On the day of the sacrifice, Damon force-feeds Elena his blood to make sure she'll come back to life; Elena tells Stefan how desperately she doesn't want to become a vampire.

2.21 "The Sun Also Rises" The sacrifice takes place: Jules and Jenna are killed, Klaus unleashes his werewolf side, and Damon is bit by Tyler after he rescues him and Caroline.

2.22 "As I Lay Dying" Stefan gives up everything to save his brother from his werewolf bite, becoming a minion to Klaus. After Jeremy is shot dead, Bonnie brings him back to life. Ghosts Anna and Vicki appear to Jeremy.

Sources

Abrams, Natalie. "Cassidy Freeman on Her *Vampire Diaries* Debut: Sage Is Not Unlike *Smallville*'s Tess," TVGuide.com. March 15, 2012.

"Alice Evans Interview," *The VRO*. May 7, 2012. www.blogtalkradio.com/vampradio/2012/05/08/alice-evans-interview.

Andrews, Terri J. "The Sacredness of Sage," angelfire.com/biz2/turquoisebutterfly/sage.html.

Ballhorn, Kelly. "*The Vampire Diaries* Star Joseph Morgan Says Caspar Zafer 'Is a Hell of a Guy,'" RyanSeacrest.com. February 2, 2012.

Baltin, Steve. "My Morning Jacket Perform on *Vampire Diaries*," RollingStone.com. November 9, 2011.

Before Sunset. DVD. Warner Home Video, 2004.

Bell, Crystal. "*The Vampire Diaries*: Candice Accola Dishes on Caroline's Birthday, Tyler's Future, Daddy Drama," HuffingtonPost.com. January 12, 2012.

———. "*The Vampire Diaries*: Zach Roerig Previews 'Dangerous Liaisons,' Talks Potential Matt and Rebekah Romance," HuffingtonPost.com. February 9, 2012.

Bernstein, Abbie. "Exclusive Interview: The Season 3 scoop on *The Vampire Diaries* from Kevin Williamson," AssignmentX.com. February 9, 2012.

Bierly, Mandi. "Best of 2011 (Behind the Scenes): *The Vampire Diaries* EP Julie Plec Talks Moments that Made her Cry," EW.com. December 16, 2011.

———. "David Gallagher Talks *Vampire Diaries* Arc (Which He Can Thank *Super 8* For)," EW.com. September 9, 2011.

———. "*Vampire Diaries* Casts *Supernatural* Star Sebastian Roché as Mysterious Vampire Hunter," EW.com. August 10, 2011.

———. "*Vampire Diaries*: EP Julie Plec on Elena Ogling Damon, Caroline Championing Stefan, and a Twist on the Rebesther Twist," EW.com. April 25, 2012.

———. "*Vampire Diaries*: EP Julie Plec on the Trending Topics She'd Like to See Before March 15," EW.com. March 5, 2012.

———. "*Vampire Diaries* EP Julie Plec Talks Season Finale Shocker and What Comes Next," EW.com. May 11, 2012.

———. "*Vampire Diaries* Preview: Cassidy Freeman and Paul Wesley Tease Upcoming Episodes," EW.com. March 15, 2012.

———. "*Vampire Diaries* Season Finale Preview: Kat Graham on Bonnie's Deal and Possible Dark Side," EW.com. May 9, 2012.

———. "*Vampire Diaries*: Torrey DeVitto Talks Dr. Fell, Enjoying Husband Paul Wesley's Turn as Bad Stefan," EW.com. January 19, 2012.

"Bio," EnishaBrewster.com.

Bonin, Liane. "Interview: Daniel Gillies from *Vampire Diaries* Talks Elijah's Next Step," HitFix.com. February 16, 2012.

Bricker, Tierney. "*Vampire Diaries* Boss Sounds Off on Elena's Transition and Dark Side!," EOnline.com. June 6, 2012.

————. "*Vampire Diaries*: Candice Accola Teases Klaus and Tyler's Fight for Caroline at the Decade Dance!," EOnline.com. April 25, 2012.

Bringing Out the Dead. DVD. Paramount, 2000.

Byrne, Craig. "Interview: Cassidy Freeman Talks About Tonight's *Vampire Diaries* & Tess Mercer's *Smallville* Fate," KSiteTV.com. March 15, 2012.

————. "*Vampire Diaries* Interview: Julie Plec Talks About This Week's Show & the Rest of Season 3," KSiteTV.com. February 8, 2012.

"Casper Zafer Interview," *The VRO*. May 14, 2012. www.blogtalkradio.com/vampradio/2012/05/15/casper-zafer-interview.

"Claire Holt as Emma Gilbert: *H20 — Just Add Water* Cast," AustralianTelevision.net. Accessed April 21, 2012.

Dangerous Liaisons. DVD. Warner Home Video, 1997.

Dean, Leonard F. ed. *Joseph Conrad's Heart of Darkness: Backgrounds and Criticisms*. Englewood Cliffs, NJ: Prentice-Hall, Inc. 1960.

Disturbing Behavior. DVD. MGM, 1999.

Dos Santos, Kristin. "Spoiler Chat: Which Couple May Be Doomed on *Grey's Anatomy*?" EOnline.com. August 15, 2011.

"Edgar Degas: The Rehearsal of the Ballet Onstage (29.160.26)." In *Heilbrunn Timeline of Art History*. New York: The Metropolitan Museum of Art, 2000–. www.metmuseum.org/toah/works-of-art/29.160.26. October 2006.

Eramo, Steven. "'Lex Schmex' — Meet *Smallville's* Tess Mercer," Newsrama.com. May 1, 2009.

Forner, Nancy. "Style, Emotion & Vamping on *The Vampire Diaries*," Magazine.CreativeCow.net. March 19, 2012.

Fox, Sue TL. "History of Women's Boxing," HotBoxingNews.com.

Furlong, Maggie. "Ian Somerhalder Talks *Vampire Diaries* Season 3: Drama, Nudity & More," AOLTV.com. September 14, 2011.

Gelman, Vlada. "Post Mortem: *Vampire Diaries* Boss on Finale Gamechanger, Elena's Choice and Who's a Goner," TVLine.com. May 11, 2012.

————. "*Vampire Diaries* Preview: Tyler's Back! But Has Caroline Been Swept Away by Klaus?!," TVLine.com. April 18, 2012.

Ghost World. DVD. MGM, 2002.

"*H20: Just Add Water* Stars Nearly Reunited in the U.S.," TVWeek.ninemsn.com.au.

Hales, Taylor and Nikolas Kazmers. "Prohibition and its Effects on Chicagoans and Organized Crime." 2004. www.umich.edu/~eng217/student_projects/nkazmers/prohibition1.html.

Halterman, Jim. "On Location: Spooning, Being Bad and Nudity with the Men of *The Vampire Diaries*," AfterElton.com. February 9, 2012.

————. "Interview: *The Vampire Diaries* Co-Stars Ian Somerhalder, Candice Accola, Joseph Morgan & Zach Roerig," TheFutonCritic.com. February 9, 2012.

"Interview: Daniel Gillies (Elijah) from *The Vampire Diaries*," TheTVChick.com. February 16, 2012.

MacKenzie, Carina Adly. "*The Vampire Diaries*: Meet Dr. Meredith Fell! Torrey DeVitto Brings a Book Character Off the Page," Zap2It.com. January 5, 2012.

———. "*The Vampire Diaries* Originals: Is Klaus Going Soft? Plus, Rebekah's Rise-and-Shine," Zap2It.com. December 16, 2011.

———. "Torrey DeVitto Joins *The Vampire Diaries*: 'For the sake of Alaric, I hope this lasts!,'" Zap2It.com. January 12, 2012.

Marcil, Monique. "*The Vampire Diaries* Consults *Beauty and the Beast* to Dress the Belles of Klaus' Ball," Zap2It.com. February 9, 2012.

Masters, Megan. "*Vampire Diaries* Boss Previews Cassidy Freeman's 'Ballsy' Role, Plus 3 More Scooplets!," TVLine.com. February 16, 2012.

———. "*Vampire Diaries* Boss Talks Offing Originals, Teases 'Major Jeopardy' for All by Season's End," TVLine.com. February 10, 2012.

"Meet NHPCO Hospice Ambassador, Torrey DeVitto," *Newsline: The Monthly Membership Publication of the National Hospice and Palliative Care Organization.* February 2012.

Melville, Herman. *Moby-Dick; or, The Whale.* New York: Penguin Books, 2003.

Mitovich, Matt Webb. "Cassidy Freeman Teases 'Sordid' *Vampire Diaries* Threesome, Reigniting Damon's Bad Boy Ways," TVLine.com. March 15, 2012.

"Music from the Series," Vampire-Diaries.net. www.vampire-diaries.net/the-tv-series/music-from-the-series/season-three.

Ng, Philiana. "*Vampire Diaries* Actor Zach Roerig: 'Matt Is a Nice Piece of Humble Pie for Mystic Falls,'" HollywoodReporter.com. February 9, 2012.

Ordinary People. DVD. Paramount, 2001.

Our Town. DVD. PBS, 2005.

"Pagan Magical Properties of Herbs," www.squidoo.com/PaganHerbs.

Pickle, Gabrielle. "The Real Nathaniel: The Man Behind the Fangs," Facebook.com/NathanielBuzolic.

Radish, Christina. "Candice Accola, Michael Trevino, Zach Roerig and Executive Producer Julie Plec Talk the End of *The Vampire Diaries* Season 3," Collider.com. April 27, 2012.

———. "Persia White Talks *The Vampire Diaries* Season 3," Collider.com. March 8, 2012.

Richenthal, Matt. "Persia White Interview: Can Abby Be a Mother to Bonnie?," TVFanatic.com. February 8, 2012.

———. "Sebastian Roché on *Vampire Diaries* Awakening: Hungry for Revenge!," TVFanatic.com. October 31, 2011.

"Robert Ri'chard Interview," CleverTV.com. May 3, 2012.

Ross, Robyn. "*Vampire Diaries* Boss: Stefan Will Lean on Caroline During Elena's Transition," TVGuide.com. June 3, 2012.

———. "*Vampire Diaries* Video: Does Michael Trevino Want to Play Klaus?," TVGuide.com. May 28, 2012.

————. "*Vampire Diaries* Wesley: Damon Is a Puppy in Comparison to What Stefan Is Morphing Into," TVGuide.com. September 14, 2011.

Rudolph, Ileane. "Jack Coleman, *Heroes*: What's Going on Behind the Glasses," TVGuide.com. November 27, 2006.

"Sage," Herbal Grimoire. CottageHerb.tripod.com.

"Sage," PaganWiccan.About.com.

Sanderson, Nicole. "Viking Runes Through Time," *Nova*. May 9, 2000. www.pbs .org/wgbh/nova/ancient/viking-runes-through-time.html.

Smith, L.J. *The Vampire Diaries: The Awakening*. New York: HarperTeen, 2009.

————. *The Vampire Diaries: The Fury* and *Dark Reunion*. New York: HarperTeen, 2007.

————. *The Vampire Diaries: The Struggle*. New York: HarperTeen, 2009.

SparkNotes Editors. "SparkNote on *Heart of Darkness*." SparkNotes LLC. 2002. www.sparknotes.com/lit/heart/.

Spiegelman, Ian. "Sebastian Roché on 'Intense Exchanges' Between Mikael and Klaus and What He Loves About Working on *TVD*," Wetpaint.com. October 25, 2011.

Steinberg, Lisa. "Torrey DeVitto: Medical Attention," Starry Constellation Magazine.

Stevenson, Robert Louis. *The Strange Case of Dr Jekyll and Mr Hyde and Other Tales of Terror*. New York: Penguin Classics, 2003.

Swift, Andy. "*The Vampire Diaries* Scoop: Jamie Will Factor into Bonnie's 'Flawed Love Life,'" HollywoodLife.com. January 24, 2012.

————. "*Vampire Diaries* Scoop: Torrey DeVitto Says Meredith's Death Is 'Inevitable,'" HollywoodLife.com. February 8, 2012.

————. "*Vampire Diaries* Scoop: Vicki & Matt Will 'Explore Their Brother-Sister Relationship' in Season 3," HollywoodLife.com. August 17, 2011.

————. "*Vampire Diaries* Scoop: Will Bonnie Pick Jamie Over Jeremy?," HollywoodLife.com. April 24, 2012.

Theo. "Kayla Ewell and Malese Jow Reveal 'Ghostly' Secrets," VampireDiaries .AlloyEntertainment.com.

The Departed. DVD. Warner Home Video, 2007.

The End of the Affair. DVD. Sony Pictures Home Entertainment, 2000.

"The New Deal," pbs.org/wgbh/americanexperience/features/general-article/ dustbowl-new-deal/.

The Vampire Diaries. TV Series. Executive Producers Leslie Morgenstein, Bob Levy, Kevin Williamson, Julie Plec. The CW. 2009–.

Thomas, Dylan. "Do Not Go Gentle into That Good Night," *The Dylan Thomas Omnibus*. London: Phoenix Giant, 1995. 128–129.

Twitter.com/CMollere.

Valenzuela, Morgan. "Chicago's Prohibition-era 'Pansy Craze,'" ChicagoHistory .org. September 30, 2011.

"Vampire Diaries," TuneFind.com.

Vampire-Diaries.net.

"Vikings: The North Atlantic Saga," Smithsonian National Museum of History. www.mnh.si.edu/vikings/start.html.

Wieselman, Jarett. "Torrey DeVitto: TV's Crazy Lady du Jour!" TheInsider.com. March 1, 2012.

Wikipedia.org.

Acknowledgments

As always, thank you to the ECW family for your support of my books and to those who designed *Love You to Death* — cover designer Rachel Ironstone, page designer Melissa Kaita, and typesetter Troy Cunningham. Jen Knoch, thank you for your thoughtful edit, your unending love for Price Peterson candle storage jokes, and for being my partner-in-crime on the Liv Spencer books. You are a wonderful co-captain and remind me to never, never, never give up. Gil Adamson, thank you for helping me through the inertia by refocusing my muddled brain. Mad love to Sarah Dunn for, among other things, her clever questions for the *LYtD* interviews. Thank you for being a fandom tourist with me and for mailroom *TVD* recaps on Friday mornings.

Thank you to J. Miller Tobin, Joshua Butler, and Price Peterson for their interviews; I cannot overstate how touched I was by your willingness to participate in my book.

Julie Plec, your support of this project, your responsiveness and generous spirit, and your unwavering awesomeness — in both how you steer *The Vampire Diaries* and how you interact with its fandom — have really done nothing but encourage me to think of you as a real-life Tami Taylor: accomplished, inspiring, and someone I wish was my next-door neighbor. Thank you.

Vee, thank you for always being an iMessage away and for agreeing to write the "Where's Meredith?" section without hesitation. Thanks to the beloved Vampire-Diaries.net family — Red, Kate, Abby, and Vee — for allowing me to contribute to your site. Excuse me, your NewNowNext Award–winning site. Thank you to all the people who comment on my episode posts there, who chat with me on Twitter, and to the *TVD* fandom at large. And to all the journalists whose articles are quoted herein, a world of thanks.

Finally to my family and the Ace Gang: I've finished writing my book and I'm ready to leave my apartment again.

GET THE eBOOK FREE! At ECW Press, we want you to enjoy *Love You to Death — Season 3* in whatever format you like, whenever you like. Leave your print book at home and take the eBook to go! Purchase the print edition and receive the eBook free. Just send an email to ebook@ecwpress.com and include:

- the book title
- the name of the store where you purchased it
- your receipt number
- your preference of file type: PDF or ePub?

A real person will respond to your email with your eBook attached. And thanks for supporting an independently owned publisher with your purchase!